King

ลิลิตพระลอ และ ทวาทศมาส

Kings in Love
Lilit Phra Lo and Twelve Months
Two Classic Thai poems

Translated and introduced by

Chris Baker and Pasuk Phongpaichit

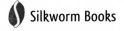 Silkworm Books

ลิลิตพระลอ และ ทวาทศมาส
ISBN: 978-616-215-161-3
© 2020 Silkworm Books

First published in 2020 by
Silkworm Books
430/58 M. 7, T. Mae Hia, Chiang Mai 50100, Thailand
info@silkwormbooks.com
http://www.silkwormbooks.com

Cover photo: Beautiful lotus from "photoroad", 123rf.com
Typeset in Gentium 10.5 pt. by Silk Type
Printed and bound in Thailand by O. S. Printing House, Bangkok

5 4 3 2 1

Contents

Introduction:
Literature, Language, Love

These two poems are among the earliest works of Thai literature, both on a theme of love, both distinctive, both controversial, and both deserving to be better known. *Lilit Phra Lo*[1] is a long narrative poem with an unusual romance, a contest of rival magic, a quest-like journey, an erotic climax, a bloody massacre, and a finale of Buddhist-inspired reconciliation. The work has been condemned as feudal, indulgent, immoral, male-centric, and technically flawed, but commands respect for its unique plot, flowing poetry, Buddhist teaching, and emotional power. *Twelve Months*[2] is a passionate and elegantly erotic lament for a lost lover. The poem was once celebrated, but over the past century has been quietly sidelined. It is now greatly admired by a small coterie and little known by others.

Both were written about a century before Shakespeare's *Romeo and Juliet*. Though rooted in Thai culture, both speak to universal themes and have echoes in world literature. We hope these translations allow these works not just to be understood but also to be enjoyed.

---

1. *Lilit* indicates a certain metrical form (see Note on Translation below). *Phra* is a title or prefix, here meaning a king. *Lo* is a personal name with a long vowel, sometimes transcribed as *Law*, *Lǫ*, or *Lor*.

2. *Twelve Months* or *Thawathotsamat* comes from the Pali-Sanskrit dvādaśa māsa.

Literature

The earliest survivals of Siam's literature are five works from the late fifteenth and early sixteenth centuries: *Mahachat Khamluang*, a chanting script for the Vessantara Jataka; *Yuan Phai*, a war poem incorporating a royal elegy; *Lilit Phra Lo*, a tragic courtly romance; *Nirat Hariphunchai*, a poem of pilgrimage and lament; and *Thawathotsamat* or *Twelve Months*, a love lament.[3] The five are varied in genre, metrical form, and content, and each is quite sophisticated in its own way, suggesting that there must have been many more works which are now lost. All five were probably composed to be heard rather than read. They were performed by a reciter in a context of either ritual or entertainment, stored in memory, and passed on by word of mouth. Such works were vulnerable to changing preferences, and disappeared when there was no demand for them to be heard. To survive, works needed to be written down and, as the old media for writing were vulnerable to heat, damp, and insects, regularly recopied every fifty to a hundred years. Siam developed no printing technology and no university. The facilities for preserving manuscripts were found among royal scribes in the palace and Buddhist monks in the *wat* (monastery). Works had higher chances of survival if they were religious or royal.

Both these poems may have survived because they were associated with kingship, but also because they were seen to be good. Both are mentioned in *Jindamani*, a seventeenth-century manual of literary

---

3.   This is a deliberately narrow definition of "literature." It is possible to expand this list to include *Ongkan chaeng nam*, an oath of loyalty, on the grounds that it is also in verse, and Sukhothai Inscription I, on the grounds of its poetic quality; and to expand it further, to include all written work that has survived, mainly other inscriptions and religious texts. In early studies, *Lilit Phra Lo*, *Thawathotsamat*, and *Nirat Hariphunchai* were all dated to the Narai era (1656–88).

arts. After the destruction of the Siamese capital of Ayutthaya in 1767, both were among the manuscripts that the Siamese court and literati made efforts to preserve through the nineteenth century, and render into print around the turn of the twentieth. Since then, however, the fate of the two has dramatically diverged. *Lilit Phra Lo* is one of the best-known works of old Thai literature. Thai children study it at school and can often recite key verses many years later. *Twelve Months* is less known, less published, less studied and less well appreciated than the other early works. Most people have never heard of it. Why this should be so is examined below.

Language

Today, these early works are rendered remote by language. At the time they appeared, the Thai language was evolving. Siam (the lower Chao Phraya plain) had a very mixed population—older inhabitants who spoke languages now called Mon-Khmer; newer arrivals who spoke several variants of the language family now known as Tai; coastal peoples now labeled as Malay; along with a sprinkling of Chinese, south Indians, Persians, and others. People probably spoke in their natal tongue but listened in many others. In the palace, court brahmans used Sanskrit, and in the *wat* the monks studied and chanted Pali. Today's Thai language has input from all of these tongues, though the Tai dialects are the dominant element. At the time these early works appeared, the language was evolving through intercourse in the court, port, *wat*, and street.

Both *Lilit Phra Lo* and *Twelve Months* were composed in metrical forms designed for a language with three tones. As the language evolved, the three tones expanded to five, these old metrical forms were abandoned, and new forms were developed. This "great tone shift" was complete by the mid-seventeenth century, but when it began is uncertain. As two of the five early literary works can be relatively securely dated around 1500,[4] and as they all share certain characteristics, probably they all date from this era, and the "great tone shift" began after 1500.

The tonal system was not the only aspect of language that shifted at this time. Old words went out of use and new ones were crafted. Syntax changed. As a result, there is a barrier in the linguistic history. Today, seventeenth-century Thai texts can still be read without much difficulty, but earlier ones are significantly more obscure.[5] The originals are read only by scholars and students who have invested in acquiring the expertise. Others know the texts through summaries, academic editions, versions in modern Thai, and reworkings as novels, plays, films, TV series, and cartoons. Those crafting these adaptations interpret, expand, contract, and modify the originals, both consciously and unconsciously.

Love

Love is the most popular theme of literary works across the world because it is the most powerful of human emotions. The portrayal of

---

4. For the year 1482/83 CE, the Luang Prasoet chronicle of Ayutthaya states: "In 844, a year of the tiger, the king held a great 15-day festival to celebrate Phra Si Rattana Mahathat, then composed the complete version of the *Mahachat Khamluang*" (*Phraratcha phongsawadan krung kao*, CS 844, 19; Cushman, *Royal Chronicles*, 18). However, large parts have since been lost and recomposed. *Nirat Hariphunchai* has a date in the form "year of the ox, ninth of the decade," which recurs every sixty years. Prasert na Nagara believes it refers to 1517/18 CE, but others have suggested both earlier and later dates (Prasert, *Khlong Nirat Hariphunchai*, 12; Lagirarde, "Un pèlerinage bouddhique," 74–76; Winai, *Ruthiratramphan*, 23–25). *Yuan Phai* focuses on a battle fought around 1475 CE and was probably written soon after (Baker and Pasuk, *Yuan Phai*).

5. As nobody is sure how the three-tone system was spoken, it is impossible now to recite these works in the original form.

love, however, is constrained by customs, conventions, and sensitivities which vary across space and time. *Twelve Months* was celebrated in the nineteenth century as a gem of the Thai literary heritage, but has been neglected and obscured since the early twentieth. *Lilit Phra Lo* remains well known but has been flayed as an example of feudal indulgence. Since the 1970s, it has been repeatedly reworked by leading novelists, dramatists, and film-makers. None of these productions follow the original plot faithfully. Instead, these artists have rewritten the plot and changed the characters to fit contemporary conceptions of love, gender relations, heroism, power, and social decorum.

Most of the new nation-states that emerged from the colonial world in the twentieth century compiled a "national literature," partly as a qualification for their new national status, and partly as a means to shape a modern, national citizen.[6] In Siam from the late nineteenth century, the royal court took the initiative in developing this national literature, both as a source of pride and as a didactic device. Chosen works had to reflect the court's conception of "Thai values" and the proper behavior of a Thai citizen. In 1914, King Vajiravudh laid down that a chosen work had to be "a good book, meaning suitable for the public to read, and not harmful, such as being a meretricious work, or inciting readers to have baseless or politically unruly thoughts."[7] Over the subsequent century, the code of values was subject to shifts and challenges, but the emphasis on a work having a didactic purpose remained. Since 1972, the rubric for the government's national book prizes has specified that "entries under all categories must be books

---

6. Hau, *Necessary Fictions*.
7. Translated from Ruenruethai, "Wannakhadi sueksa choeng pramoen khunkha," 125. The term translated as "meretricious" is *thuphasit*, from Pali *du bhāsita*, literally "bad speech," not a term now in use but clearly an antonym of *suphasit*, "good speech," the term for a proverb or moral saying.

that do not contravene morality and do not affect the security of the country," and should also have "beneficial utility" (*sanprayot*). As a result, such prizes excluded several genres, including detective fiction, science fiction, fantasy, and *love stories*.[8]

Love stories could be problematic in two ways. The first concerned the portrayal of physical love. When Prince Damrong Rajanubhab[9] edited the Thai folk epic *Khun Chang Khun Phaen* in the 1910s, he rewrote the tryst scenes, explaining that such passages "made readers dislike [the poem], and in the past women were even forbidden to read it."[10] This delicacy over women betrays the Victorianism behind Prince Damrong's thinking. Over subsequent decades, this Victorianism faded, but was replaced by an idealization of women as good wives and good mothers. In the 1970s, a prominent literary academic, Suphon Bunnag, claimed that a work like *Lady Chatterley's Lover* could not appear in Thai literature because Thais "never do anything sexually dirty, and authors will not portray anything titillating because they don't titillate themselves." She added: "The Thai do not believe that men and women are sexually equal, because women are the gender that own the womb, the origin of new human life .... Thus, the womb must be kept pure and free of promiscuity."[11] These attitudes still linger. In 2017, Samoe Bunma explained that *Twelve Months* had been sidelined because "people call it 'erotic literature' as it deals with inappropriate matters such as the private organs of men and women,

8. Ruenruethai, "Wannakhadi sueksa choeng pramoen khunkha," 136, 143–44. Publishers responded by creating specialists awards for some categories.

9. Prince Damrong (1862–1943), a son of King Mongkut, was the leading administrator of King Chulalongkorn's reign (1868–1910), with a major role in education and provincial administration. After his retirement in 1915, he authored a prodigious output of studies in Thai history, literature, and culture.

10. Baker and Pasuk, *The Tale of Khun Chang Khun Phaen*, 1363.

11. Suphon, "Kan yatyiat pom wiparit rueang phet hai kae wannakhadi thai," 20, 37, 39, 40.

and uses words for erotic effect in some verses. This is too much for Thai society."[12]

Love stories could also be problematic because by definition they celebrated strong emotions. From traditional Buddhist teaching through to modern codes of manners, there is advice to resist or repress strong emotions. Early Buddhist scriptures, including the *Siṅgāla sutta* and many *jātaka* tales, warn people to avoid the four "bad courses" (*agati*) of desire, fear, anger, and ignorance. The *Dhammapada*, an eternally popular collection of short sayings of the Buddha, states: "The wise are controlled in bodily action, controlled in speech, and controlled in thought. They are truly well-controlled."[13] While the many manuals of behavior published since the mid-nineteenth century have slid from a Buddhist framework to a more worldly morality, and from a courtly and distinctly Thai mode to something more middle-class and international, their ideal person remains someone who is humble, calm, restrained—in control of body, mind, and speech.[14]

All portrayals of love, especially physical love, in literature and other forms of expression have had to negotiate this environment. The histories of the two poems presented here are outstanding examples of this process, because they are outstanding examples of poems of love.

We hope these translations help to liberate these works from the obscurity of their original langage, the assumptions of a didactical approach to national literature, and anxieties over the expression of love.

---

12. Samoe, "Thawathotsamat wipak," 21.
13. kāyena saṁvutā dhīrā atho vācāya saṁvutā manasā saṁvutā dhīrā te ve suparisaṁvutā. *Dhammapada*, 17 (v. 234).
14. Jory, "Thailand's Politics of Politeness" and "*Khunatham jariyatham thai* (Thai Morals and Manners)."

Note on Translation

In these translations, we aim to convey the meaning accurately, to reflect the beauty and drama of the originals, and to be readable. How successful we are, the reader must judge, but we have attempted to do justice to these works as literature.

We intend to accurately convey the meaning by adopting strict rules for translation, by drawing on all the prior work of translation and explication, and by tapping the expertise of colleagues. We recognize that both works would have been primarily consumed by listening rather than reading. We use blank verse for three reasons: because it is a stylized form of everyday speech, like the metrical forms used in the Thai original; because it has a track record in translation of non-English poetry; and because it is relatively easy to craft without complicating the task of accurately conveying the meaning. In the translations, we favor iambs but allow the line length to vary to accommodate the meaning. As *Lilit Phra Lo* is essentially a drama, we have drawn inspiration from playwriting, especially Shakespeare. For *Twelve Months*, we have drawn on the enormous heritage of love poetry, especially the elegiac strain.

The two works use two metrical forms, *rai* and *khlong*.[15] Both forms are built with a basic unit of five stressed syllables composed of two phrases (2+3 or 3+2), and both have rhymes from the final syllable of some lines to a mid-line syllable in a line below, creating a strong forward momentum.

In *rai*, the final syllable of each unit is rhymed to a non-final syllable in the next unit; the passage can be of any length; and the ending is

---

15. This discussion of meter is based on the work of Robert Bickner.

usually announced with a shorter unit of four syllables, and sometimes a final two-syllable flourish.

Khlong has variants of two, three, and four lines. In the four-line variant, each unit may have a 2–4 syllable tailpiece; there are rhymes from the final syllable in certain lines to a non-final syllable in a line below (in various patterns); and tones are used to add rhythm to the lines, especially to create some drama in the final line of the verse. The two- and three-line versions are constructed on similar principles. Scholars have codified the rules for several variants of the form, including the *wiwitthamali* (วิวิธมาลี) variant most commonly used in *Twelve Months*, and graded them in terms of their aesthetic quality, but probably this codification came later, and poets simply varied the meter to suit the content. As Bickner notes, *rai* and the various forms of *khlong* are "simply different variations on the same poetic phenomenon, a five-syllable unit," which in turn is derived from the patterns of everyday speech.[16] Modern printing lays out *rai* and *khlong* in different ways which exaggerate their difference. In old manuscripts, the text was written continuously with only spaces separating lines and a circular "oil-bubble" to mark the beginning of a verse.

A *lilit* is a poem that uses both *rai* and *khlong*. In *Lilit Phra Lo*, *rai* is used more for narration and *khlong* for dialog, but the distinction is far from strict. The *khlong* are mostly the four-line variant. In our translation, we do not identify the meter of each verse, but it can be derived from the line length of the translated verse.[17] *Twelve Months* is in four-line *khlong* except for six lines of *rai* at the end.

16. Bickner, *An Introduction*, 202.

17. If the translated verse is three lines, the original is *khlong song*; if four lines, the original is *khlong si* except for nine verses in *khlong sam* (50, 87, 294, 335, 362, 396, 427, 577, 592); and anything longer is *rai*.

9

We make no attempt to add rhyme, except (for fun and where possible) in a few passages of *Lilit Phra Lo* where a song is being sung. Both works bristle with other figures of speech, especially alliteration, often of high complexity, assonance, and onomatopoeia. Where the opportunity exists, the translation attempts to reflect these devices, but not at the expense of the meaning.

The translations are line for line. We make an exception for forms of address, which may be shifted between lines and even omitted if the sense is not compromised. Any other departure from the line-for-line rule is flagged in the notes.

In the original of *Lilit Phra Lo*, there is no indication of which passages are dialog and who is the speaker in each case. These facts have to be determined from the context, and are sometimes unclear or ambiguous. We have added quotation marks to indicate dialog, and sometimes added a form of address to help identify the speaker.

In *Twelve Months*, the phrasing is extremely terse, perhaps imitating the Pali-Sanskrit verse that literati would have studied. Pali and Sanskrit are inflected languages in which the case, number, and gender of a noun and the tense and person of a verb are indicated by the endings of the words. The meanings are very precise. Thai, however, has no inflection. Variations such as the tense of a verb and the case of a noun are supplied through syntax, especially through supplementary words and through word order. In the compressed form used for this poetry, these supplementary words are often omitted, and the word order adjusted for the sake of the meter or euphony. As a result, the lines often require some expansion by the reader or listener. Renderings of *Twelve Months* in modern Thai are generally two to three times longer than the original in syllable count because of these additions. For some lines, the imaginative expansion by the reader may have several results. Possibly a reciter would have reduced the ambiguity by the way the line was read—through pause and emphasis.

In our translation, some words have to be added to be readable in English, but we have restricted these to prepositions, conjunctions, articles, auxiliary parts of verbs, and pronouns. We do not add or subtract nouns, verbs, adjectives, or adverbs, though sometimes verbs and adjectives are expanded to convey multiple shades of meaning in the original, and sometimes the subject is repeated from an earlier line for clarity. Where these rules occasionally are broken to make the English readable, the additions are confessed in the footnotes. Punctuation is minimal.

Because of this need for expansion, because many words are unknown today or capable of more than one interpretation, and because errors may have been introduced during the copying of manuscripts, many lines of *Twelve Months* can be interpreted in multiple ways. Where possible we have retained some ambiguity in the English, but in practice this is usually difficult. Where there are significantly different interpretations of a line, we mention these in a footnote.

As those working in meter often do, we have invented several new words and mangled old ones, but hopefully with meanings that are easily understood. We have also invented names of flora and fauna to approximate the similes in the original.

The section headings do not appear in the originals of either work. In the footnotes, Thai words from the text are given in the spelling found in the original, which sometimes differs from the modern spelling. Where there is a note on a Thai term derived from Pali-Sanskrit, the note gives the Thai version, followed by English transcription in italics, followed by the Pali-Sanskrit transcription in roman, for example, อริยสัจ, *ariyasat*, ariyasacca. In cases where the transcription seems closer to Sanskrit than to Pali, the transcription is preceded by "S:". Transcription of Thai words follows the Royal Society/RTGS system with the exception of using "j" for จ, *jo jan*. Thai personal names are given in the owner's preferred English form where that is known.

In respect for both works' origin in a tradition of oral performance, we have tried to make the translations "read well." We have repeatedly read the English translations aloud, alongside the original Thai. To free the text of academic clutter, we have borrowed the notation system from the Oxford editions of world classics.

This translation of *Lilit Phra Lo* is based on Cholada Ruengruglikit's edition of the Fine Arts Department text, while taking account of variations in the manuscript versions noted by Chanthit Krasaesin and Robert Bickner, and the interpretations by Plueang na Nakhon and Phra Worawet Phisit.[18] The Ministry of Education edition divided the text into verses and gave them numbers, which have become canonical. We follow this layout. Bickner has identified some verses that appear in most manuscripts but not in the Ministry edition. We include these verses, with a note.

This translation of *Twelve Months* is based on the 2017 edition by Trongjai Huntangkura while taking account of the earlier work by Chanthit Krasaesin and Maneepin Phromsuthirak.[19] The team producing the 2017 edition included Winai Pongsripian, Trongjai

---

18. The editions by both the Fine Arts Department and Ministry of Education have no explanation of what manuscripts were used. According to Bickner, the Ministry of Education edition contains some wording that cannot be traced back to any of the manuscripts. In the Fine Arts Department's 1997 printing, the spelling was updated "to conform to the Royal Institute dictionary, 1982 edition" (Fine Arts Department, *Wannakam samai ayutthaya lem 1*, 11).

19. Panit and Maneepin made an English translation for an ASEAN project in 1999, and Winai contributed an English translation to Trongjai's 2017 volume.

Hutangkura, Samoe Bunma, and Natthaphon Yurungruangsak.[20] Samoe is a Sanskritist while the other three are historians with an interest in literature and literary history. This team has an impressive command of languages, including Pali, Sanskrit, Khmer, Old Khmer, Lao, and Lanna Thai. They are able to unscramble several lines where the obscure vocabulary has crippled earlier attempts. *Twelve Months* has a particularly large number of words from Khmer, not so much the royal and technical terms found in other Thai works but everyday words.

Acknowledgments

We owe a special debt to the editors of the principal editions that we have used, namely Cholada Ruengruglikit for *Lilit Phra Lo*, and Trongjai Hutangkura and Winai Pongsripian for *Twelve Months*. We also honor the memory of Chanthit Krasaesin for his pioneering work on both texts.

In 2011, shortly after meeting Robert (Bob) Bickner in Madison, Wisconsin, we read his working translation of *Lilit Phra Lo* and sent some comments, though at that stage we had not studied the Thai original. In 2016, we decided to make our own translation, and completed the first pass without consulting his version again. In mid-2017, we told him of our project and urged him to publish his translation first. He responded very warmly to this suggestion, and we have cooperated since. We are very grateful to him and Khun Patcharin Peyasantiwong.

---

20. Other members of the team are Sayam Phathranuprawat (anthropologist), Phongsathon Buakhampan (epigrapher), Wannawiwat Ratanalam (linguist), Nichanan Nanthasirison (folklorist), Sasithorn Sinvuttaya (anthropologist), and Jakkri Phothimani (anthropologist).

We owe special thanks to Xiong Ran, co-translator of *Lilit Phra Lo* into Chinese.

We owe a great debt to those who have helped an economist and historian in the world of literature, especially Niyada Lausunthorn, Duangmon (Paripunna) Jitjamnong, Rachel Harrison, Caroline Hau, Susan Morgan, and Ruth Morse. We are very grateful to Peter Skilling, Samerchai Poolsuwan, U Thein Lwin, Elizabeth Moore, Lilian Handlin, Piriya Krairiksh, Cholthira Satyawadhna, Justin McDaniel, Arthid Sheravanichkul, and Noor Azlina Yunus for their technical help and their encouragement. Thanks also to Craig Reynolds, Soison Sakolrak, Nathan McGovern, Patrick Jory, Sun Laichen, Simon Creak, Thanapol Limapichart, David Atherton, Umaporn Soetphunnuek, Parkpume Vanichaka, and Claudio Sopranzetti. Thanks as ever to Trasvin Jittidecharak and Silkworm Books.

Lilit Phra Lo

Introduction

Invocation

May fortune, victory, power, success befall   1
the city great whose peerless power spans the skies.
The world does quake in awful dread
and cower 'fore its might,
which subjugates directions all,
attacking forcefully,
destroying cities great,
dispatching Lao and Kao,
heads lopped by sword
and writhing bodies strewn around.   /10
The Yuan face defeat!
The Lao are killed!
The Thai, with victory won,
return to their great land.
The people celebrate success.
The royal wealth is swelled
by more auspicious properties
in every region of the earth.
The populace is joyful and content.
The world entire exults!   /20

1/1   **May fortune ...** ศรีสิทธิฤทธิชัย, *si sitthi ruetthi chai*, S: śrī siddhi ṛddhi jaya. Similar strings of "auspicious words" are found at the start of *Ongkan chaeng nam*, the early Ayutthaya text of the water oath of loyalty, and on several inscriptions from Cambodia ("Lilit ongkan chaeng nam," 7; Coedès, *Inscriptions du Cambodge*, I, 19; VI, 133).

1/8   **Lao and Kao** ลาวกาว, *laokao*. It is not clear whether this means two groups or one. Lao is a word used loosely by Siamese to refer to Tai-speaking peoples outside Siam (roughly equivalent to the Central Plain of Thailand today), particularly those in Lanna and modern-day Laos. Kao is a name used by the early Tai settlers in and around Nan and also by some around Luang Prabang.

1/11-2   **Yuan ... Lao** Yuan is a term for the people of Lanna, probably derived from an old name for the region, Yonok. From the 1430s to 1540s, Ayutthaya fought sporadic battles with Lanna.

1/15   **royal wealth** ราชสมบัติ, *ratchasombat*. A term that includes the realm.

The city, Si Ayodhaya,
the acme of the world,
the nine-gem royal seat,
abode of joy,
utmost in rank across the earth,
is perfect as the heavens made anew.

By merit made the sovereign king sustains the world 2
with lasting joy and happiness in large degree.
The pleasures of Ayodhaya exceed what's told.
All lands admire and oft-times sing its praise.

On man and woman knowing all the arts, 3
here's told in verse of excellent Phra Lo
more sweetly than has e'er been told before,
alike a flute that soothes and snares the heart.

The sound when sung, none can compare. 4
Just hear its music—rivals none are known.

1/21-4 The city … joy พระนครศรีอโยธยา มหาดิลกภพ นพรัตนราชธานีบุรีรมย์, *phranakhon si ayotthaya mahadilokphop nopharattana rachathani buriram*. These four lines appear in the title of the city in *Phrakat phraratchaphrarop*, the preface to the Three Seals Law and elsewhere (*Kotmai tra sam duang*, I, 1; Winai, *Ayutthaya*, 29, n. 2). The capital's name was originally spelled Ayodhaya, following Rama's capital in the Ramayana, but is believed to have been adjusted to Ayutthaya, meaning "undefeated" or "invincible," as a show of defiance after the fall of the city to Pegu in 1569.

1/23 nine-gem นพรัตน, *nopharat*. A conventional term conveying extreme riches. The nine are usually listed as diamond, ruby, emerald, topaz, garnet, sapphire, moonstone, zircon, and lapis lazuli.

1/26 heavens made anew ฟ้าฟื้น, *fa fuen*, "heaven/gods revived/made anew." This refers to the regeneration of the world after a Buddhist era has ended in a cataclysmic fire. Among the regalia of Khun Borom, the hero-ancestor of Lao legend, was a pike of this name, provided by Phya Thaen, the creator-god. The term is also used for thunder and lightning, especially prior to a storm. In *Khun Chang Khun Phaen*, Khun Phaen gives this name to a powerful sword he forges (Baker and Pasuk, *The Tale of Khun Chang Khun Phaen*, 320; Souneth, "The Nidān Khun Borom," 126).

3 flute ปี่ลู้, *pi lu*. *Pi* are blown woodwind instruments, and *lu* is perhaps a Lao version often called *khlui* (ขลุ่ย).

> This verse, well-buffed to lure and lull the heart,
> is offered to Your Majesty, king meritful and great.

Two cities and their rulers

> Here's told about a valiant lord   5
> by name Maen Suang,
> a sovereign, royal ruler
> of Suang City, king of rank,
> who has a beauteous major wife
> by name the Queen Bunluea
> of perfect noble lineage;
> and consorts young and beautiful;
> and palace ladies, every branch;
> a host of ministers;   /10
> a mass of elephants and horse;
> and troops throughout the realm,
> all soldiers brave,
> attending on the king in throngs;
> and many subject cities of high rank.
> This monarch has one son, a youth,
> by name Phra Lo, a gem beneath the sky.
> Within this world, towards the west
> this territory is found.

> There is one more great lord,   6
> a king by name
> Phimphisakhon,
> the city-lord of Song.
> The wealth of these two kings
> is vast and equal both.

5/2   **Maen Suang** For notes on all the names, see Cast of Characters below.

5/8-9   **consorts ... palace ladies** พระสนม ... กำนัล, *phra sanom ... kamnan.* These two terms are sometimes considered synonyms but appear to be different here. The *sanom* consorts are referred to below as the king's "friends in joy." The *kamnan* are ladies in the palace staff.

Towards the eastern side,
this king of rank holds sway.
He has a son, renowned as brave,
by name Phichai Phitsanukon.   /10
And when this son is grown,
the king sends men to ask
a lady born of noble line
by name Darawadi,
a maiden beautiful,
to be the prince's queen.
This son thus has a loving wife,
attractive to the eye,
and soon has daughters, two,
the darlings of the royal pair,   /20
both pretty as the moon,
called Lady Phuean and Lady Phaeng.
To tell, they look sublime,
in every detail, beauties seen
that touch and snare the heart.

There comes a time, Maen Suang,   7
great king, does summon forth
the lords of subject cities, says:
"Song City's king's too bold.
Without delay we'll go to war
and seize his realm as subject state.
Have troops called up at once."
The unit chiefs convene
and, once the army is prepared,
the king leads out the troops   /10
proceeding from the capital
in columns marching forth,
comes quickly to the battleground

7/6 **subject state** เมืองออก, *mueang ook*. A dependency.

with hordes of tuskers, horse, and men
that swamp the surface of the earth.

Now lord and king   8
Phimphisakhon,
when he hears word
that King Maen Suang
has brought his forces to attack,
he sends out troops
in streams to mount defense
and goes himself without delay.
The vanguards clash,
cleavers brandished, hack and slash,   /10
sabers brandished, cut and thrust.
In unison, the pikemen hurl.
In unison, the pikemen swarm ahead.
To left they fight without retreat,
to right they fight without reverse,
the brave against the brave compete to kill,
the bold against the bold compete to win.
At quarters close, they hurl, they stab,
attack, defend, deploy, assault,
and loudly cheer for victory.   /20
The sound of gunfire booms around
and shakes the earth's own crust.
From bows and crossbows massed
fly arrows, darts, and shafts.
The strong assault the strong with force.
Tuskers clash with tuskers.
Horses swirl to join the fray.
Their troops now charge with stabbing spears,
advance at speed in massive force
towards Phimphisakhon,   /30

8/21   gunfire ปืนไฟ, *puen fai.* Chinese gunpowder technology reached mainland Southeast
Asia by the early to mid-fifteenth century (Sun, "Military Technology Transfers").

who's slashed down on his tusker's neck.
His army chiefs come wheeling round
to shield the royal corpse,
and speed back to his capital
to bring the royal corpse inside,
then throw the bolts to close his gates.

The capital is saved   9
by Phichai Phitsanukon's defense.
He makes Maen Suang withdraw;
installs himself as ruler of the realm;
cremates his royal father's corpse;
and sends his pretty daughters two
to occupy one palace with the dowager
along with two smart, clever maids,   /10
to whom the king gives cheerful names
as Ruen and Roi,
to take care of the princesses.
Their majesties, the royal pair,
reside within the major royal residence.

Introducing Phra Lo

And then Maen Suang,   10
great king of high repute,
requests the hand of Laksanawadi,
a lady bright and beautiful,
to give sublime Phra Lo,
exalted as his major wife,
with retinues of consorts,
and palace ladies, every branch,

9/9 **dowager** The widow of King Phimphisakhon, never named, referred to as ย่า, *ya*, a paternal grand-relative, though we learn in the finale (v. 607) that she is not the mother of Phichai Phitsanukon and thus not the grandmother of the princesses.

9/11 **cheerful names** Ruen (รื่น) means happy or fresh and Roi (โรย) means cheerful or outgoing in Northern Thai.

and all accouterments in full.
Then when his father, ruling king,   /10
retires to heaven's realm,
Phra Lo ascends to rule.
His fitting handsome mien
both earth and sky eternally admire,
his beauty more sublime
than lords of any other land.

Had Indra dropped down from the skies   11
to show his body to the world
for people to admire?

His body rounded, slender, slight,   12
slim-waisted, elegant,
is beautiful in every part.

His looks excel in all three worlds,   13
superb in every facet, aspect, prospect—
a captivating sight.

Word spreads across the world   14
as traveling traders, every one,
recount his looks with praise:

"The shining moon that lights the sky—   15
if you've not seen Phra Lo's fine face,
just view the moon, they are the same.

His eyes are like the eyes of golden deer.   16
O, see his eyebrows shaped
as finely curved as arched bows.

12   **rounded** กลม, *klom*. Fleshy and robust, not scrawny.
13   **three worlds** สามแผ่น, *sam phaen*. The cosmology of Theravada Buddhism divides the
universe into three parts: the world of desire, the world with form, and the world
without form (Reynolds and Reynolds, *Three Worlds*). The term is also used loosely, as
here, to mean "everywhere."

O, see his pretty ears as neat   17
as petals of a lotus flower,
his cheeks like gold *maprang*.

His nose, as fit for royalty,   18
seems conjured by a deity
to be like Kama's goad.

His mouth is fairer than if drawn   19
and seems to smile eternally.
So beautiful, his mouth!

See his chin, so fitting, fine.   20
See his neck, as rounded as if cast;
two shoulders luring love;
his breast alike a lion's chest;
his arm, a tusker's trunk;
his fingers, long with curly nails.
Superb is he, each limb, each part,
from foot to top of head,
with hair of beauty, every strand.
His looks are fitting for a king   /10
in every way."

The princesses fall in love

In cities all they sing his praise in chants,   21
and spread Phra Lo's repute across the land.
The young king's handsomeness astounds the world.
Young folk who hear can only yearn, made mad.

---

17 **maprang** (มะ)ปราง. *Bouea macrophylla*, a fruit related to the mango, the size and shape of a small chicken egg, with a fine smooth skin that turns from yellow to orange when ripe; sometimes called a Marian plum or mango plum; common simile for a good complexion.

18 **Kama's goad** ขอกาม, *kho kam*. Kama, the god of love, uses a goad to draw couples together.

The news about his beauty spreads to Song,   22
and to the ears of sisters two, who wilt
just like a golden vine, heartsore to see his face,
lamenting in their room, ears pricked for news.

The Princess Phaeng and Princess Phuean, love-struck,   23
their minds absorbed in thoughts of him,
suspect they have been dazed by some device,
made limp and languid, faces sunk in gloom.

When Ruen and Roi come up to visit them,   24
they find the couple dark like fever-sick.
"Most days you look as bright as shining moons.
Please tell us why you're gloomy in this way."

"A fever can be cured with physic easily.   25
But fevers strange as this no one can treat.
A fevered heart—'tis better just to die.
Please ponder this, and wait to see our pyre."

"We hear but cannot understand.   26
O sisters two, your majesties,
explain please what is up.

If something's troubling you,   27
O ladies two, your majesties,
tell us the task to do."

"The pain is graver than the earth is wide.   28
Should news be spread across the world,
where could we show our faces—tell.

---

22   **golden vine** (เถา)วัลย์ทอง, (*thao*)*wan thong*. The image is a climbing plant that has been uprooted or torn from its support.

23   **suspect** ... A difficult line. Bickner (personal communication) proposes, "they even imagined that they could see him, and so were bewildered." Chanthit (*Prachum wannakhadi*, 39) proposes, "they want to see him but feign so others are confused."

No one could ease the shame—
the shame at those who laugh.
To die is better than such infamy.
Don't question us, you two.
The pain's too much to talk about.
O, if you care for us,
don't ask again and make us die as one."   /10

"We beg to pledge our lives!   29
We've served you close and faithfully.
Why then do you trust us
less than one strand of hair?
Or do your highnesses
not care for us at all?"

"The news that's talked about is news of what?   30
The news is praising who across the land?
Were you asleep, not wont to wake, you two?
Go think it out yourselves. Don't question us!"

"About this thing, our mistresses, don't fret.   31
We beg to undertake to sort it out,
to somehow bring this lord to tryst with you.
We'll send a message so he knows somehow."

"That thinking breaches custom! 'Twould bring shame—   32
the lady asks the man to her abode!
'Twould cause us pain. We'd rather die.
We love the lord; the lord does not know us at all."

"We erred, but we can think again.   33
We'll find a scheme that's right and suitable.

---

30 **The news** ... This verse is quoted in the seventeenth-century manual of prosody *Jindamani* (32) as an example of *khlong si* verse. Today, literary scholars assume it has the ideal pattern of rhyme and tone for the *suphap* (genteel) form of this verse, and schoolchildren learn it by heart.

We'll seek somewhere a doctor weird with power
to slyly charm the lord so he can't stay away."

The ladies inwardly approve,   34
but outwardly, they say they don't,
forbidding them: "That's very wrong!
Your thinking is not good.
If people knew—then terrible!
Disgrace for daughters of a king,
found fault across the world.
Where could we show our faces then?"
The maids can understand this well,
can see the meaning of the pair,   /10
that in their hearts they do not disapprove.
"We'll do what should be done
about what's troubling them,
and any fault may fall on us."
They say, "Your highnesses serene,
you both won't know a thing.
Leave us to get it done.
This time we'll do no wrong.
If two of us can't think it out,
then why should your two ladyships   /20
still keep us as your maids?

We'll have some palace staff,   35
close friends and good at heart,
go off to buy and sell,
and on their travels round
to praise the beauty of two princesses
throughout the city of Phra Lo,
to sing the glories of

33   **doctor weird** มดหมอ, *mot mo*. *Mo*, doctor, is a term for anyone with expertise and learning; *mot* may come from the Pali mata, meaning "dead" and be a reference to spirits; "weird" is used here in the sense that the witches in Macbeth call themselves "weird sisters."

two daughters of a king, a lord of elephants,
whose truly winsome charms
there's none can match."

/10

"All cities have king's children numerous,   36
but with these royal sisters, none compare—
the Princess Phaeng of great felicity
and Princess Phuean as pretty as the moon.

They look like droplets come from sky to earth,   37
like Indra's lovely angels visiting.
Wish not, hope not for what is hard to have.
Admire these buds of merit with a smile.

O lords and nobles all from cities all,   38
let not your thoughts be fired by love.
'Tis merit past that makes this pair shine bright;
a king of merit, thus, is fit for them."

The praises of the pair are sung   39
in every place, in every land.
Phra Lo thus hears the news.

And having heard their fame,   40
he quickly has the singers brought
into his hall of audience.

There learning of the youthful pair,   41
his highness yearns for them,
his heart abrim with pride.

35/10 **lord of elephants** เจ้าช้าง, *jao chang*. An epithet for a king, perhaps meaning the
lord of the *white* elephant, the palladium of kings.

36 **"All cities ...** The next three verses are the song sung in praise of the princesses,
though this is not announced in the text.

37 **angels** อัปสร, *apson*, S: apsara. Heavenly maidens, a metaphor for beauty.

41 **pride** He is proud to be identified as the king of great merit in the song.

He muses to himself,   42
"If I have made great merit then
perhaps I'll go to tryst with them."

The praising of the sisters two   43
has touched the monarch's heart.
He gives rewards
of courtly cloth and clothes.
"I thank you greatly for this news.
Your words do captivate.

What shall I do   44
to tryst with two
young lovely princesses?"

The lord composes verse,   45
a royal verse so pleasing
that truly none compares:

"I've heard them tell the news so earnestly,   46
I feel as if I see your loveliness,
two perfect golden lotuses of mine,
lain flesh to flesh each side in sweet caress."

One hand he rests upon his brow;   47
one strokes his breast with tenderness.
He acts this play for them to see.

Then after this charade,   48
he has them victualed well,
and they take leave. On reaching home,
with faces bright and fresh,
they go to tell maids Ruen and Roi

43/4 **courtly cloth** สนอบ, *sanop*. Cloth presented by a king.
48 **them** Meaning the singers who brought news of Phra Lo.

what happened, everything.
The two maids then
attend upon the two of silken skin
and tell the news in full.

Old Lord Tiger Spirit

Finding an adept

The maids then seek a sorceress.   49
They contact those with fearful medicine,
select one having sacred power,
an adept skilled in charms,
and tell the scheme to her in full,
that if she helps achieve success,
they'll give great wealth,
reward her handsomely;
and once Phra Lo has trysted with the pair,
the sorceress will live in state   /10
far better than the rest,
beyond compare.

On hearing this, the woman shakes her head.   50
"Enchanting—I've done only common folk.
A world-lord, if I try,
it will not work, my child."

"But do you know of one who could?   51
Please help, please point
the proper way and we will go."

She says, "I've met them all,   52
know each and every one,

49/2   **fearful medicine** ยาย่ำ, *ya yam*, "medicine-fear." Here meaning the supernatural arts in general.

50   **world-lord** เจ้าหล้า, *jao la*. An epithet of a king.

all hopeless, lacking skill,
except we three, the aged ones,
the ancient crones, the great adepts.
If we enchant someone, he comes;
if we send someone off, he goes—
except the lords of sky and earth.
They know the skills, the arts.
They have the merit and the power.   /10
Our sorcery may not come close.
For these two princesses—cannot.
We likely won't succeed.

But then I know   53
three doctors of real power,
who know the potent lore—
the pupils of Lord Tiger Spirit."
The woman tells the way,
takes them to a lane, then leaves.
The maids go in to meet
Old Sage, a great adept.
They pay respect, and tell him all,
then beg him help their cause.   /10
He speaks just like the sorceress:
"My standing is still low.
Enchanting only common folk,
my spells and ghouls are just enough.
Lords of the land, kings of the world—
there's no one who'll succeed."
Dismayed at hearing this, the maids

52/4 we three. The next three phrases can be read as descriptions of three different
people, or (as here) a collective description of all three.

53/1 But then ... These opening lines can be read as a further plea by the maids ("What
can we do to meet three doctors ...").

53/8 Old Sage ปู่หมอเฒ่า, *pu mo tao*, "grandfather-doctor-old." This could be a description
rather than a name, and he is often referred to using the same prefix as Old Lord Tiger
Spirit (ปู่ *pu* or ปู่เจ้า *pu jao*), but in this translation is called Old Sage throughout.

implore, "Please let us know
of someone with the power, the skill,
the strength, the potency,   /20
who maybe can enchant a king.
We'll offer wealth in heaps.
We'll offer gold in crores.
Who gives the name will profit too.
Please tell us quickly now,
so we may know his face.
And speak sincerely, sir."

He says, "Beneath the sky,   54
throughout the world, there's none
that bears comparison
to him—Old Lord Tiger Spirit.
If he says, 'Die!', they die before your eyes.
If he says, 'Live!', they come to life at once.
Who he enchants, they come as called.
Who he seeks out, cannot stay still
and comes to him as bid.
Leave it to me to lead you there.   /10
The way is far and takes some time.
It's evening now, go home, you two.
Tomorrow morning hasten here."
The two maids take their leave
and go to tell the princesses,
who both are very pleased.

The two young beauties, once they hear the news,   55
are glad as if the lord were on his way.
They laugh like lotus blooms in sunny beams,
but fear their plan may leak with bad result.

The pair act smart to keep things under wraps   56
by using tricks to mask and hide

---

53 **crores** โกฏิ, *kot*. A unit of ten million.

their secret deep by slyly acting properly
in open sight so bad's disguised as good.

The maids, who have a plan, are still unsure,   57
and so pile ploy on ploy in no small way.
They *wai* the dowager: "The grandmisses
are strangely sad, both faces sunk in gloom.

A seer looked, advised, 'Call back their souls.   58
Their souls are weak; they wander 'cross the sky;
they tour all hills and forests. Quickly now,
call back their souls. Tomorrow morning's good.' "

Upon this news, the dowager's distressed.   59
"Make haste, you maids. Attend upon the king,
their father, sovereign lord of solar race."
The maids pay court and tell him everything.

Once told, the king is troubled and concerned: 60
"Whate'er the seer wants, provide at once."
"We'll fetch him from his mount to call their souls.
The seer's said he'd like a speedy elephant."

The maids return from audience   61
and tell their highnesses, the pair,

---

56 **The pair** ... Worawet, *Khumue lilit phra lo* (I, 41–42) interprets this verse and the next
differently, roughly: The princesses still pretend they do not like the maids' plan, hide
their own hopes, and state openly that the plan is wrong in order to put on a proper
appearance; the maids are perplexed; the princesses thus try another scheme by
going to see the dowager, looking sad, and telling her about the seer.

57 **dowager** See v. 9.

58 **call their souls** รับขวัญ, *khwan.* In Thai traditional belief, the body and its various
elements, usually numbered as thirty-two, all have a *khwan* or spiritual representation.
In cases of illness or psychological trouble, the *khwan* are believed to have deserted
the body for some reason and have to be called back by ceremony.

58 **good** วันดี, *wan di.* A good day, meaning an auspicious time according to astrology or
some other predictive method.

60 **We'll fetch** ... The last two lines of this verse are spoken by Ruen and Roi.

who listen, hearts awash with joy.
"Go quick tomorrow! Help us fast, you two!

Request the royal tuskers, Like-the-Wind   62
and Holy Storm, who live up to their names.
You'll like their pace which truly is superb.
The more you drive them, faster they will go."

At cockcrow, quickly harnessed up,   63
an elephant is brought each side
along the ladies' mounting stage.

Before the streaks of dawn, the maids   64
say, "Mistresses, get everything prepared
for when Old Lord will come.

We take our leave, your highnesses.   65
If we delay till dawn,
'twill be too late. The way is long."

They mount the elephants, set off,   66
and fade from sight along the road.
At midpoint on his lane,
Old Sage is there and sees them come.
At speed he conjures how he looks
to be a young and handsome man.
The two arrive and ask about Old Sage.
He laughs and smiles a smile,
then says, "You pretty pair,
what place have you come from?"

Agog to know, they speculate: 67
"Is this the son or grandson of Old Sage?
Or who? So handsome! Oh!"

---

62 **Like-the-Wind and Holy Storm** เทียมลม พระพายุ, *thiam lom* and *phra phayu*.

In part, they're stirred by lusty thoughts.   68
In part, they fret that if they're late,
their mistresses will sicken.

But soon, the semblance that they see   69
becomes Old Sage's ancient form.
This revelation stuns the two.
"None else can rival you, Old Sage!
Please help two daughters of the king,
so we don't need to look elsewhere."

"When there's no fire, who'd stoke a firefly.   70
My knowledge and my power are small.
Did you not know?"

They call Old Sage to mount   71
and ride their elephant behind.
All three then go at speed,
towards the verdant hills.
They look and see the road far off,
a-wending through the woods and hills,
among wild sugar, kans-grass, vetiver,
margosa groves, and rosewood trees,
and stands of *yung* and *yang*,

---

68 sicken ป่วย, *puai*. Chanthit (*Prachum wannakhadi*, 88) assumes this is short for ป่วยการ, *puai kan*, making the line, "their mistresses' plan will come to nought."

70 **When there's no fire** ... Proverb, meaning "don't do something pointless out of frustration."

71/4 **verdant hills** เขาเขียว, *khao khieo*. This could be a proper name, Green Hill.

71/7 **wild sugar** ... แฝก, *faek*, *Vetiveria zizanioides*, vetiver grass; แขม, *khaem*, *Saccharum arundinaceum*, a reed in the sugar family; เลา, *lao*, *Saccharum spontaneum*, kans grass. All three are tall, coarse grasses.

71/8 **margosa** ... **rosewood** ประเดา, *pradao*, usually สะเดา, *sadao*, *Azadirachta indica*, margosa or nim; and ประดู่, *pradu*, *Pterocarpus macrocarpus*, Burmese rosewood.

71/9 **yung and yang** ไม้ยางไม้ยูง, *mai yang mai yung*. *Dipterocarpus grandiflorus* and *Dipterocarpus alatus*, a conventional way of referring to the various dipterocarps found in the dry forests.

tall ironwoods that pierce the haze,   /10
phayom in flower, as high as clouds,
and plants of many types
with vines entwining twigs
and budding leaves on many trees.
Wind blows in gusts.
Plants put out blooms in strings and sprays,
and buds encase the pollen dust.
Flowers blossom everywhere,
their scents allure, inspire,
and fruits are luscious yellow-ripe.   /20
Young leaves and sturdy trunks
have twig and branch entwined so prettily.

They travel on and soon   72
they reach the foothills' base;
see monkey, lemur, gibbon, colugo;
hear spirits' frightful cries,
that make their hair stand up in fear.
Here tigers prowl and peer around;
horn-tossing ox and rhino block the way;
herds of gaur tour the woods;
wild cattle crop on leaves;
bears roam in packs;   /10
cow elephants come past
in countless numbers, trailing males;
a deadly snake unfolds its hood;
a python coils a buffalo;
serow climb up a slope;

71/11   **phayom** พะยอม. *Shorea roxburghii*, white meranti, a tall dipterocarp.
72/3   **colugo** บ่าง, *bang. Cynocephalus variegatus*, similar to a flying squirrel.
72/8   **gaur** กระทิง, *krating. Bos gaurus*, a massive wild buffalo of dark gray or black color,
          weighing around a ton when fully grown.
72/10   **bears ... packs** หมู่หมี, *mu mi.* Some manuscripts omit the tone mark on *mu*, so this
          means "boars and bears."
72/15   **serow** เยียงผา, *yiang pha. Naemorhedus sumatraensis*, goat antelope, southern serow;
          a small goat antelope found mainly in steep limestone terrain.

and deep within the hills,
more beasts of many species lurk.
Old Sage walks on without a fear,
through the forests, further in,
fast forging 'long the way.   /20

Have pity for two frightened maids,   73
as, breasts a-shiver, heads a-shake,
and hearts a-thump,
they hurry-scurry after him.
They see the waterways and ponds,
the lakes, canals, and streams,
where crocodiles lurk by the banks,
heads poking up and peering round;
and water-tuskers stab at shadow-shapes;
and serpents drag men down below,   /10
with bodies wriggling, squirming,
eyes a-goggle, rolling, wide,
choked dead with their own hair.
From tops of trees
come sounds of barn owls' angry hoots,
of fish owls muttering,
of scops owls calling out in pairs
to echo through the forest like a roar,
that heard afar and faint still scares.

73/9   **water-tuskers** ช้างน้ำ, *chang nam*. It was believed that there was an aquatic species
       of elephant.
73/10 **serpents** เงือก, *ngueak*. A mythical water creature, sometimes with a human body
       and fish tail.
73/15 **barn owl** แสก, *saek. Tyto alba*; "Voice: long screech" (Boonsong and Cronin, *Birds of
       Thailand*, 104).
73/16 **fish owls** ทึงทูด, *thingthut. Ketupa zeylonensis*, brown fish owl; "Voice: a succession
       of deep mutterings, rising to a maniacal chuckle" (Boonsong and Cronin, *Birds of
       Thailand*, 109).
73/17 **scops owls** เค้ากู่, *khao-ku. Otus bakkamoena*, collared scops owl; "Voice: short
       descending hoot ... repeated for hours; strange human-like quality" (Boonsong and
       Cronin, *Birds of Thailand*, 106). The author of this passage clearly knew the calls of
       various owls.

Old Sage just laughs, /20
consoles the two: "Don't be alarmed.
It's nothing, miss.
These tricks were done
by our Old Lord himself!"
Old Sage is not afraid of anything.
He drives the tusker fast uphill.
They come not far behind.
Arriving at the mountain's foot,
Old Sage dismounts the elephant
and leaves the maids far off, /30
while he goes in to meet
Old Lord Tiger Spirit.
He raises hands, prostrates,
and tells about the princesses,
good Phuean and golden Phaeng.

"These two, as sick as sky is high, 74
came begging me
to bring their two maids here."

Old Lord replies, "Old Sage, 75
go call them close.
There's nothing here to fear."

Old Sage informs the pair, 76
"Old Lord has asked you in.
Please go to meet him now."

They see a tiger, crouching there. 77
Alarmed, both bow and kneel,
prostrate to pay respect.

---

77 **a tiger** Chanthit (*Prachum wannakhadi*, 103) suggests there are two tigers, but the text
is not clear how many there are.

They stare unblinking at the beast,   78
and see the tiger change into a cat
with beautiful bright stripes.
And then they see Old Lord
become a gray-haired man,
eyebrows and lashes white,
then change into a handsome youth,
as shapely as if crafted, made,
with body slender, tall, and fine,
alike a smiling rogue,   /10
with looks to make one laugh or weep.
He turns again to one of middle age
of good physique
and manner humble and refined.
The pair then offer up
all things prepared and brought,
and pass the message from two princesses:
"Our ladyships prostrate to pay respect
here at your feet, O lord.

Their hardship's heavy as the sky.   79
They look to you, O sire,
to you and you alone, Old Lord.

They had us hasten here since morn   80
to ask you, sire,
to purge the pain of both.

Please carry out this task   81
and heaps of silver, gold,
and varied gems they beg to give.

78/3   beautiful bright stripes แถวจราสศุภลักษณ์, *taeo jarat suphalak*. Here *jarat* may mean
"whole body" rather than "bright."

78/10   rogue ลักเลง, *lakleng*. Usually *nakleng* and meaning a ruffian or gangster, but here
clearly positive. The term *leng* comes from an old Khmer word meaning to joke, flirt,
show off, deceive, or act rashly.

Desire for love is burning them.   82
Please help entice the king,
Phra Lo, so they escape from death."

Old Lord does not reply one word,   83
but spends a little while
to look with insight, questioning:
"Should I help them or not?"
He knows then everything,
that fruit of karma from the past
has made things tight and loose,
and what's to come cannot be stopped—
the end is quick, the death is quick,
a fruit of karma of their own.   /10
But both, he sees, in times before
made merit to safeguard their lives
and asked to count upon his merit too.
With this insight Old Lord then says,
"You ladies should not talk
of payment and reward.
I'll go to meet the pair
where they reside.
Return there first, you two,
and let them hear this news.   /20
I'll go there later, 'fore too long.
If not within today,
tomorrow I'll arrive."

Two maids appreciate his words   84
and *wai* acceptance endlessly,
then offer their reply:
"Our thanks, Old Lord, your words

83/7　**tight and loose** ทำหย่อนหย่อนตึงตึง, *tham yon yon tueng tueng.* Literally, "make loose-loose tight-tight," meaning "be uneven."

are like a hundred nectar cups
that bathe us in content.

O sire, when we came here,   85
we felt as numb as buried dead—
the birds and beasts along the way,
the spirits and the owls.
May we depend on your own merit, sire,
to free us from this fear."

Old Lord just smiles and laughs,   86
then says, "You pretty pair,
don't be alarmed.

While daylight still, you two   87
must reach the way out from the woods,
then tell your mistresses to wait
if they have things to say."

Soon after, Roi and Ruen   88
pay homage happily, take leave,
and mount the tuskers with Old Sage,
through the foothills wend their way
along the route they came,
chit-chatting, looking round
to view the trees and fine bamboos,
resembling massive palaces,
celestial abodes,
festooned with flowers in red,   /10
that shine like ruby gems
among the fresh green leaves,

---

84 **nectar** อำมฤต, *amrit*, S: amṛta. Divine liquid, the nectar of immortality created during
the churning of the sea of milk; one drop removes all sorrow (Worawet, *Khumue lilit
phra lo*, I, 60).

85/4 **spirits and the owls** สาง, *sang*, either a spirit or a mythical creature similar to a
tiger; แสก (ทิ้ง)ทูด คูดเค้า, *saek, (thing)thut, khutkhao*, barn owl, fish owl, hawk owl.

that gleam like emeralds,
and yellow blooms like pristine gold,
and lots of pearly white,
so bright and colorful.
The varied landscapes passed
are captivating, beautiful.
Descending down to lower land,
they see more plants,   /20
attractive to their watching eyes,
while dulcet to their listening ears
are bird calls to and fro
that echo sweetly through the woods,
like calls to friends and kin.

The sounds of lory, lorikeet,   89
of magpie, coel in flocks,
of starlings, parakeets,
of mynas grouped in pairs,
of drongos, barbets,
ostlers, spying gulls,
of storks in mating mood,
of magpie robins flying, tail-spread,
of martins, eagles, sparrows, coucals, tailorbirds,
of peacocks dancing, feathers fanned   /10
and tails a-bobbing up and down
with peahens gathered round.
Some sand deer nestle close in pairs.
Lamang look round for mates.
The herds and packs are scattered round
with countless elephants,
magnificent and fun to see,
while turtles, tortoise pass unseen,

89/6   **ostlers** โคกม้า, *khokma*. A bird found only in old literature. The name has gone out of use and cannot be identified.

89/14   **lamang** ละมั่ง, *thamin*. *Cervus eldii*, a brow-antlered deer, Elds deer; named after a British Indian army officer in 1844; facing extinction in Thailand now.

and fish and crab of countless types
and birds are everywhere. /20
Some swans swoop down to swim in lakes,
and ducks descend to drift around,
and pelicans pass by a pond.
A parting duck sits hatching eggs.
A cottonteal swims with its mate.
A lotus-stork on lotus lands,
while drowsy, drunken bees
bathe deep in pollen dust.
So many flowers bloom.
Red lotuses that catch the eye /30
are hid among white lilies, smiling wide,
the sacred lotus seven-leafed,
nymph lotus' fragrant blooms,
the lilies red and deepest blue
and white and purple pale.
The former forest fearful is now fun
and full of joy, contentment, happiness.
They drive the tuskers, pacing fast,
arrive close by the palace residence,
and hold a calling for the ladies' souls: /40
"O souls, return, and stay
with their two ladyships.
May they not burn from sun or fire,
and not be fever-struck.

89/24 **parting duck** จากพราก, *jakphrak*. A bird found only in literature with a name meaning "parting" and a fable that the pairs are forced apart and call out to each other at night.

89/26 **lotus-stork** ดอกบัว, *dok bua*. *Mycteria leucocephala*, painted stork; same word as "lotus."

89/32 **seven-leafed** สัตตบรรณบงกช, *sattabongkot* nowadays, but perhaps here the correct original, from Pali: satta paṇṇa paṅkaja, "seven-leaf-born-of-mud." *Nelumbo nucifera*, sacred or Indian lotus.

89/33 **nymph lotus** จงกล, *jongkon*. *Nymphaea lotus*.

Whate'er they wish for, may they have.   90
And may they gain their hearts' desire
to live beside their lover and not part!"

The princesses meet Old Lord Tiger Spirit

Meanwhile the princesses   91
have placed a golden royal seat,
a canopy arrayed above,
fine cushions to recline,
silk drapes with dazzling 'broidery,
rare fragrances and scents,
and flowers of every kind,
in place of popped rice, gems,
and gold and silver flowers,
with foods of every sort—   /10
rice liquor, pleasing snacks—
all done to greet Old Lord,
but made to look like calling souls.

Before they've spoken, suddenly   92
Old Lord arrives
and comes up to the palace first.

The sky looks dark and overcast,   93
as if above were raining dust.
The princesses, unsure at heart,
both raise their hands in *wai*:
"Perhaps Old Lord of ours has come."

They look round for the maids,   94
and, spotting them afar,
feel happy as a city-lord.

91/2 golden royal seat Old Lord Tiger Spirit is received like a king. He is often addressed with the honorific *phra* and with the pronoun *ong*, mostly reserved for royalty and gods.

94 happy as a city-lord ดั่งได้กินเมือง, *dang dai kin mueang*. As if they ate (ruled) a city.

Attendant ladies sit around in flocks.   95
The maids dismount, approach,
prostrate before the princesses.

Their hands in *wai*, the pair look round.   96
"With things this way, perhaps,
Old Lord of ours has come?"

The maids reply, "For sure,   97
Old Lord has come.
Please have no doubt."

To welcome him,   98
all raise clasped hands above their heads,
prostrate to pay respect,

bestrew popped rice and flowers,   99
and offer incense, candles gold,
while speaking words of praise:

"Your glory tops the sky, O lord.   100
Have mercy for us, please,
and let us see you now."

They *wai* a welcome to the guardian god.   101
"Please show your sacred powers, unhid.
Please be our refuge ever more,
Old Lord, and help us to live on."

Forthwith Old Lord reveals himself,   102
his form and face both beautiful,
his figure neither stout nor thin, not young
nor old, his hair, skin, eyes, brows, mouth all elegant.

The princesses admire Old Lord,   103
prostrate and bow to pay respect,

present the offerings prepared:
"Accept these, please, Old Lord."

He sees the pair's intent and loyalty.   104
His kindly heart desires to help.
He takes the gifts they made and gave with care.
On seeing this, the sisters feel content.

The pair prostrate to honor him,   105
and tell in full their deep distress:
"Please help relieve this pain and woe,
achieve, if can be done, what we are longing for.

Nine crores of silver, gems, and gold, we'll give,   106
of each a cartful brought to you,
gilt-horned white cows and buffalo, pig, swan,
duck, chicken, liquor, rice as your deserved reward."

On hearing this, Old Lord responds, "For shame!   107
Don't beg me. This I hate. I'm not for hire.
Your loyalty alone is good, is very good.
Your hardship will be overcome. Fret not.

I'm not some hungry spirit on the prowl,   108
just roaming round and turned up here
to blurt out lies and tales to make you beg,
committing sins for gold in wicked, shameful ways.

I am a lord divine of mountain peaks.   109
The title they have given me, 'Old Lord,'
does mark the mass of merit I have made.
I'll live this world a million years until the era ends.

My gloried powers are fruit of merit made.   110
Good works are capital that cools the heart.
My faculties resemble flowing streams,
that fill the world with perfect excellence.

On seeing you two princesses, my pity's great.   111
I'll help this royal pair. Don't be upset.
I'll call Phra Lo to come and meet you two.
Don't hotly beat your breasts. Just wait for news."

The two prostrate to pay respect, and ask,   112
"How long until this handsome man will come?"
Old Lord replies, "He is no common, lowly type—
a sovereign prince, a man of merit, lord of lands.

Old doctors skilled in thwarting lore are rife.   113
I cannot warrant what you ask.
O children, I will try, and doubt he can escape.
Before too long this king will come to us.

You two young ladies, wait,   114
and should this king seem slow,
send word to let me know."

He tells the pair to wash their hair   115
in water he enchants,
then takes his leave.

They set their eyes to watch Old Lord depart,   116
and in one tick he vanishes from sight
as taken by a puff of wind.

Old Lord Tiger Spirit lures Phra Lo, 1: the wind-ball

Once whisked to home,   117
Old Lord brings bamboo canes
and weaves a wind-ball;
midmost draws the king;

---

113   lore คุณ, *khun*. Supernatural or magic power.
117/2   bamboo canes ไม้เลี้ยงไม้ไล่, *mai liang mai lai*. Two species of thin, thornless bamboo.
117/3   wind-ball ลูกลม, *luklom*. Perhaps something like a takraw ball.

a princess either side,
with both embracing him
and luring him to come;
and yantra circling round,
four pairs around the rim.
Old Lord intones a mantra, sees a tree,   /10
a *yang* tree seven arm-spans girth.
Fist clenched, he flicks to bend
the treetop down to touch the ground.

And when the tree hears Old Lord's words,   118
then Phra Lo's heart's awry.
Old Lord now spears the wind-ball top of tree,
removes his hand, and instantly
the tree's peak rises up,
its leaves all fluttering,
then springs upright.
The ball is spun by breeze
alike a windmill's sails.
Phra Lo, the lord of elephants,   /10
is spun as if by wind.

In dreams he sees the noble Phuean and golden Phaeng,   119
each lying pressed close by his side,
their arms entwined around him tight,
inviting him to speed to Song.

The golden lord awakes from sleep,   120
and shakes as if in tears,
lamenting, lonely, lost.

117/8   yantra ยันต์, *yan.* A graphic device, made by an adept, combining several powerful
symbols: numbers, words in Khmer or Pali, images of gods and powerful animals,
symbols for the Buddha, etc.

117/11   arm-spans อ้อม, *oom.* The distance from fingertip to fingertip with arms
outstretched, a method for measuring the circumference of a large tree.

And when he won't revive,   121
his consorts nudge their friends to look
and see the monarch's freakish state,
then take this strange report
to tell the blessed dam,
his mother, of the news.
With troubled heart,
she goes to find her son,
and sees he's wrong with her own eyes.
She says, "O, lotus foot, beloved,   /10
what's up? It troubles me."
He greets her highness, says:
"Today, my body shakes,
my mind is spinning round.
Last night I clearly dreamed
that Phuean and Phaeng, two princesses,
were lying close on either side,
my face against theirs pressed,
their arms around me tight,
caressing and inviting me to go.   /20
My mind is shaking fit to fall.
My breast is spinning fit to flip.
Distressed a countless thousand ways,
I wish to go in search of them.
Were I to beg to take my leave,
your highness, mother, please,
have mercy on your son."

The royal dam hears out her son's address,   122
and feels her love-burnt heart will break.
Her tears flood down like streams in spate.
She sobs from sadness, cries and cries again.

121/5 blessed dam ภควดิ, *phakhawadi*, bhagavati, "blessed one." A term of address for
royal and divine females; "dam" and "royal dam" are used throughout the translation
for Bunluea, the queen mother.

She beats her breast, "O son, your mother's best beloved,   123
how did you come to be like this?
Whatever wealth there is within our realm
I'll use to treat you, countless crores.

Where's Kaeo? Go fetch him quick!   124
And bring the chief astrologer forthwith.
Seek out the spirit doctors, medic staff,
the sorceresses, all that counter lore.

And Khwan. Go bring them all, quick, quick!   125
Each *muen* and *khun* and overseer can help.
Send hunters out for forest herbs,
and have the storemen bring the foreign cures.

My treasury, and my beloved son's,   126
will pay for all this treatment of my child,
and though both son and mother lose the realm,
it's only wealth—may he regain his strength."

When all have tried as best they can,   127
whatever doctors say has all been done,
'fore long Phra Lo revives, feels well.
The queen rewards each doctor handsomely.

The royal dam is cheered.   128
His wife and consorts brighten up.
The ministers and cityfolk are glad.
Phra Lo, world-lord, revives, his gloom is gone.

---

124 **Kaeo** and **Khwan** (in the next verse). Phra Lo's aides who have a major role in the story.

125 **foreign cures** ยาเทศ, *ya thet*. Foreign medicine, where *thet* often means "from the West," and may here mean from India, Persia, or Arabia.

Old Lord Tiger Spirit lures Phra Lo, 2: the flag

Two lotus flowers still wait.   129
On hearing news Phra Lo is slow,
their breasts are hot as fire.

They send to tell Old Lord,   130
who says, "They have an aged sage
who thwarts our lore quite well."

Old Lord takes up a triple-victory flag,   131
instills more yantra than before,
at center draws Phra Lo,
two ladies close on either side,
embracing tight the lord of elephants,
and pulling, urging him to come.
Old Lord then blows upon a great ironwood,
nine arm-spans round, no common tree.
The treetop bows down low.
He puts the flag and pushes up.   /10
The tree now trembles—
leaves all flutter, flap—
then springs up straight.
A whipping wind vibrates the flag,
and flaps it back and forth
to stir and stimulate the brew,
and blow the physic hard
to hit the lord and king,
who seems to see two ladies stroke
and fondle him.   /20

131/1 **triple-victory flag** ธงสามชาย, *thong sam chai*. A triangular pennant with three
notched points, used in processions.
131/7 **blows** He intones a mantra, blowing it onto the tree.
131/7 **ironwood** ตะเคียน, *takhian*. *Hopea odorata*, Malabar ironwood.
131/8 **arm-spans** See v. 117.

He feels it stronger than before,   132
as if the pair were there before his eyes,
inviting, tugging him to go
towards their home, their residence.
His mind slips into dreams.
His body shivers, shakes.
He kneads himself and pushes up.
His face is turned
towards the east.
Some people tell the Queen Bunluea,   /10
who hurries to her son,
a-grieving as she comes
with sorrow in her heart.
She sinks to sit and scans his face,
the excellent Phra Lo,
then beats her breast and cries,
hands hammering her chest,
"O mother's best beloved son!

Your fever caused me pain—a mountain high.   133
And when your pain declined, I brightened too.
But now I see you quieter, darker than before,
the pain on pain weighs worse than sky felled on my breast.

The many men and women in our land, I do not see.   134
I see just you and me—two people paired in death.
But how have you and I become like this?
Were you to die, I'll die as well, beloved.

Now, Khwan and Kaeo, go off to seek   135
for every adept, doctor everywhere,

---

134   **The many men** ... The first couplet can be read in other ways: the many men and
      women in our land do not suffer / only you and me, two people paired in death; the
      many men and women in our land do not understand / see you and me only as a
      couple paired in death.

to have them quickly come and treat my treasured son.
Don't dawdle, help with all your heart."

Each doctor, every sorcerer is found.   136
Throughout the realm no more remain.
They treat Phra Lo but no relief is seen.
The dam, his mother, views her son, perplexed.

She summons all the nobles high to meet.   137
She has the curtain opened, then she speaks:
"His majesty our sovereign king
has not been cured of lovesickness. And I'm enraged!

Go check with care the doctors weird;   138
there may be good ones still unfound.
Give thought again to what might help,
and anything that's fit, do fast. Be quick!"

The nobles grasp the royal writ,   139
and search for doctors of all kinds.
They learn that Master Sitthichai,
who's gone to live within the woods,
knows more than all the rest,
has fearful capabilities
and expertise in lore,
along with special powers
of might and mastery.
She makes a royal ordinance   /10
to have the master fetched.

---

137 **She has the curtain opened** A senior royal female would not normally be seen by
such nobles. She is emphasizing the unusualness of this state of affairs.

137 **enraged** This line could be read as "His fever has not gone. Love ails his heart."

139/7 **lore** These three lines have several terms for supernatural ability: คุณ, *khun*
(virtue); ศาสตราคม, *sastrakhom* (knowledge of formulas, spells); สิทธิสามรรถ, *sitthisamat*
(power, ability); ฤทธิ์, *rit* (power, mastery); ประกาศิต, *prakasit* (command).

He sets a sacred fire,
makes offerings to gods of power,
intones the sacred formulas,
composed with arts occult,
to make Phra Lo's enchantment disappear.
He has him bathe in water sacralized
to bring him light and ease,
and take effective medicines
with special powers,   /20
and wash his royal body, royal hair.
He makes a three-ring mandala,
invites inside the guardian-gods,
at center places ogre guards,
fierce spirits at the outer doors,
and gangs of ghouls in skies above,
so every place is taken care.
With all decked splendidly,
he then performs the rites,
with *baisi* placed, to call the monarch's souls.   /30
The queen provides rewards
and all the ritual articles
for Master Sitthichai.
For other doctors in their turn
she offers sets of cloth
to all of those adepts
who came to treat the king.

139/12 **sacred fire** กลากูณฑ์, *kalakun*, k(r)alā, heap, and kuṇḍa, a fire-pit.

139/15 **arts occult** ไสยศาสตร์, *saiyasat*.

139/22 **mandala** มณฑล, *monthon*, maṇḍala, circle. An enclosed space for ritual, often in a symmetrical design, here being used to give protection.

139/30 **baisi** บายศรี. A representation of a food offering, often crafted from folded banana leaves and flowers, and resembling a tree; used in many ceremonies, especially soul calling.

139/30 **call ... souls** See v. 58.

139/31 **The queen** ... Sitthichai's methods have clearly worked, though that is not stated in the text.

Old Lord Tiger Spirit lures Phra Lo, 3: the attack

The princesses, meanwhile, are pitiful.   140
Not seeing him, they pine, their breasts on fire.
"Phra Lo will come or will he not?"
They weep and wail and wait for him alone.

Then urgently they send the maids   141
to ask Old Lord why things are thus.
The maids go there, salute, and ask,
"Old Lord, how long until the king will come?"

"I've looked at everything, mistress.   142
News is they've thwarted us and guarded him.
Weird doctors par to theirs are hard to find.
Leave it to me to counter them myself.

Fear not that it may take some time.   143
The pair will see his face 'fore long.
The king will come, mistress."

Old Lord gives thought to spirits.   144
He seeks them from the woods,
from landings and from waterways,
from caverns and from caves.
They come from every side to sit in court,
the spirit lords of every spot,
the heads and all their retinues,
who oversee each place.
Old Lord appoints a Forest Chief,
Sri Brahma Raksa, ogre prince,   /10

144/9 Forest Chief Sri Brahma Raksa ogre prince พระพนัศบดี ศรีพรหมรักษ์ยักษ์กุมาร, *phra phanatbodi si phrommarak yak kuman*, S: vanasa pati śrī brahma rākṣasa yakṣa kumara. The same sequence of words appears in *Ongkan chaeng nam*, a chant to accompany an oath-taking ceremony of loyalty to the king, believed to date to the early Ayutthaya era. These names appear there in a list of spirits invoked to punish

with retinues of ghosts and ghouls
in massive quantities.
And each and every chief,
a leading spirit, brave and bold,
profuse with splendid powers,
is made the captain of a troop.
He has the leaders ride on elephants,
and some on tigers, lions,
and some on boars and bears,
on serpents and on snakes,   /20
on horses albino,
and some rhinoceros or buffalo.
Their fearsome roars and cries resound.
The spirits change to many forms,
with some as types of crow,
or with a head as vulture, crow,
as tiger, elephant,
as deer or antelope,
and bodies strangely different.
They quickly arm themselves   /30
with weapons and missiles.
They war-dance, leap, and run,
all making fearful sounds.

---

severely anyone who breaches the oath and shows disloyalty to the king ("Lilit ongkan chaeng nam," 9–10). Sunait Chutintaranond thought this referred to three spirits (Sunait, "Lilit ongkan chaeng nam," 42–43). Sri Brahma Rakshasa ogre prince also appears in a similar enforcement role in Inscription 45 from Wat Mahathat, Sukhothai, dated 1393 CE. Griswold and Prasert interpreted this to be a single spirit. The inscription says he lives on Mount Vipula, suggesting he may be confused with Kumbhira, ogre chief of the Kumbhandas (Griswold and Prasert, "Pact between Sukhodaya and Nān," 79, 89). A rākṣasa (ราทษส, raksot) is a fierce and malevolent spirit, often associated with water, sometimes attendant on Yama, the god of death. Sri Brahma Rakshasa probably originated from India as the demon spirit of a brahman or scholar who did evil things in his life, and reached Siam via Cambodia where he appears as a minor deity in late ninth-century inscriptions. He appears in *Samutthakhot khamchan* as a matchmaker, and in *Anirut khamchan* as a helpful spirit (Maneepin, "Thawathotsamat," 86–87; Cholada, "The Thai Tale of *Aniruddha*," 175–76). *Phanatbodi* may be an epithet of the spirit, signaling that he likes to live in trees.

Some rip up bamboos, rocks,
come rushing in a mass,
all shouting back and forth
so loud the earth vibrates.
And when the spirit horde is all prepared,
Old Lord gives out commands,
instructing what to use   /40
of mantra, physic, medicine,
of strategy and ruse,
to make the foe's own physic fail,
their mantras shrivel, void of power,
their guardian spirits run,
their phantoms fail and flee.
"And then I'll send a flying betelnut
across the sky to him
to draw this lord and king
to come to this pair's home.   /50
Don't stray from words I've ordered here."

A sight to see—the army of the mountain lord,   145
a rowdy crowd that fills the sky, now moves.
Hill spirits, packs of ghouls, amassed in crores,
quick-march across the heavens high.

The gangs of ghouls look like a demon horde.   146
Whole forests full of trees are trampled flat.
When soon they reach the borders of the realm,
the border spirits know and summon others fast.

These come in swarms to guard the land.   147
The foreign spirits strike at once.
The local ghouls fight back in force.
They charge, engage, war-dance, and leap;

144/47 **flying betelnut** สลาเหิน, *sala hoen*. Betelnut (areca) was chewed as a mild stimulant, and used in ritual encounters such as welcoming to a home or negotiating a marriage.

but some soon hide away, some flee,
and don't put up a fight.

The spirit horde attacks the local ghouls.   148
They strike and chase and stab at speed,
their bodies changing shape, and roaring loud
to urge the foreign force to finish off the locals fast.

The spirit masses fight.   149
The uproar echoes round.
They strike and chase and stab,
attacking hard and roaring loud.
Lord's spirits raid repeatedly,
and shout to urge the troops
to strengthen the attack.

The spirits conjure up a maze of fires   150
so smoke obscures the sky,
and cast strong mantra medicine
the border spirits cannot bear,
and hence send news upon the wind
that echoes loudly cross the sky
and travels fast full-tilt
to tell the city's guardian gods:
"The sky is yellow, ominous.

The air is dark with smoke,   /10
and thunder blasts the sky.

---

148 This verse does not appear in any manuscript and is undoubtedly a late addition, but
is retained as it has been included in the conventional numbering sequence (Bickner,
personal communication).

150/4 border spirits The spirits guarding the borders of Suang.

150/8 city's guardian god เทพดาเสื้อเมือง, *thephada suea mueang*. The spirit of the city's
lineage, representing the ancestors or the city's founder, generally resident in a pillar
shrine near the city center.

150/9 sky is yellow ฟ้า ... เหลือง, *fa lueang*. A yellow sky is traditionally believed to predict
a disaster, especially a natural disaster.

The city's heart is mad, as if to fall.
The city's breast is fit to break apart."
The guardian gods that hear the news
are shocked, confused, and shake
in fear of Old Lord's mastery,
this man of mammoth power.
Then Sitthichai, the doctor, looks:
"There'll be a great disaster here."
He looks inside his mind,   /20
and sees his teachers indicate:
"All this has clearly come about
through powers of spirit ghouls."
He tells the queen, the royal dam,
who hears about these wondrous things,
and says, "We can't defend ourselves.
We'll see disaster here.
It's pitiful in every way."
She beats her breast, both hands.
"Who now can succor me   /30
and my beloved son,
the sovereign of my heart?

O sage, how did this come about? Alas!   151
Please look and scrutinize again.
O sage, please pity me and give me help,
and should that work, I'll give you half the realm."

He looks again and says, "It's past my powers.   152
They have a god with sacred might.
Our spirit guards have lost and fled.
The physic their lord adds subdues our own.

The time to fight and fend them off is past.   153
Our gods and ghouls are routed, every one.
Our medicine of every type has failed.
Our mantras, physic can't repel their lord's."

The royal dam is pitiful. On hearing this,   154
her sorrow deepens, fires in thousands burn,
her eyes are stung by floods and streams of tears
so oft, her voice is hoarse and heart is dry.

The spirits in the city flee away,   155
while those outside storm in.
The deities Old Lord commands
now come to act as he instructs
to weaken every force,
then send out messages
with news to reach
Old Lord Tiger Spirit.
And once Old Lord has heard,
he sends the flying betelnut   /10
traveling through the sky
to drop among
the betelnuts the king will take.
And when he picks and eats,
'fore long the king, Phra Lo,
his heart is hot and fit to break.
He thinks about the sisters, his beloved,
nonplussed not knowing what to do,
and sinks in grief and gloom.

Departure

Queen Bunluea's pleading

The lord salutes his mother-queen,   156
pays homage, lifts her foot upon his head.
"While I stay here, my heart is weary, ma'am.
I wish to leave to tour the forest now."

155/5 **weaken** To weaken all the forces protecting Phra Lo.

On hearing him take leave of her, she says,   157
"O son of mine, what's making you this way?
The doctors who are treating you report
their powers are spent and all is truly hard.

They sent so many spirits, more and more,   158
with mantra, physic, medicine.
The day you walk away from here,
my breast will shrivel, sicken. I'll collapse."

Phra Lo can't leave, must stay and bear the pain.   159
He sits, then lies, then rises, sighs.
To rule gives him no joy. He sinks in grief.
He pines for winsome beauties, cannot find content.

His queen sits close beside the king,   160
and lifts his lotus foot upon her head.
The consorts fan them back and forth.
The royal dam soft-strokes and soothes his soul.

Phra Lo can't ease his grief and gloom.   161
He sleep-talks to the youthful pair,
distracted, doting, fearful he will fail.
He pines. He yearns to hold his breath and die.

He wakes and begs, "I wish to go   162
to see the forest, hunt some elephants;
to view the woods and hills and hunt some deer;
to view the forest, great and wild, and caves, and lakes."

The dam, who hears her son, is worried sick.   163
"He speaks of viewing flowers and trees,
but if he goes he'll tryst with two young girls.
Deceitful, begging thus, can he be stopped?"

She summons seers, summons ministers. 164
She summons elder Sitthichai. They come to her.
She tells them every word the king has said.
A seer says, "A king who does not hear cannot be stopped."

And Sitthichai informs the dam: 165
"Should gods oppose him, it won't work."
A minister declares: "All ways seem blocked.
Should word be sent to ask the king of Song?"

She thanks the noble for his words. 166
"A good idea. True thanks.
As other ways have failed, this should be done."

She goes herself 167
to see Phra Lo and speaks:
"Have pity on your mother, son.

I've heard you say 168
you wish to tour the woods and hills,
and yet I doubt your words are true.
Your thoughts are otherwise.
Please tell the truth
to me with honest heart."

"My mind is elsewhere, yes. 169
I'll tell the truth,
but don't oppose your child."

"Whate'er you want, beloved. 170
Have ever I stood in the way
and made you feel displeased?

---

165 **Should word** ... Meaning, should they send an envoy to ask formally for the hand of the princesses, as Bunluea proposes in v. 176.

I'll follow what you wish,   171
do things as you will,
and not oppose my orphaned son."

"My heart, O mother dear,   172
desires to see the faces of
princesses Phuean and golden Phaeng.

And if my wish is not fulfilled,   173
I will not see your face,
O sovereign queen.

I take leave of your lotus foot   174
to go to meet the pair,
then will return with speed."

"Once gone will you return, O son?   175
A deer that meets a tiger, is he spared?
On hearing you I don't know what to think.
I see none else but grief, unhappiness.

Were we to take the path that is correct,   176
we'd send to beg these sisters' hand,
and welcome these two beauties here.
An easy thing. No snag of e'en a spider's thread."

"I fear your plan will take too long.   177
I fear the maidens' father won't consent.
The road to send requests is long and hard.
To go myself is simpler every way."

"But once you go, will you return alive?   178
You won't survive, O king. Don't go!

---

171 orphaned กำพร้า, *kamphra*. This can mean deprived of one parent.
176 **No snag ...** No difficulty, even one as small as a single strand of a spider's web; a
conventional metaphor.

Their medicine is sharp, their mantras too,
their spirits, people fierce. Will you survive?

Our city is ill-fortuned greatly, son.   179
The powerful ghouls they sent defeated us.
Will you survive, young lord of all three worlds?
If land and life is lost, lost is the realm and I."

She tells the royal foot whose merit's famed: 180
"We killed their grandfather, cut off his head.
They harbor hate and scheme to take revenge.
Will you go there to stew in their hand's palm?"

"If karma wills it, how can I survive?   181
But if no karma pends, they can't kill me.
Reward of good works done is happiness.
If sins mean I must fall, it can't be helped.

Perhaps I'll go and meet my karma,   182
fall to hells with umpteen arrows, umpteen fires.
Perhaps I'll live to savor joy and heaven high.
But I'll not stay. I farewell you to go."

She beats her breast as were her time of death.   183
"Your mother's warnings are no use at all.
Perhaps your karma fools you, lures you on.
I know this but I'll yield—engulfed in gloom.

I kept the precepts fully seven days,   184
gave treasuries of alms for fruit sky-wide,
and begged to have a goodly dhamma-minded son,
thus I had you, world-lord, my best beloved.

182   **umpteen arrows** ... At the lower levels of the Three Worlds cosmology are several
      hells with various forms of torture, including fire and piercing, often graphically
      illustrated in *wat* murals.
183   **I know this** ... In this line it is not clear who is the subject. She could be referring to
      him rather than herself.

Ten months my belly held your excellence,   185
with care to not forget myself one mite.
And after birth, O lord of all three worlds,
I bathed you, fed you, held you, took good care.

I fed you thrice a day always,   186
not letting others do a different way.
I tended my life-mate with nothing changed,
always the same till you could feed yourself.

Intent I was to make the food you ate,   187
not laxly slacking in the slightest way.
Your every dish I made and checked, O son,
not letting others lift a little-finger joint.

Since you were small I raised you, cared,   188
and taught you all until you'd grown,
become a king, the ruler of the realm.
Now will you leave me here to die of grief?

While I'm alive I'd hoped to bank on you,   189
and planned on death to trust you with my corpse,
but hearing you'll desert your mother's breast,
when dead who can I trust to tend my pyre?

To stop you is beyond me now, O king.   190
I warn but you won't listen. You will leave.
My worries weigh my heart with massive woe.
Though living, I'll know only pain and grief.

O son, what karma makes you leave me here?   191
Henceforth, now you've resolved to seek these belles,

---

185 **ten months** The old form of counting time (and some other things) began with one
at the *start* of the first unit, and thus reached ten at the end of the ninth.

187 **little finger joint** ก้งก้อย, *kueng koi*. Half a little finger.

alone and pining, sadness I must bear.
Come, let me gaze on you to ease my mind.

I praise your cheeks, your forehead, hairline, hair,   192
admire your mouth, your pretty eyes,
your moon-like face that charms the eye.
O handsome king, I kiss your cheek, caress your ear.

I kiss your nose, beloved—your scent's unmatched.   193
I kiss your chin, and neck—my heart capsized.
I kiss your skin, your breast—in bliss, my son—
your shoulder, back, your breast again, your side, your arm."

She wants to pet her son all over, every limb.   194
He lifts his hands in *wai* and speaks:
"It's only fit to kiss the head, the crown.
The cheek and hair are fit when taking leave."

"Beloved son, please have a care for me.   195
I lift your lotus foot upon my head.
Why does your highness hamper me?
I beg to kiss your lotus foot farewell."

"You say you love me, place me 'bove your head.   196
I fear that I'm committing here a sin.
Through mother's virtue, I was born, was taught.
I've not repaid that debt one spider's thread.

Perhaps some karma makes me leave your majesty.   197
Perhaps past sin pulls us apart, O queen.
Your virtue still unpaid, I anger you like this!
Their medicine has led my heart astray."

---

196 **repaid that debt** แทนคุณ, *thaen khun.* Repaid the virtue/goodness.
196 **spider's thread** เท่าเส้นใยยอง, *thao senyai yong.* Equal to a filament (of a spider's web);
a conventional simile for smallness.

And then the queen   198
the mother-royal, in distress,
her heart a hollow, desolate,
now says, "O handsome lord,
your mother's best beloved son,
loved more than my own eyes, my self;
loved more than my own heart, my life;
but now, world-lord, you part from me,
from me and from the city-realm.
A splendid king has seven attributes.   /10
Remember this, my most beloved.
Recall these words, and hold to them.
Stray not from noble custom.
Do not, through negligence, forget yourself.
Do not consort with faithless folk.
Give all-round thought before you act.
Weigh up each word before you speak.
Don't stress the minds of common folk.
Decide on cases honestly.
Maintain the coolness of the realm.   /20
Quell troubles both outside and in.
Attend to every ministry.
Do not be taken in by lies.
Do not, from rashness, be unjust.
If stopping something, stop it well.
If doing something, have the means.
Be mindful of your leading staff.
Choose those with honest minds.
Ensure your ministers act right and straight.
Inspire your men to bravery.   /30
Destroy the pests that rot the realm.

198/10 **seven matters** Chanthit (*Prachum wannakhadi*, 250–51) claims these are old
sayings inserted by the author. Both Chanthit (*Prachum wannakhadi*, 240–48) and
Worawet (*Khumue lilit phra lo*, I, 136–37) organize the thirty plus sayings into seven
categories to comply with this line.

Chastise the populace's negligence.
Prohibit those who'd help a foe.
Snuff out a spark before it flames.
Don't act before the time is ripe.
Don't rein a horse's mouth both sides.
Don't leave a poison trail behind.
Don't act so people slyly hate and curse.
Conduct yourself so people love.
Spur folk to seek the heavens high, /40
so later gods will praise.
Conform to what is thought correct.
Don't think amiss,
and keep in mind always
you must not lose your good repute,
so when the sky, the world, and heavens die,
the era ends, your name is not destroyed.
O king, remember this advice,
and follow mother's warning words.
O mother's best beloved, /50
be blessed with fortune, sire!

O may you thrive with fortune, fame, and might; 199
escape all hardship, sadness, and disease.

198/32 Chastise … อาญาเรื่องเรื้อยราษฎร์, *aiya rueang rueai rat*. An obscure line. Bickner (personal communication), "Punish subjects who violate our laws"; Cholada (*An lilit phra lo*, 194), "Use power bestowed by the people to protect the realm"; Worawet (*Khumue lilit phra lo*, I, 138), "Display sacred authority before the people."

198/36 Don't rein a horse's mouth So the horse cannot turn its head. Don't over-manage.

198/37 Don't leave a poison trail Don't do something wrong that damages people later.

198/47 the era ends At the close of an era in the Three Worlds cosmology, seven suns rise in succession, starting a fire that burns not only the realm of mankind but all four realms of loss and woe below and ten of the realms above (Reynolds and Reynolds, *Three Worlds*, 305–11).

199 Chanthit (*Prachum wannakhadi*, 99) suggests this verse, along with 208, 209, 217, 218, and 257 are late additions, authored by Phra Paramanuchit Chinorot in the 1840s (Bickner, personal communication).

May foes and villains fail before your power.
May you be happy, trouble-free, serene.

Achieve your wish to meet two princesses.　　　　200
Avoid becoming fooled by charms of love.
Do not forget your mother's guiding words.
Return at speed to guard this land and capital.

May I entrust the gods who rule the earth,　　　　201
the air, the plants, the rivers, forests deep,
Iswara, Indra, Brahma, and Narai
to guard the lord of elephants from harm.

When you return alive, your majesty,　　　　202
we'll put out victory flags and pretty shades,
fine golden candles strung with charming gems,
and *baisi*, chicken, duck, at every place."

He listens to her speech,　　　　203
and bows, prostrates, and *wais,*
accepts her guiding words.

He takes her blessings on his head,　　　　204
lets down his hair and wipes her feet,
the queen and royal dam.

He clasps his hands above his head　　　　205
to take leave of her majesty,
and goes inside the hall of audience.

201　**Iswara ... Narai** In Thai, Siva is generally called Iswara (*issuan*) and Visnu is called Narai.

204　**blessings on his head** A gesture of raising the clasped hands over the head and then lowering them palm down onto the crown, as if placing the words there.

Phra Lo's departure

He gives commands to ministers,   206
his trusted loyal men:
"Be watchful in my stead;
take care of government;
sustain my city well;
ensure the people are not irked;
repel the city's foes;
as for the queen, her majesty,
attend her lotus feet,
the same as I would here."   /10

He orders then the officers   207
and troops, all fierce and valiant:
"Prepare the army column now,
the four-limbed fighting force,
all units, all brigades.
Inspect all stringently.
Arrange the cavalcade complete.
We'll start the march
tomorrow morning dawn.
Have everything prepared at once."   /10

He walks inside a palace room   208
to soothe his wife and take his leave:
"Stay well, my dear.

I go away.   209
Stay here and don't be sad.
'Fore long I will return to you."

207/4   **four-limbed** จัตุรงค, *jaturong*, caturanga. A conventional Indic term for an army. The four limbs are elephant troops, cavalry, infantry, and chariot troops.

Laksanawadi aches inside her breast,   210
so sad her eyes near-drip with blood
and swell in floods of tears.

She asks the world-lord, fingers clasped: 211
"You're leaving me.
to be alone, my lord?

The way is lonely, long. The beasts are fierce.   212
Unruly ghouls will trickily
display themselves in changing forms.

I fear the foe ahead of you.   213
Left here I'll die of grief,
like blacking out two gems.

Let me forbid you, lord.   214
Stay here to shelter me.
O lord and master, do not go!

I lost my father, mother, all my kin.   214a
With grace you brought me here to settle, keep
as servant of your foot, much loved, content.
Your parting's like my head is severed, sire."

"Impermanent are all things in this world.   215
The only lasting ones are merit, sin,

---

213   **blacking out two gems** ดับแก้วสองดวง, *dap kaeo song duang*. An obscure line, seemingly
meaning that both of them will die.

214a   This verse was omitted from the standard edition yet appears in most manuscripts
(Bickner, personal communication). When Laksanawadi was introduced above (v. 10),
there was no background.

214a   **servant of your foot** บาทบริจาริก, *batborijarik*, pāda paricārikā, "serving the foot." A
term for a royal wife or consort.

215   **Impermanent** ... สิ่งใดในโลกล้วนอนิจจัง, *sing dai nai lok luan anijjang*. The verse, expressing
a basic Buddhist concept, is one of the most famous in the poem.

which stick to people tightly, shadow-like.
From sin and merit made come succor, care.

To leave you, I am sick at heart, beloved.   216
From tryst I go to tryst, yet full of doubt.
Were I to stay my lovesick breast would burn.
Depart I must, but soon I will return."

"You go from me to tryst with two!   217
No way will you return to husband me.
I don't dare dream those two will let you go.
They'll sweet-talk you and keep you palace-caged."

"I have to leave but not because of hate.   218
Though parting now, I'll not break off our love.
A lotus picked still leaves a fiber strand.
Though gone I'll not forget you. Don't you fret.

I leave you, leave my queen, my love.   218a
Their mantra, physic makes me leave and go.
Were I to stay, would we still couple, wife?
Not dead and gone, I'd be like one made mad."

"Since I was small and knowing nil, naive,   218b
you nurtured me and made yourself
the pin upon my head, my mother,
father, god, and teacher, day and night."

---

215   **From sin** ... Alternate reading: All goes by sin and merit made. Take care of this.
218   **A lotus picked** ... The image of a plucked flower still attached to the stalk by a strand
      of fiber is a conventional metaphor for a break that is not final.
218a   Alternate version found in twelve of the fifteeen texts which have this portion of
      the story, yet omitted from the standard edition (Bickner, personal communication).
218b   Extra verse found in twelve of the fifteeen texts which have this portion of the
      story, yet omitted from the standard edition (Bickner, personal communication).
218b   **pin upon my head** ปิ่นปักเกศา, *pin pak kesa*. The pin fastening a topknot, the highest
      point, most sacred, with overtones of protection.

Her pleas and warnings done, her merit spent,   219
she sadly weeps, bends down her face
upon the royal feet, grieves back and forth,
lets down her hair and wipes his feet for fortune's sake.

She bends her face down on the world-lord's lap,   219a
embraces him with arms fast tight,
inhales him time and time again, uncloyed,
and with his footsole's dust anoints her head.

To see his sweetheart's sorrow swells his own.   220
Caressing her, consoling her, he says,
"Don't grieve, 'twill bring bad luck while in the woods.
Snuff out your anger, grief. They'll mar your looks."

Consoling done, he meets his consorts, says: 221
"Stay well. Don't grieve with breasts on fire."
They take the order, *wai* his lotus foot,
bow heads and loudly weep till strength is gone.

The palace sounds with weeping, wailing cries—   222
the ministers and nobles sick at heart.
In homes all people sob and beat their breasts.
The city's chilly damp with tears of grief.

On seeing every man and woman weep,   223
his heart is shaken up, his body wilts.
"Come now. Don't be so sad, so sorrowful,
as grief may lead to fever, fever lead to death."

His sorrow now subsides.   224
He's taken leave of consorts, queens,
and all the palace lady staff,
but not yet gone to rest.

219a Alternative version (Bickner, personal communication).

The moonshine bright
and stars that strew the sky
dim down at dawn's approach.
The morning star invests the sky.
A cock awakes still bleary-eyed,
then flaps its wings and crows. /10
A coel makes an early call.
He enters the latrine.
Water's brought by duty-maids.
He goes to where he bathes
and quickly cleans himself,
applies a rousing scent
and lotion fused with gold.
He puts fine britches on,
a gleaming lowercloth,
a waist-sash beautiful, tied tight, /20
with tails that swing and sway,
chai khraeng in vine design,
a shirt of many shades,
a bright breast-binding cloth,
a breast-chain and a *tap* as ornament,
a shimmering breast-plate,
whose gems compete to shine,
bright bracelets on the wrists,
and armlets shaped as dragons intertwined,
some pretty finger rings, /30
a sparkling jeweled crown
and, lastly, arms in hand.
The monarch walks with grace

224/11 **coel** ดุเหว่า, *duwao. Eudynamis scolopacea*, which habitually calls before dawn.

224/18 **britches** สนับเพลา, *sanap phlao*. Close-fitting trousers ending below the knee, often with a flared cuff, now seen mostly in costume for traditional dance.

224/22 ***chai khraeng*** ชายแครง. A cloth hanging from the waist in front of the upper legs.

224/25 **tap** ตาบ. An ornamental plate, often lozenge-shaped, worn at the throat or center of the chest.

224/26 **breast-plate** ทับทรวง, *thap suang*, "breast-cover." Much the same as the *tap* above.

alike a royal lion-lord,
who leaves his jeweled mountain cave,
to quickly reach the mounting stage.
Mahouts and expert officers
escort an elephant beside the stage.
He mounts the tusker's neck
and starts the army's march. /40

Ensemble, trumpet, conch, and gong 225
strike up the music, echoing
across the city and the realm.

Phraya Chayanuphap—superb— 226
with expertise in war, the scourge of foes,
all features fine, is lodged within the royal heart,
with tassels, fore-strap trimmed with golden stars.

Two goads extol the king's great rank. 227
He looks like Indra visiting the world,
his mount a tusker-lord alike the king of gods',
his army world-acclaimed as dropped from heaven down.

At front, a standard leads the troops. 228
Above, flags wave as signaling
to move the army fast,
all units, all brigades.
Inspectors, officers, and guards
arrange the infantry in pairs,

224/34 royal lion-lord พระยาราชไกรสร, *phraya rat kraison*, "lord-king-lion." *Kraison* is a mythical form of a lion; a conventional simile.

226 Phraya Chayanuphap พระยาไชยานุภาพ. Lord Victory Power; the official name of one of the king's principal elephants, especially the elephant known for his role in King Naresuan's famous elephant duel in 1593. Chanthit (*Prachum wannakhadi*, 281) has an alternative version of the verse: Phraya Chayanuphap trumpets loud / in musth, roars, sways head slowly / all features fine, dwells in the royal heart / garlands strung with shining jewels, like Erawan.

226 fore-strap รัด(ประ)คน, *rat(pra)khon*. A strap round the front of an elephant's chest.

the cavalry in ranks and lines,
all properly spaced apart,
with officers who brandish spears,
red tassels blowing in the wind,   /10
great arrow quivers shoulder-slung.
The horses' splendid finery
is sparkling prettily,
all gems combined with gold.
The mounts of Sindhu breed
prance round and look superb,
their neighs and whinnies loud,
in battle tested, never known defeat.
The officers ride robustly,
all holding royal ranks and posts,   /20
as *khun* and *muen* of cavalry,
and *nai* and *phan* of cavalry, a mass,
all splendid to the eye,
well dressed, in numbers great,
arrayed behind the king.
At front, the vanguard's large;
at back, the rearguard overflows;
to left, a mass;
to right, a multitude;
all looking beautiful,   /30
too many men to count,
the horses each with qualities superb,
the best to see throughout the world,
all looking still more beautiful
than horses in the world above.

The army looks magnificent.   229
A waving standard leads the troops.

228/15   **Sindhu** สินธพ, *sinthop*. In old Indian texts, the best war horses are said to come
from Sindh, and this origin became conventional in Thai poetry.

229/1   **The army** ... This verse seems to be a redrafting of the previous one. This text may
have originated as a reciter's notebook. See Afterword.

Behind come companies and regiments,
attack brigades, defense brigades,
all packed with *khun* and *muen*,
a stirring sight, quite grand,
impossible to count:
shieldmen, swordsmen,
poison-arrow archers,
pikemen, all brave,   /10
lancemen, all fine,
and buckler troops behind the shieldmen,
and troops with guns and javelins,
all brave and brash,
and bold and beautiful.
Men march behind their officers.
And those most valiant
are riding lofty, gutsy elephants,
swords raised, in full Garuda-wing array.
The infantry in columns comes: /20
the swordsmen multitudinous,
the swordsmen of the left, the right,
the swordsmen of the front, the rear.
The swordsmen of the four fine feet,
who guard his majesty the king,
a swordsman at the elephant's four feet,
the royal elephant's defense.
The swordsmen of the guard and royal guard
surround and keep close watch
around the royal mount   /30
named Thawiratha Rattanat.

229/13 **javelins** โตมร, *tamon*. A throwing pike.
229/19 **Garuda-wing array** สลาบครุฑ, *salap khrut*, usually *bik* (ปีก) *khrut*; *salap* is Khmer. This is a battle formation found in old military manuals.
229/24 **swordsmen of the four fine feet** จัตุลังคบาท, *jatulangkhabat*. Men posted by the four legs of the king's elephant.
229/31 **Thawiratha Rathanat** ทวิรทรัตนาสน์, S: dvi rada ratna āsana, "two-tusked jeweled seat."

The vanguard looks so bold,
its tuskers finely decked
with royal emblems and
the king's regalia,
so fine they look perfect,
regalia and circling troops both fine.
The king is on the march.

See many pretty parasols,   230
refulgent *chumsai* shades,
and tiered umbrellas, pretty, peacock-type,
kanching aloft for all to see,
waving fans and yak-tail fans,
that flap back-forth to fan the king
on both sides of the royal mount.
To serve the king, the lady staff
attend with sundry royal articles,
a golden palanquin and chair.   /10
The service units numberless:
brave officers and men in force,
the vanguard first, beyond belief,
the rearguard last, beyond account,
the left-side flank, beyond all bounds,
the right-side flank, beyond esteem,
and off the road both sides
more units to protect the flanks.
The cheering of the troops
and sounds of trumpet, conch, ensemble, gong   /20
echo around and shake the earth.
The king is on the march,
his massive horde
still finer than all ever known.

230/1 In the manuscripts, v. 229 and v. 230 are continuous, missing the last three lines of
v. 229, a late insertion (Bickner, personal communication).

230/2 *chumsai* ชุมสาย. An article of tall regalia with a triple umbrella.

230/4 *kanching* กรรชิง. Another ceremonial umbrella, often with a fringe.

230/5 **yak-tail fans** จามร, *jamon*. An article of tall regalia shaped like the tail of a yak.

Journey

Phra Lo travels

The king shines brightly like the moon,   231
and marches as the moon moves 'cross clear sky.
Like stars whose patterns fill the firmament,
the troops surround the world-lord as he goes.

He sees the people, houses, gardens, fences, fields.   232
On viewing paddyfields, he thinks about the queen.
"Right now she'll pine for me, her body gaunt,
breast limp, resentful, listless, no one to console.

I've left though loth to leave you, angel mine.   233
I would turn back, but think of those ahead.
To go, or not to go, that is the nub.
This thinking desolates—I fear ahead, I miss behind."

Behind are all his ladyfolk and loves;   234
ahead their medicine of mighty power.
Could fine Phra Lo turn back? Who could?
The world-lord shuns return, resolves to go.

The troops march on ahead,   235
intent to make good speed,
past paddyfields and upland plots,
on royal roads and other ways.
They reach upcountry settlements,
where locals name the place.
He halts the troops to camp.
At once the men take up their tasks,
in line with practice of the past.
The king stays in a golden lodge.   /10
The officers all sit in audience
arrayed around their king,
the lord supreme.

The aides, the servants of the foot, 236
and pages wait on him
in numbers as ordained.
The sun falls low,
approaching dusk.
A woman's scent wafts on the breeze.
The monarch's thoughts
then turn towards his queen,
Laksanawadi, friend in joy,
and to his consorts' youthful miens. /10
His hands caress his breast: "O,
I rushed to leave, but now am sad.

I see the moon looks like your lovely face. 237
I call for you to come to where I wait.
I look and see the lonely rabbit's shape.
The moon smiles on—I want to choke and die.

I see the stars strewn 'cross the sky 238
so like my consorts when they all attend.
I look again—they are but strings of stars.
O fresh-faced consorts, how I miss my loves!

I sleep alone in loneliness, 239
with arms around my breast, I weep
far from my wife and loves.

I view these sprays of forest flowers, 240
inhale their scents that seems like yours,
here wafted on the wind.

237   **rabbit's shape**. The pattern on the moon is seen as a rabbit. In the Sasa Jataka, a monkey, otter, jackal, and rabbit each resolve to perform an act of charity on a fasting day, believing the most generous act will earn a great reward. While the others give gifts of food, the rabbit offers its own body by throwing itself into a fire, but is not burned. The old man reveals himself as the god Sakka, and draws a picture of the rabbit on the moon to be visible to all. This story is retold in many places, including the Grimm Brothers tales and the Japanese collection, *Konjaku Monogatarishu*. In Thai poetry, the moon is often called *sasithon*, sasidara, the holder of the rabbit.

A bird there feeds its mate by beak,   241
just like you do, my sweet,
to coax me to caress.

I think about your tender looks.   242
I seem to see your face,
my maiden best beloved.

Why do you two, my aides,   243
not speak a single word
like mutes? This should not be.

I beg you, make me smile.   244
Why are upcountry folk like this?
Please take a look at them.

These houses, see, aren't like our city ones.   245
The rabble's dwellings are so badly shaped,
not good to look at, not one bit,
best left alone, not lived in—such a sight!"

"O sire, to cool they bathe in cloudy streams.   246
So poor, they chew on smelly salty fish.
Sometimes for lust a wench's a must when lacking else.
Not eating when you crave, how can you live?

Bad times, a grassflower's picked to deck the hair   247
or tuck behind an ear, good scent or not, as madmen do.

---

246   **salty fish** ปลาผอกหมก, *pla phok mok*. Fish pounded with salt and baked by burying
      under a fire.
247   **grassflower** ดอกหญ้า, *dok ya*. Not a genus but a figure of speech (grass has no flower).

Lamduan, happyshade are sweet to smell, my lord.
For me, the scent of jasmine grabs my heart."

Two aides thus banter with their lord.   248
Though chatting yet his mind is on his loves.
While one mind yearns for Phuean and Phaeng,
another's on his queen and consorts young.

The handsome lord and king   249
wraps arms around a pillow, fevered, lone,
his heart bereft of love.

A pristine moon lights up the sky.   250
Phra Lo, world-lord,
sets out along the way.

The army marches on,   251
at times through paddyfields,
at times 'cross grassy plains.
The leaders enter kans-grass fields.
Foot soldiers pass through vetiver,
wild sugar mixed with lalang grass,
to forests thick and forests dry and red,
see earth in places cracked apart,
and many trees of many types.
The lord, refreshed, now points: /10
"What tree is that, and this?
What are their names?"

---

247   **lamduan** ลำดวน. *Melodorum fruticosum*, devil tree, white cheesewood; small, very
       fragrant flowers.
247   **happyshade** สุกรม, *sukrom*, "happy-shade." *Shorea roxburghii*, a dipterocarp with
       fragrant white flowers; also called *phayom*.
247   **jasmine** แก้ว, *kaeo. Murraya paniculata*, orange jasmine.
251/5 **vetiver** See v. 72.
251/7 **forests ... red** ป่าดง, *pa dong*, thick, jungly forest; and ป่าแดง, *pa daeng*, "red forest,"
       dry deciduous forest.

A forester, whose memory's good,   252
reports the names, tree after tree,
to tell the lord, each one.

And once he knows them well,   253
Phra Lo admires the lovely trees:
"Just like those gems, my loves.

This nestle-tree is like you nestling me.   254
The scents I sense remind me of your scent.
Phayom or happyshade now captivates my heart,
alike young ladies' scent—I'm overcome.

This smilinglady's like your happy smile;   255
the touchflower like your hands I touched;
those falling-tresses like you loose your hair.
Amora—loving you, and knowing you love me.

The followfern is like you following,   256
leaves waving like you beckoning to me.
I see a hairwood, yearn to see your hair.
The vine entwines that tree like your arm round my waist.

---

254 nestle-tree แอ่นเคล้า, *aen khlao*, "lean-caress." Unknown.

254 *Phayom* or happyshade See v. 247.

255 smilinglady นางแย้ม, *nang yaem*, "lady smiles." *Clerodendrum fragrans, Volkameria fragrans.*

255 touchflower (มะ)ต้อง, *matong* = กระท้อน *krathon. Sandoricum indicum; tong* also means touch.

255 falling-tressses ช้องนางคลี่, *chong nang khli*, "hairbun-lady-releasing." A name for various tasselferns and clubmosses of the *Lycopodium* genus.

255 Amora รัก, *rak. Gluta usitata*, lacquer tree; same word as "love."

256 followfern ยมโดย, *yomdoi.* A tasselfern.

256 hairwood เกด, *ket. Manilkara hexandra*, an evergreen ironwood tree, and a homophone of a word for head or hair.

These lady's fingernails are just like yours. 257
I see a lady's drape but think of yours.
Roseapples hint your breastcloth slipping down.
The forest's fine! Yet, tree rings rival not
the rings around your neck."

Phra Lo goes on, 258
admires the many different trees
both sides along the way,
admires a flock of egrets on a *yang*,
and peacocks teasing on a *yung*, /5
an odd greenpigeon on a pigeon tree,
a stork upon a storkwood,
and nestbox trees with rows of nestbirds' nests.
A cock creeps up a plumed cockscomb.
A boo-bird bumps its mate on bamboo cane. /10
A purger picks a purger plant.

---

257 lady's fingernails เล็บมือนาง, *lep muea nang*, literal translation. *Quisqualis indica/ conferta*, Rangoon creeper, a climber with very fragrant pink flowers.

257 lady's drape ม่านนาง, *man nang*, "lady's curtain." A type of *Caladium*.

257 tree rings … neck A dewlap or fleshy ring around the neck, considered beautiful, was called by the same word as the rings dividing sections of bamboo (ปล้อง, *plong*). An extra line has been added in the translation to accommodate the meaning.

258/4–5 yang … yung See v. 79.

258/6 greenpigeon เปล้า, *plao*. The name of both a greenpigeon (*Treron curvirostra*) and various croton.

258/7 stork upon a storkwood กระสา, *krasa*, a stork; and กระสัง, *krasang*, *Peperonia pellucida*.

258/8 nestbirds' nests รัง, *rang*, a nest, also *Shorea siamensis*, a dipterocarp; and (นก)รัง *(nok)rang* or กะรัง *karang*, hoopoe, *Upupa epops*.

258/9 plumed cockscomb หงอนไก่, *ngon kai*. *Celosia argentea*, plumed cockscomb, a herbaceous plant, named in both Thai and English because of its resemblance to a cock's crest.

258/10 boo-bird ไผ่, *phai. Erythrura prasina*, pintail parrotfinch, usually called กระติ๊ดเขียว, *kradit khieo*; homophone for bamboo.

258/11 purger … purger plant ตอดต่อ, *tot-to*. Unknown; plant is ตอด, *tot*, a poetic name for สลอด, *salot, Croton tiglium*, purging croton.

A lala flies through lalang grass.
A rushbird rushes mat-rush plants.
A jambo-pheasant peers from jambolan.
A cottonteal alights upon a cotton tree.   /15
A lotus stork admires some lotuses.
A traveler travels seeking travelers.
A goldtree teems with goldsmith birds.
A cocky parrot greets a cockatoo,
both strut along a branch.   /20
The countless types of birds,
he watches as they fly around
and call to others, back and forth.

Crows grab cawvines that twine round cawnut trees.   259
Crows swoop through cawrush, cawing loud.
On cawpod trees, crows crowd to perch.
Crows quit cawferns for cawflower boughs.

258/12 **lala** ตับคา, *tapkha*. Unknown.

258/13 **rushbird rushes mat-rush** คล้า, *khla*. Both an unknown bird and *Schumannianthus dichotomus*, a reed-like plant used for making mats.

258/14 **jambo-pheasant ... jambolan** หว้า, *wa*. Both *Argusianus argus*, argus pheasant, and the jambolan tree.

258/15 **cottonteal ... cotton tree** คับแค, *khapkhae*, a cottonteal or cotton pygmy goose; and แค, *khae*, various *Pterosperium* trees.

258/16 **lotus stork** นกดอกบัว, *nok dok bua*. *Mycteria leucocephala*, painted stork.

258/17 **traveler** กระเวน, *kraven*. An unknown bird found in literature and a verb meaning to travel.

258/18 **goldtree ... goldsmith birds** ช่างทอง, *changthong*. Unidentified bird, literally "goldsmith," and ทอง(หลาง), *thong(lang)*, *Erythrina fusca*, coral tree.

258/19 **cocky parrot ... cockatoo** แขกเต้า, *khaektao*, a parrot; and กระ(ตั้ว), *kra(tua)*, cockatoo.

259 **cawvines ... cawnut** กาฝาก, *kafak*, a general word for parasitic vines; and ตุมกา, *tumka*, *Strychnos nux-blanda*. All the plants in this passage contain กา, *ka*, meaning a crow.

259 **cawrush** กาลา, *kala*. Unknown.

259 **cawpod** เพกา *pheka*. *Oroxylum indicum*, known for its massive seedpods.

259 **cawferns ... cawflower** มัดกา, *matka* or *maka*, *Bridelia ovata*, a fern; and กาหลง, *kalong*, *Bauhinia acuminata*, a tree with white flowers.

In tiger's eye a tiger waits to watch the way.   260
Deer stick by deer's-ear trees where barkers hide.
The tuskers tug at bong cane, muddled with *masang*,
and thread through tusker-ash to fade among the trees.

Some monkeys monkey round in monkey vines,   261
and watch their young below who fight for fruit.
Wind monkeys race the wind and leap away,
and monkey kids chase, play and swing in monkey vines.

huat hiang hat haen han   262
jak juang jan jaeng jik
pring prong prik pru prang
khui khae khang khae khet
tree groups *phlet phlong*
tree groups *fong fai*
tree groups *phai pho*
tako taku
lamphu lamphaeng
tree *groups daeng dan*
somphan saraphi
nontri trabun
khun kamkhun kamyan
phiman khlo khlai
kamjai krajap-bok

260   **tigers eye** ตาเสือ, *ta suea. Dysolxylum cochinchinese*, direct translation.

260   **Deer ... deer's-ear ... barkers** กวาง, *kwang*, deer; and หูกวาง, *hu kwang*, literally deer's ear, *Terminalia catappa*, a large leadwood tree; ฟาน, *fan*, another word for เก้ง, *keng*, barking deer.

260   **bong cane** บง, *bong, Bambusa tulda*, a bamboo that elephants eat; and (มะ)ซาง, *(ma) sang, Madhuca pierrei*, a fruit tree.

260   **tusker-ash** อ้อยช้าง, *oi chang*, "elephant sugar." *Lannea coromandelica*, Indian ash.

261   **Some monkeys ... monkey vines** ลิง, *ling*, monkey; ลางลิง, *langling, Bauhinia scandens*, pinanga vine.

261   **wind monkeys** ลิงลม, *linglom*, literal translation, *Nycticebus coucang*, slow loris.

262   A display of versification, fitting tree names into the meter, as found in several old poetic works.

katok-rot sak son
So many types of trees.
Above are those recalled,
but there are many more.

Here vines and little *kum*   263
entwine around a modest tree
with pretty curling leaves atop.

"These blooms in pretty sprays   264
whose scent now fills the air
direct my rueful thoughts to you.

I ponder what's behind; I hope on what's ahead.   265
My mind is almost mad
for having left my loves so long."

He travels through the woods   266
for many nights and days
to reach the borderlands,
the frontier of the realm.
They make a lodge and army camp,
all scattered through the woods,
a sight well worth to see.
The officers of every branch
stand guard around the area.
Phra Lo, the lord of elephants,   /10
gives out commands,
as follow here.

"I'll quickly forge ahead   267
while all of you
return home first most happily.

---

263   **kum** กุ่ม. *Crateva magna*, a shrub found beside streams.
267   This verse is a modern insertion, not found in any manuscript (Bickner, personal
          communication).

We've traveled long and hard to this frontier. 268
It's fit I send the mass of troops back home.
I pity all who miss their wives and kids.

I think of noble Phuean and golden Phaeng."
Lieutenants *wai* the royal feet, 269
and take the dust upon their heads.
"Pray take your pleasures first, your majesty.
In three-four days then have us journey home."

"'Twill take a longer time, my officers. 270
Tomorrow you should go without delay,
so that the realm is not long left alone.
I fear the dam is waiting, keen for news."

They bow and *wai* the feet of merit's fount, 271
hands clasped and looking elegant as flowers.
"We are like beings sire has raised,
and all we have comes from your grace.

We beg to 'tend upon your righteous majesty 272
until returning home to rule the realm.
To go and die is better, sire, than turning back.
Whatever hardship's had, we beg to serve."

He will forge on, but thinks of what's behind, 273
concerned about the land, about the dam.
"Go do as you once did when I did rule the realm;
guard every part so none can criticize.

I trust to you the city, horses, tuskers, troops, 274
and people, out and in, the land entire.

---

269 **lieutenants** ต่างเนตร, *tang net*, "alternative eyes," i.e., overseeing in his place, *lieu-tenant*.

272 **righteous** ทรงธรรม, *song tham*. Upholder of the dhamma.

Fail not in strictly judging right and wrong.
I trust to you the dam and my beloved queen."

He orders all the officers, each branch.   275
They take the royal mandates on their heads
in floods of tears from love of this their king.
"Your majesty, return before too long."

"When you attend my royal mother's feet,   276
inform her that his majesty her son
is hale and happy, well content;
and say he bows his head before her feet.

Then go to *wai* her majesty my queen.   277
Inform her I am well, without disease;
I'll hasten home to join my treasured wife;
do not lament but wait to welcome me."

He has arrangements made   278
to single out those close
and loyal to their lord,
about a hundred men,
to journey on with him.
He sends the other officers and men,
the elephants and horse, back home.
He bids his pair of aides,
"Give thought to how we'll go.
Have some left here to wait for news.   /10
Have those who know the ways of border guards
befriend them, draw them close,
and once they're on good terms,
they'll tell us what we want.
Then give them silver, gold, and cloth,
to have them on our side;

275 on their heads See v. 204.

converse to make them well-disposed
and firmly in our camp,
by telling them, 'His majesty
will recompense you royally   /20
with silver, gold to fill your hearts.
Don't be concerned to keep things hid.'
Then tell them all a tale
that I'm a border chief,
that you two aides are district heads;
the swordsmen, sergeants;
the servants, common troops.
And change the names of everyone.
Call one another as do border guards.
Go stealthily, keep watch, and don't get lost.   /30
Conceal this subterfuge.
Don't let the secret spread.
Put on disguise.
Greet anyone you meet
in any forest village site.
If people question you, be smart,
state clearly your false name,
you've come on boundary patrol,
and to the city will return.
If they're not happy and at ease,   /40
then tell them this is true
according to this tale,
with nothing kept concealed."

"O may the merit of the king protect us all!   279
His majesty's planned subterfuge
is truly good in every way!

If sire requires to go at speed,   280
leave all behind except two aides
and start along the way.

When at the gateway to the woods,   281
just act as if you've come
to look for forest goods.

We *wai* your highness in farewell."   282
They leave two aides attending on
the royal foot, and go their way.

Thenceforth he travels on   283
past paddyfields, past settlements.
The two aides lead the way.
He sheds his kingly look,
and dresses as a border chief
in fitting shirt and hat,
so none will recognize a king.

He travels through the forest great,   284
a hundred men, and horses, elephants,
three with the king.

His two aides in the lead,   285
the king proceeds
in stage by stage,
with stays in villages.
They reach the gateway of the woods,
the border guards' main post,
and speak as he has said,
bluff as he has taught.
On seeing him arrive to stay,

281   **forest goods** Articles collected from the forest were a major part of Siam's exports, especially to China. The goods included fragrant timber, resin, metals, and exotic animals.

284   **three with the king** The parsing of this verse is difficult. The number three may mean there are three elephants or they are traveling in three groups. Cholada (*An lilit phra lo*, 258) has รอย, *roi* (tracks) in place of ร้อย, *roi* (hundred), meaning they are making tracks of only three people (Phra Lo and his aides), but in v. 315 below there are still a hundred men.

the forest people greet and question them.   /10
They tell their names and say
a border chief's on boundary patrol
and will return.
The people come to pay respect
and meet the chief, each one.
They pass the forest gateway there,
continue on, one village to the next,
and make good time.

Omen at the Kalong River

They reach the Kalong River,   286
release the tuskers by the bank,
and sit together, laughing merrily.
He has them cut some wood
and bind to make a raft,
then travel 'cross the stream.
He has them clear a camp
as for a border chief,
then goes to bathe,
scrub off the dust,   /10
and wash his hair. When done,
his mind slips back
to thoughts about his mother-queen.

He thinks of her with great concern.   287
"Perhaps you weep and pine
about your son, my sovereign.

The hurt of love, the hurt of parting too—so hard.   288
The hurt of wanting me to turn back home.
The hurt because your son has gone abroad alone.
The hurt you feel makes me, your son, hurt too.

286/1   Kalong River แม่น้ำกาหลง, *maenam kalong*. See Afterword.

The hurt about my father—and now me.   289
The hurt of watching, pining all alone.
The hurt of being slighted, scorned by foes.
The hurt that deepens, making death preferred.

A hundred loves don't match a first wife's flesh.   290
A thousand wives don't match a mother.
To bear a child, give birth is not an easy thing.
To raise a child is hard, O virtuous mother-queen.

Should I not go ahead to meet the pair   291
but travel back instead to Queen Bunluea?
I shillyshally here. O, help me think!
What sin now makes me fret about her so?"

Thereon two aides, without delay,   292
raise hands in lotus shape,
pay homage, say:
"Your humble servants here
implore our sovereign lord
to give commands
that he, his highness, will return
back to the blessed city now.
We humbly hold it right
that he should not go further furtively,   /10
return instead to rule the realm, content,
beside her majesty the queen,
beside your mother-royal, sire."

"If I go forward I'll be alone mid foes.   293
If I go back, I fear some folk will say,
'This king is cowardly,' accuse, defame,
and stir up slandering. I'd rather die."

The two aides gently say,   294
"There's none would dare berate

93

a sovereign king and lord
as little as one strand of hair."

"I'll go a little while and then return,   295
enjoy both what's ahead and what's behind.
I only fear their ghouls will capture me,
and I'll not see the worthy dam again.

I'll seek an omen where the river floods its banks.   296
This river named Kalong flows truly fast.
If I'm to go and not return alive,
may now the waters swirl—or else flow straight."

Upon his words the waters swirl around.   297
His own eyes see them dyed blood-red.
He trembles in his heart in great distress,
as if a hundred arm-span tree fell 'cross his breast.

He lets none know of this, and steels himself,   298
walks up from river's side towards his royal bed,
goes in the golden lodge. "Why is this so?"
He shuts the curtains, cries, "O mother mine, Bunluea!

Were you to die, your son should see your corpse.   299
Were I to die, my mother-queen should then
cremate the corpse so there's no shame.
Or shall not I burn yours, nor you burn mine?

If I'm to die, then let me die,   300
but I will hurt if I don't see the face
of her who gave me life."

His tears flood down. He weeps enough   301
for blood to fall, his breast on fire.
"My mother may not see her son again.

---

297 arm-span See v. 117.

On seeing there the omen in the stream,   302
my breast was close to caving in,
O mother merit-heart of son.

I am a king with rank beyond the sky.   303
Does sin ordain I wander in this world
to sink in mud and die alone?

I will turn back. I cannot turn.   304
I've stepped on foreign land
with both my feet.

I once was sovereign ruler of the world,   305
and city princes, all one hundred one, paid court.
Alone I've fallen mid an ocean deep,
and may not see my mother's face nor she her son's."

His pain feels great as sky is wide.   306
He thinks of what's ahead and what's behind,
afraid about himself,
but hides so none can see
how much he is distressed.
He parts the curtain, feigns good cheer,
and calls the border guards to talk:
"Please take my two
heart-trusted aides to see
where we should stop and stay,   /10
where we should keep concealed,
so all is right and good,
where we'll steal in, slip out,
so all is done with skill and art.
And memorize the roads,
the names, the turns,
the names of places where
the tuskers, troops, and horse can meet.
Inspect both back and front,

make checks both near and far.   /20
And as you go and look, you two,
give careful thought
to every stratagem."

They take the king's commands   307
and *wai* his lotus foot,
then hasten on their way.

Not straying from his words,   308
they look at every route and place
and memorize in full.

Two aides are led to see the lairs,   309
and act like brothers, friends,
at villages along the way.

They carry cash as bait and bribe   310
to silver-soften people hard as iron
to be compliant as required.

And when these folk are friends, onside,   311
then Khwan and Kaeo deceptively
seduce them with sweet words.

Once told about the plans in full,   312
these people say, "Do not disdain.
Just leave the work to us."

The aides go in to see the park,   313
to find the wardens there
and pay them off as sweetener
with silver, gold to close their mouths
and have them do all things.

---

313   park As we learn below, this is a royal pleasure garden outside Song.

The aides inspect the city palace gates
and two princesses' residence.
At barriers, they look for chinks.
At open roads, they note the way,
inspecting every spot,   /10
committing this and that to memory,
not letting people see,
by keeping hidden out of sight—
an undercover job.

And when they've traced the route,   314
the villages and roads, the names of lairs,
the two aides go by forest paths,
heads down, bent over,
pushing through,
until before too long
they come upon their lord.
They *wai* and tell the trickery,
so he now knows the hideaways.
And once they've told it all,   /10
they draw a map for him
with every detail shown.

The king gives matters thought.   315
He leaves two elephants, four horse
to stay behind with border guards;
selects some thirty men,
all bold and strong, to go with him;
and leaves the other seventy
to be with all the elephants and horse.
The world-lord stays in comfort there,
awaits a day that's good.
His two fine aides   /10
attend to hear each royal writ,
and wait to serve his needs.

315/9 day that's good วันดี, *wan di*. See v. 58.

The cock

Meanwhile the pair of princesses 316
await the time they'll see the king.
"O Ruen and Roi, he comes too slow!
For love, please go to *wai* and warn Old Lord."

They go to tell Old Lord, the mountain god. 317
He says: "Phra Lo has reached the river bank,
Kalong, in our domain, but still laments.
I'll speed him up once more."

Old Lord gives thought to forest cocks, 318
and when he does, the cocks appear
in countless flocks and flights.
Old Lord selects a gorgeous one,
both young and strong,
red feathers round the neck,
plumage glossy green,
and wings of five mixed shades,
as lustrous as a *sibbat* swan,
a pretty crimson rim around the eye, /10
a bright and striking crest,
a sweet appealing crow,
with arcing spurs in flashy shades,
two feet like nine-grade gold,
and legs that look as painted rouge.
Old Lord instils a spirit in the cock.
The splendid bird, not scared at all,
then holds his head up boldly high,
flaps his tail and beats his wings,
and calls out loud and long, /20
a sound of crowing, crisp and clear.

318/9 *sibbat* swan หงษ์สิบบาท/สบาท, *hong sibbat/sabat*. Either red and purple or red and
yellow.

Old Lord commands on every point,
and soon the cock takes off and flies,
descends along the waterway,
arrives where famous Phra Lo stays,
uplifts his throat and crows,
beats his wings and struts around,
while crowing shrilly on and on,
then preens his tail and wings.
The cock looks bold and beautiful. /30
The king peers out and sees.
His royal heart then blooms.
The beauty sates his eyes and heart.
No time to put on scent,
or don his crown and clothes,
or grasp his royal weaponry,
he straightaway gives chase,
intent to have this splendid cock.
The army marches after him.
If he lags back, the cock will stop and wait. /40
If he goes slow, the cock crows out a call,
and looks him in the eye.
If he draws close,
the cock walks on ahead a bit,
stepping slowly foot by foot,
the gait of swans.
If he falls far behind, the cock stops still.
They reach the forest rim,
about to enter village land.
The cock pretends to tire. /50
On seeing this, the lord speeds up.
The cock flies up and disappears.
The king looks every way,
then thinks to self alone,
"O, I've been tricked!
This spirit cock has lured me on."
He turns to see his aides.

The two speak words that soothe,
each and every one.

In Song territory

"From here we should be on our guard,   319
and not forget ourselves.
Instruct the men, each one,
and once they know, we'll leave."
They reach a friendly village where
the people nudge and talk.
The villagers approach
and *wai* the lord,
escort him to a fitting place,
then offer food and say,   /10
"Enjoy one night."
They leave behind ten men,
and at the village next along,
they leave the elephants and five,
so those remaining with the lord
amount to fifteen men.
Ten more are left ahead of there.
They reach a place
with only unused gardens, people none,
fir trees in rows,   /20
and one quiet, empty house.
They urge the lord to stay:
"The garden of the princesses is close."
They raise clasped hands in *wai*,
and sit around attending him.

People come to pay respect   320
and bring a set of food,
some scented water for his bath,
clean bedding, covers, pillows,
a coverlet of silk on top.

They ask his aides on every point.
And once his dressing's done,
his majesty the king
adopts a brahman guise,
Si Kesa as his name,   /10
someone from Siva's land,
who wants to see this realm.
The aides pass off as householders
with names of Rat and Ram.
Then he warns everyone:
"Do not forget yourself, forget your mouth."
To show their love,
the villagers invite the aides and men
to go inside their homes.
They lay on liquor, food, and rice,   /20
and call the master's men:
"O brothers, come and eat!"

The villagers feed everyone,   321
as happens every place.
They stay a while till evening comes.
The lord, who wants to see the ladies' park,
departs forthwith.
The others lead the world-lord
on his way.

The staff on guard   322
are told Phra Lo has come
to see the charming gardens there.

They gather round to sit and *wai,*   323
invite the lord and king
to tour the park.

320/10 **Si Kesa** ศรีเกศ, *si ket.* Holy/glorious head/hair.
320/11 **Siva's land** สยมภูวนาถ, *sayam phuwanat.* The one who is self-created, Siva (or Brahma); meaning India. This line and the next have been transposed in the translation.

The king, with face a-bloom,   324
admires the flowers and trees
and fruits that please him well.

And when he's viewed the place,   325
he smiles and says:
"I thank you very much.

I wish to know whose park this is."   326
"Their majesties, the princesses,
who love the golden lord."

They then compose a verse,   327
presented to the king of elephants,
the lord of merit:

"Your servants *wai* your holy foot sublime,   328
invite you, sire, to see the flower sprays,
the two princesses' pleasant, shady park,
enjoy the couple's trees and place to play."

The lord admires the *karaket*'s rare scent,   329
that rouses him like fragrant hair,
inhales the scent of jasmine, kindling love,
and prizes blooms to wreathe the hair of Phuean and Phaeng.

The smilinglady's like a lovely smile.   330
The leaves are waving, calling to the lord.
A falling-tresses brushed by breeze waves too.
The boughs bow, beckon him to view the trees.

The birds are perched on branches, row on row,   331
and call out songs in welcome to the lord.

---

329   *karaket* กระเกด. *Pandanus tectorius, furcatus,* screwpine, pandan.
330   **falling-tresses** See v. 255.

A stork that sings the king a plaintive song
alights on storkwood, draws his mate beside.

A parakeet in welcome dances up,   332
and calls out to the sovereign king.
A parrot sings out loud inviting him.
The rushbirds fuss and fondle with their mates.

They urge the king to view a lake,   333
bestrewn with blooming lotus flowers,
with many turtles, tortoise, terrapin, fish, crab.
Bees probe the flowers to bathe in pollen scent.

He walks, sits down,   334
and thinks about the sisters beautiful,
the lady Phuean and golden Phaeng.

The aides invite their lord to sleep.   335
At dusk a breeze blows low through leaves.
He yearns to see their ladyships,
lamenting in a verse:

"Two fragrant ones I love as my own life,   336
I left the splendid city, came at speed,
not seeing you my heart is desolate.
I pine and yearn for two young lady-loves.

A sweetscent flower is my desire.   337
Lamduan's fragrance feigns your own,

---

331   **stork ... storkwood** See v. 258.
332   **parakeet** แขกเต้า, *khaek tao. Psittacula alexandri*, red-breasted parakeet.
332   **parrot** สัตวา, *sattawa.* A large green parrot, sometimes identified with *Eclectus roratus*, found in Indonesia but not in Thailand.
332   **rushbirds** See v. 258.
335   **blows low** ลาดไม้, *lat mai.* An idea that wind in the evening drops closer to the ground.
337   **sweetscent** เสาวคนธ์, *saowakhon*, su-gandha, "beautiful scent." *Tetracera loureiroi*, bee flower, a vine with a very sweet scent.

blown by the god of wind to make me yearn.
Moon lights the sky yet I tryst not with you.

The rousing scent of climbing jasmine spreads.   338
The *pru* and perfume trees stir senses five.
I scent my soulmate's fragrance, my beloved,
yet seeing not your face, I wish to choke and die.

The scent is only flowers—my heart now wilts.   339
I see so many birds throughout the woods.
O birds, please send the princesses some word,
to give the noble sisters news of me.

I beg you, magpie, send them word.   340
Please take this message to the sisters two:
I've suffered, struggled much to seek these beauties out;
I see but singing birds, yet cry for them.

I beg you, parrot, go at speed to say: 341
Phra Lo feels far apart his fragrant loves;
he's come to stay inside the royal park.
And let them know, he longs for them.

I beg you, lory, fly away at speed   342
to find their golden residence,
invite their royal ladyships to come,
enjoy the trees, the place of joyful play.

---

338   **climbing jasmine** มลุลี, *maluli*, *Trachelospermum jasminoides*, confederate/star jasmine, a climber; and มะลิวัลย์, *maliwan*, generic term for vine-type jasmine. Both words refer to climbing jasmines.

338   ***pru* and perfume trees** ปรู๋, *Alangium salvifolium*, sage-leaved alangium, with fragrant white flowers; ประยงค์, *prayong*, *Aglaia odorata*, rice flower, perfume plant.

338   **senses five** ที่นท้า, *hoen ha*, meaning กามคุณ, *kamakhun*, kāmaguṇa. Five sensual aspects: form, sound, odor, taste, and touch.

O coel and barbet, singing clear and sweet,   343
your voices captivate in no small way,
for love, go quick and find these beauties two
to come and cheer me in this lovely park.

The birds fly to and fro and sing,   344
or land in trees and tuck themselves away,
but bring no news for me about the pair,
just dance and sing and hide below the trees."

Phra Lo regards the birds,   345
and listening, knows they do not care.
His aides massage the royal feet,
prostrate to pay respect,
and say, "Don't be distressed.
Tomorrow sire will tryst the princesses,
his friends in joy."

They call their lord to grace a crystal bed.   346
The sound of cicadas, both clear and sweet,
lulls the lord and lights his mood.

Winds waft the scents of flowers.   347
He ponders on the fragrances
of these two princesses.

A bright moon lights the world.   348
He longs to see their faces,
young and lotus like.

Phra Lo, his heart   349
replete with joy,
appreciates his aides' sweet words.

---

343 **barbet** พระโดก, *phuradok*, usually โพระดก, *phoradok*. General name for barbets, *Megalaima*, which have a distinctive, piercing two-note call.

The two recite fine verse
that lulls the lord to sleep.

They fall asleep beside his feet. 350
Phra Lo then dreams,
while also Khwan and Kaeo
each sleeps and dreams a dream
beside his royal feet.
And when the lord awakes,
he stirs the aides,
recounts his dream forthwith,
and asks them to interpret it.

"Please listen, Kaeo and Khwan. 351
You lulled me then I dreamed like this:
I wore the lovely ladies' breastchain bright.
Two snakes coiled round my form and, shocked, I woke.

I dreamed I saw myself embracing my beloved. 352
I dreamed I saw them coming to my bed.
I rose bewildered, babbling, seeking them.
I dreamed they snared me tightly with desire.

I dreamed I wore a vivid lowercloth, 353
a lotus in my hair that scattered scent,
and walked towards the very lucky east.
I dreamed the maidens played all round a lake.

My right hand stroked a royal lily flower. 354
My left arm clasped a lotus nymph in bloom.

351 **snakes** อุรค, *urakha*, uraga. Literally, something creeping on the breast, a snake.
352 **snared** แร้ว, *raeo*. A noose to trap animals.
354 **lotus nymph** See v. 89.

A swimming carp caressed a channa fish.
A frisky goldbarb swam around a pond."

The aides decode their master's dream: 355
"'Twill be as wished. Do not be sad.
Tomorrow sire will tryst the pair
of noble budding princesses."

Then Kaeo interprets his own dream: 356
"I dreamed the lord caressed two shining moons,
that brightly lit the sky, both beautiful.
O sire will tryst with two young lotus loves!"

And Khwan has dreamed the lord was like a moon   357
an angel took and placed upon her head.
"I dreamed that sire enjoyed them, as desired.
O sire will tryst the princesses 'fore long!"

When these two aides   358
relay good omens to their lord,
his mind is put at ease.
He likes the two aides' dreams,
and feels as if the silk-skinned pair
have come to lull him, light his mood.

The princesses wait and dream

Have pity for the perfect blooms,   359
two royals, Phuean and Phaeng.
Within their jeweled bedchamber,
both downcast, desolate,

---

354 **carp** ตะเพียร, *taphian*. *Puntius javanicus* and related species, variously called carp or
barb in English.
354 **channa** ช่อน, *chon*. *Channa striata*, common or striped snakehead.
354 **goldbarb** พรวนทอง, *phruan thong*, *Labeo pruol*. *Cirrhinus microlepis*, small-scale mud carp.

107

they hug their breasts and yearn.
Their lover takes so long to come.

They think they won't achieve their wish.   360
Their cheeks are dark, their hair loosed down.
Both desperately distressed,
they long for him to hurry there,
and countless times
tears flood their eyes.
Upset and sad and sorrowful,
they whisper words
to their two maids:
"Our wish is not fulfilled.   /10
Should we not tryst our lover yet,
tomorrow we will die."

The two maids pay respect,   361
with clasped hands raised,
console the princess pair:
"O, we two maids of yours
believe the time has not yet passed.
Have patience. Wait a while.
For, not long now,
your lord and lover comes to tryst.

Don't fret, don't be upset;   362
if not today, tomorrow morn,
Phra Lo will come,
will reach the treasured park."

"How do you know?   363
Who came to tell
this news about the king, world-lord?
Now answer quick, without delay:
he's come for sure, or not?"

The two reply with clasped hands raised: 364
"Your golden highnesses,
old men of sacred power
have taught us omens from the birds,
which ones are good, which bad.
Right now they promise joy.
Forthwith, no time at all,
your hearts will be awash
as if the handsome lord of elephants
had come to nestle by your sides—   /10
your highnesses, before our eyes!"

Two princesses are pleased.   365
They thank the two maids for their words:
"They're fit to place upon our heads.
The goodness you two show to us
is great as sky is broad.
We sisters two just wait
to compensate the goodness of you two.

You raised us both since we were small.   366
The goodness of you two surpasses words.
If now you help fulfil our wish
to tryst the lord of elephants, your goodness will excel!"

When gratified by these sweet words,   367
the pair of precious maids
speak solace to the pair:

"Your golden ladyships, don't be distressed.   368
Retire to bed in comfort now.
'Fore long, your highnesses,
Phra Lo will come
to be received by both of you.

364/3   old men of sacred power ผู้เฒ่าผู้ศักดิ์สิทธิ์, *phu tao phu saksit*. Worawet (*Khumue lilit phra lo*, II, 2) thinks this means Old Lord Tiger Spirit.

Be not downcast, your ladyships. 369
Please sleep while waiting for Phra Lo.
We'll sing a lullaby."
At that the pair lie down.
The maids embrace their feet
and sing a lullaby:
"Now sleep, pray sleep,
two mistresses of ours.

The golden jeweled bed shines bright, 370
a pad of jeweled silk with pretty broidery,
pillows soft, a canopy bestrewn with stars,
a net and curtain closed to hide you both.

May sisters two now sleep, 371
soft souls, untroubled, undistressed.
Phra Lo will soon arrive to tryst you two.
Carefree, await his soft caress.

O winds that blow the lord along, 372
come racing 'cross the sky with him!
O guardian-gods of nature, speed him on!
O moon and stars, be torches, light his way!"

The couple hear the two maids sing 373
that soon the famed Phra Lo will come.
So sweet and pleasing to their ears,
the dulcet sound sends sisters two to sleep.

And once they sleep, 374
two treasured maids,
who lullabied, sleep too.

At once all four have dreams, 375
and see amazing auguries,
that strike and stay in memory.

On waking up, the princess
Lady Phuean remembers, can recall
and tell what she has dreamed:

"I dreamed celestial blooms came to my hand,   376
supreme in scent, in beauty without par.
These best of blooms that ornament the world,
the heavens' pride, were tucked in we two's hair."

Then, happier than words can say,   377
young Phaeng, reclining close beside,
relates the dream she had:

"I dreamed the sun drew near,   378
became a pin in my head's hair,
and like a glass, the moon reflected back my face,
while many stars adorned my hair like flowers."

The maids review the ladies' dreams: 379
"You'll gain your hearts' intent,
fulfil what you desire,
be bathed a thousand streams,
as queens, as ladies of the realm,   /5
beside Phra Lo, the world's famed gem,
whose glories garner praise.
The handsome lord of elephants,
Phra Lo, will soon embrace
two princesses, and join with you in love."

---

376 **celestial blooms** ดอกฟ้า, *dok fa*. Chanthit (*Prachum wannakhadi*, 471) suggests this is
มณฑารพ, *montharop*, a mythical flower; also a name for *Talauma candollei* in the
Magnolia family.
378 **glass** See v. 460.
379/4 **bathed a thousand streams** อาบสหัสธารา, *ap sahat thara*. A reference to *abhiseka*,
the bathing rite at a marriage or royal installation.

"O may it be as you maids bless!   380
On hearing what you say,
you make us savor heaven."

Now Roi, awash in joy,   381
and Ruen raise clasped hands high,
pay homage at the two princesses' feet.
Two maids with hands in *wai*
now give their own accounts.

First Ruen explains the dream she had: 382
"I dreamed you placed the stars around your heads,
and dreamed a coiling snake near swallowed you.
Phra Lo will shortly come to be your guest!"

Then Roi addresses them: "I dreamed   383
that you will savor heaven's joys,
together sup the nectar sweet of senses five.
Tomorrow Lo, the great world-lord, will come!"

These readings of the dreams, well-liked, are done, 384
the pitch-dark night has passed,
and dawn is coloring the sky,
yet for the maids and mistresses
daybreak's a thousand years away.

The coel cries,   385
then partridge, barbet, dove,
while ostlers peer around,
and all birds sing out loud and clear.
Wild cocks crow on and on.
When dawn's dim light allows,

---

383 **nectar ... senses five** อมฤตปัญจ์รส, *amrit pan rat*, amata pañca rasa. See v. 338.
385 **partridge** กระทา, *kratha*. General name for small partridges such as *Francolinus pintadeanus*, Chinese francolin.
385 **ostlers** See v. 89.

they'll go to find the lord
within the royal park.

The moon no longer shines.   386
The sun comes up.
The woodpecker and laughing thrush
fly wheeling round and perch treetop,
spreading news the lord has come.
The sound of cawing crows
announces that the lord's arrived.
The two princesses' maids
are pleased these signs are good.
They *wai* their ladyships and say,   /10
"We had some omens from the birds.
We saw with our own eyes they're good.
Perhaps you'll meet the world-lord now,
your highnesses."

The two are truly cheered.   387
They urge two maids to hasten on:
"Go quickly! Don't delay!"

The park

The servants meet

The maids devise a plan: 388
they dress themselves up well,
farewell the princesses,
and mount an elephant to go.
Meanwhile that morn, the king
commands the garden's guards,
"To anyone who comes to ask,
'Are persons staying in the park?'

386/3 **laughing thrush** (กระ)ลาง, *(kra)lang, Garrulax* (various).

please answer them:
'Two men from somewhere else,   /10
a brahman too, so three in all,
came by and asked
to sleep here until dawn.
They viewed the trees,
lamenting with deep sighs,
then left this morn,
went out a moment past.'"
And having ordered thus,
the lord walks off.

Two aides are watching out,   389
and, looking back, they see two maids
approach along the road,
dismount, come in the park,
and straightway ask the guards:
"Has anybody come?"
The guards reply as they were told.
The maids weigh up this news.
"Pray tell us what you saw:
how young or old,   /10
how handsome? Tell us please."
The guard's reply is: "Peerless!
A god, perhaps, is not on par.
He's young and handsome—very.
This brahman's lovable.
As for the two attending him,
don't set your sights—they're peerless too."
On hearing this, the two maids fume.
"Ho hum! How dumb of us,
to waste time dressing up.   /20
Had we come here a bit more quick,
we'd not be left in doubt."

The two feel rueful, sore at heart.   390
"O, being just a little late
has let us down.

What can we do   391
to catch a glimpse,
which is our dearest wish?

O, we have merit and so soon!   392
That's them for sure. The world-lord's come
with servants two in tow."

They strain their eyes to peer ahead,   393
espy afar the slender forms
of those attending him.

"Come quick! Just look from here.   394
You told us just a tick ago—
is that those men or not?"

The guards now see and say, "For sure.   395
That pair of fellows over there
accompanied this brahman here."

At speed the two sweet maids   396
approach towards the men,
then artfully conceal themselves
so that they can't be seen.

"Now this is really easy here,   397
fulfilling our desire.
O friend, I'm thrilled!"

They go down to a lake to hide.   398
"We'll spy on them from here,
and not let them see us."

The aides arrive before too long   399
and when they near the lake,
they slowly saunter there.

They stride with arms hung loose   400
across the park,
the gardens of the princesses.

"We saw some people walking here,   401
but now they've disappeared,
they're nowhere to be seen.

That's strange, a real surprise.   402
We've looked and looked all round,
but nothing anywhere."

The aides go down towards the lake   403
and come upon two maids,
who laugh and smile and wait
until the men are close,
then slyly question them.

"What country are you from, you two?   404
You're bold and truly without fear
to dare to come down here, this royal lake.
Now go back quick, or there'll be trouble here!"

"We'll go back miss. No need to chase us off.   405
We walked here from a distant place,
and saw the lake looked fun and worth a try.
We did not know you're here. Don't scold.

This garden when we came, fair miss,   406
we looked but found no-one on guard.
We saw the lake looked fun and wished to bathe,
but you are here and gripe—we feel ashamed.

We'll take our leave, you lovely pair.   407
To stay around would make us more ashamed—
as men that ladies force to flee away.
We came because we did not see you first."

"You get too hot so quickly, sir.   408
Your slip was small. You multiply it thousandfold.
I feared some rogues had come and so complained.
My fault. I failed to look. Forgive me, sir.

If us you'd seen, our anger would be fair.   409
As you did not, our huff's a hairsbreadth's small.
On hearing you, our hearts are nectar-washed.
If we offended you, pray please forgive.

You wish to bathe, sir, come on down   410
and douse your heat in this fresh lake,
scrub dust and dirt, wash sweat and scurf,
then pick the lotus, peel the seeds to eat.

Eat the lotus—truly it is good,   410a
like eating something heavenly
as you will see."

The men take in the women's words.   411
They change their cloths, come down to bathe,
behave as gentlemen
with words polite to please:
"For us to bathe here in this lake
is like a dip in heaven's pond
with ladies so sublime!

410a This verse does not appear in the standard edition but is found in several of the manuscripts, positioned after v. 411. Chanthit (*Prachum wannakhadi*, 504) suggests it should appear here.

This lotus, oh so tasty, good to eat!   412
The white one, how is that, I'd like to know."
"Please go ahead. It's over there.
No need to go to heaven—nectar's here!"

"O Roi, for love, please don't be dim.   413
Pray take our guest and go that side
to pick and eat whate'er he wants,
and help make sure he's satisfied."

Then Roi invites him with sweet words,   414
and Khwan concurs like Kama's soul, all smiles.
They duck in duo through thick lotus leaf.
He breathes the lotus scent and, better far, her cheeks.

"The lotus leaves conceal us. Thanks to them!   415
The flowers seem to laugh and call us close
to touch, caress the lotus, rapt with joy,
as I enjoy you here to play with me.

Your breasts like lotus buds. Your face a lily bloom.   416
The lotus scent so sweet my senses are aroused.
This lotus lady spurs and sparks my heart.
A lotus truly beautiful from head to toe.

Lord Kama's lovely lotus, lily mine!   417
The sweet nymph lotus conjures up your scent.
O lustful lady, come and share a taste.
Come close. Don't slip away. Strike up the sport!

---

414   **and Khwan concurs** ... This line has a play on words between Khwan's name and its
      meanings as "soul" or "beloved," and can be read several ways. Worawet (*Khumue lilit
      phra lo*, II, 34) thinks *khwan* here refers to Roi luring Khwan by smiling like Kama, the
      god of love.
417   **nymph lotus** See v. 90.

Let's play, my lotus hid inside your lotus bloom."   418
A snakehead slips across the lake of flowers.
A leaf-fish, carp and catfish jostle close.
A mudfish feeding by the bank stirs foam.

This side, they play, clung close: "O bliss!"   419
That side, another pair, same game.
What fondling feels as fun as this!
Like hide-and-seek, again, again—like war!

They play in water then on land.   420
Two loving couples climb the bank,
wrapped breast to breast, caress and kiss,
till earth and sky erupt with Kama's spume.

The maids escort their guests inside the garden house,   421
slap the mattress, lay a cloth, call their lovers up.
Two trysts, two laughing sounds, two feasts.
Two hearts enjoy the tastes and tricks together.

Lovemaking done, the plots of passion played,   422
the maids lean forward and ask their lovers' names.
"Where are you from? How are you called? Pray tell.
So we may know your names and city home."

The men, on hearing these two maids,   423
conceal their names and say,
"Our names are Ram and Rat.
We jointly came to trade.
By chance, where roadways cross,
we met a brahman,

418 **snakehead** See v. 354.
418 **leaf-fish** สลิด, *salit. Trichogaster pectoralis.*
418 **carp** ตะเพียน, *taphian.* See v. 354.
418 **catfish** (เท)โพ, *(the)pho. Pangasius larnaudii,* black-eared catfish.
418 **mudfish** พรวน, *phruan. Labeo pruol* or *Cirrhinus microlepis,* small-scale mud carp.

Si Kesa, by name.
He wants to see this country too.
By chance we saw the lovely face
of you, our best beloved.   /10

We live in Rommaya,   424
a charming royal capital,
a town of joy. But speaking straight,
we'll stay with lissome you,
not leaving from now on."

The maids, surprised, have doubts: 425
are these then not the men they thought,
and what should they do now.

"When you came to this town,   426
what goods had you for sale,
in what amounts, I beg to ask."

The handsome men, now far apart,   427
cannot combine to meet
the maids' quick questioning,
so dither back and forth.

"Do tell us quick what goods you have.   428
You cannot say? O my!
I want to laugh.

So you've disguised yourselves like this!   429
Your faces are not tricksters' faces, yet
you spin us with these tricky words.

---

424 **Rommaya City** รมยนคร, *romayanakhon*. Either a fictitious name or meaning "city of pleasure."

424 **charming royal capital** โมนหรราชธานี, *manohan ratchathani*. Alternatively, this is a proper name, "the royal capital of Manohan."

Perhaps the goods were just too dear?   430
Perhaps the buyers lacked the cash?
You will not say, so tell untruths.
Your cloths are noble stuff;
your skin's a palace man's, not low;
your looks are not a trader's type;
your faces aren't of common men.

Come on! Let's laugh to make the hunger go.   431
Please tell the truth.
Don't hide a thing from us."

The aides address the ladies' points.   432
"We'll tell you now the truth,
but please, no making fun of us.

His majesty the king   433
Phra Lo has come
and we're his retinue."

And when the men relate this news,   434
the two maids feel
they've gained a realm to rule.

"The sun has dropped from heaven to our hands!   435
And should we want the moon, it can be ours!
Or golden Meru—it won't 'scape away.
O sirs, invite your lord and highness here!

The king has come to stay in what locale?   436
In someone's garden, sir? We'd like to know."
"Our master's at an empty park,
alone and lonely, without friends."

---

431 **laugh to make the hunger go** หัวให้หายหิว, *hua hai hai hiu*. Perhaps a catchphrase like "pull the other one." Chanthit (*Prachum wannakhadi*, 523) suggests "We've laughed; now tell us the truth."

They beat their breasts and say, "O sire!   437
How could he stay like that? It's pitiful.
He's never suffered so. I'm mortified."
They sob and slowly tears begin to flow.

"Go quickly, please, you two,   438
pay homage to the lotus foot,
invite his majesty to come,
and we'll invite the princesses at once.

But first we'll wait to *wai* the lotus foot   439
and bow our heads before his majesty,
receive the nectar of his spoken words,
and take the news for which young ladies wait."

Two men coil arms around two maids,   440
slip hands round slender waists, caress
their bellies, kiss and cuddle, say, "You two,
we're loath to part from you one bit."

Two maids clasp tight the two men's flesh. 441
"O sir, you leave me, go away.
To part from you will be like dying once.
For love, return to save me soon."

They leave two paces, three, and then turn back. 442
"Beloved, though I part from you,
my body only goes to fetch the king,
my heart's with her I love as my own life."

"For me, it is the same, good sir.   443
My body only here, my heart with you.
Return at once for making love with me.
Be quick. For should you dally, I will die."

Phra Lo and the princesses come to the park

The aides go fast 444
to meet his majesty, the world-lord,
and pay respect, relay their news.

They tell him every point, 445
reporting from the start
events in full detail.

"We met the maids, two ladies fine, 446
the loyal staff of their two highnesses.
Now they invite your sovereign majesty
to travel there without delay."

Phra Lo proceeds with graceful gait, 447
as handsome as a lion-lord who leaves his cave.
On seeing him arrive, the waiting maids
rush up to greet one dropped from sky to earth.

Once there, prostrate, they *wai* the royal feet. 448
"Your highness, sovereign majesty,
please grace the pleasure palace, sire,
abode of joy of two princesses fair."

Phra Lo responds to them: 449
"Are these two silk-skinned ladies
well or not in any way?"

---

445 This verse does not appear in any manuscript version (Bickner, personal communi-
cation).

447 **lion-lord** See v. 224.

448 **pleasure palace** รมยพิมานสถาน, *rommaya phiman sathan*.

449 **Are these** ... A brief allusion to the formal style of diplomatic greeting, asking about
health, the journey, the city left behind. A reminder that the characters are royal.

"The two young highnesses   450
endure no fever but a fevered heart,
that pines and yearns for you, my lord."

The king, with graceful stride,   451
ascends the couple's lodge.
With scented water from a golden jar,
his royal feet are bathed
and dried with flawless cloth.
He steps on drapery laid down
up to a sleeping place,
and mounts the bed, reclines,
his lotus feet at rest.
He greets the maids,   /10
who pay respect and say:
"Your highness, lord divine,
is used to riding horse or elephant,
or having palanquins awaiting you,
all draped with cloth, with slippers gold
to fit the royal feet, so soft and smooth.
Yet here you've walked on earth like common folk
by forest paths through undergrowth.
Our breasts are fit to break apart
to hear your lordship's suffering."   /20
They bow their heads to pay respect.
"How did your highness come
through hardships fathomless like this?"

The king replies the maids: 452
"You are so kind, you two,
like loving royal kin.

However hard, it had to be,   453
as I desire to see the lovely face
of two young ladyships.

124

Be kind to me, without delay 454
make haste that I may see the face
of this young noble pair."

"Your golden highness, stay right here. 455
Your aides will take good care of you.
We raise our hands to leave the royal foot
and lock the door to hide you from the world."

"My breast is almost breaking, you can see. 456
I feel my heart inside is like a lunatic's.
Don't dawdle please, you two, go quick
to tell the gentle pair, my best beloved.

If they desire that we should meet, 457
invite their ladyships to come at once.
Too long will be too late to see me live,
but just a corpse whose burning's left to them."

The maids salute the royal foot farewell, 458
and two on two they fondly eye the men,
two pairs of eyes that slyly seek the other's gaze,
and nearly meet His eyes while watching them.

The maids walk from the room. They yearn. 459
From corner eyes, they bid their loves farewell.
The aides caress own breasts with groaning hearts,
as if such parting none had known before.

With poise they walk outside. 460
Once there, the two
lock fast the golden door
and take the key with them.
With spirits high, they stride ahead
to mount an elephant,
return right through the city gate,

intent to see the royal pair,
dismount inside the palace ground,
and scan the tower above.   /10
They see the princesses
within a lion window frame,
like angels come to earth,
their faces like the moon
or mirrors in the sky.
Two pairs of eyes that watch the road
espy the pair of maids.
Their faces lighten up as if
the lord himself had come.

"They're here! Let's call on down   461
to ask if they have news
to cheer us up.

On second thoughts, we'd better not.   462
For if the news leaks all around,
the dowager will hear—not good.

We'd better beat ourselves to death.   463
Why do the two beloved maids
walk here at such a gentle pace?

The inner palace gates are near.   464
How come today
they've shifted far away?"

460/12 lion window สีหบัญชร, *siha bunchon*, sīha pañjara. An aperture where the king
appears at audience, often on the palace front to receive people gathered in the
courtyard, but perhaps the term is here being used loosely for any palace window. The
term comes from a design where the frame is shaped like a lion's claw.

460/15 mirrors แว่น, *waen*, ring. Meaning a round piece of glass or polished metal used
as a mirror.

The couple reach the stairs and climb,   465
and at their ladies' tier,
approach the royal pair,
pay homage, state their news
in detail, everything.
With clasped hands raised, they say,
"Right now, your very soul
has made his way here, highnesses.

O mistresses beloved, your merit's great!   466
He's handsome as a bar of purest gold!
He's like a god who's flown to meet with you.
In all the world, this king alone's supreme!

He sent with us his words conveyed to you: 467
make haste to meet his lordship with all speed;
if you take long, you'll only find his ghost,
his royal corpse consigned for us to burn."

"A gem has dropped from heaven to our hands!   468
We love him more than life, won't let him slip.
But haste may make the matter talked about.
We must farewell the dowager, then speed!"

They 'tend the dowager and pay respect.   469
They raise her royal foot upon their heads,
embrace her while reclining on a throne-divan,
behave with humble grace to win her heart.

She praises: "Young grandmisses, fairest flowers,   470
each like a lovely lotus newly bloomed,
both young and beautiful in every way,
massage me now for strength as you know how."

---

469 **throne-divan** แท่น, *thaen*. A bench throne, a low dais.

She lifts their youthful faces to admire.   471
"You both are beauties, greatly good at heart,
so perfect who is worth to partner you?"
They knead her long and slow to lull her mood.

"Don't think about massaging me too long.   472
The strain may make you loyal two fall sick.
Now, Ruen and Roi, take care of them. Make sure
they bathe, eat well, put powder on their skin."

"For us to *wai* your lotus feet,   473
no other happiness compares.
To see your face, a lily bloom, why would we go?
It's like we're nectar-bathed, we're loath to leave."

"I'm glad you love me so, you two.   474
I like to hear your voices, clear and young.
The words you speak are sweet beyond compare—
alike a nectar shower that cures and braces me.

I love you, wish that you stay near at hand.   475
I give advice from fear you may fall sick.
More than my very heart, I care for you.
I caution you a lot but don't feel hurt.

You must observe the noble poses four—   476
to lie, to sit, to stand, to walk.
My perfect pair, my golden lotuses,
you must display each pose the same always."

"We have no wish to venture far away.   477
When we're apart we think of you.
But let us now take leave and go
to revel in our lovely royal park."

---

476   **noble poses** อิริยาบถ, *iriyabot*, iriyāpatha. For standing, sitting, lying, walking; traditional deportment.

"Do go along, you sisters two.   478
Bathe in the lake, admire the forest flowers.
Set off and travel back at eventime."
On hearing this, they *wai* to take their leave.

"O bliss beyond all words!   479
We'll meet the lord of elephants
just as we wish!"

They reach their residence,   480
go in the royal bath and bathe,
then dress themselves,
do up their faces like the moon,
coil their hair like heaven's nymphs,
don lowercloths of fine design
in lustrous, pretty silk,
and breastcloths beautiful.
Once decked they walk
with angels' graceful gait   /10
and arms poised ladylike
to reach a golden mounting stage
and mount a female elephant
with saddle tooled
in shapes of graceful walking beasts
and howdah decked in gems,
the elephant itself arrayed
in splendid, gleaming ornaments.

Above flap peacock flags and golden parasols,   481
umbrellas jeweled aglitter,
fans and yak-tail shades.
Court ladies come in crowds,
the maids behind the princesses.

481/2 **umbrellas** กรรชิง, *kanching*. A form of tall regalia with the shape of an umbrella.
481/2 **fans** พัดโบก, *phatbok*.
481/3 **yak-tail shades** See v. 230.

They leave and in no time
they reach the park, its gates.
A golden palanquin receives the princesses,
proceeds till near the royal lodge.
The maids go boldly on ahead   /10
to speedily unlock the door.
As for the king, he's dressed
in crown and lowercloth
of fabric rich and rare,
as fine as Indra from the skies.
Concealed inside the jeweled lodge,
he waits to clasp the royal pair.

His aides are hid beside the bed.   482
In haste Ruen drapes a seat
for royals two to sit outside
in audience, while all around
the ladies of the court
pay homage ranged by rank.
Then Roi bows down and says,
"The dowager commands
that we be sure to warn
your ladyships to take some rest."   /10
The princesses take up this ruse:
"Soon now we'll lay us down."
Ruen adds, with hands in *wai*,
"Her majesty the dowager
commanded everything.
Court ladies are our witnesses.
Should you neglect her words, ere long
it's us who'll she have flogged."
Roi quickly draws the curtain closed,
invites the royal pair inside,   /20
informs the ladies of the court,
"If you stay here, they will not sleep,"
and shoos them all away to play:

"Go off to see the vines and blooms.
We two alone will wait upon
their highnesses, the royal pair."
And once the flock of ladies leaves,
the pair of treasured maids
close each and every door.

Without delay the maids   483
pay homage to their lotus feet,
invite the princesses inside.

At heart the pair feel bright as sky,   484
but when they hear the maids,
deep down they shyly pause.

"O please, since we were born, were small,   485
we have no knowledge, not one bit.
To go in, just like that? Please help!
I'm shy and getting shier out of fear."

"You're not a child, your highness, now.   486
Some things not done you have to do to know.
My golden mistress, dilly dally not.
Or don't you care for this great king at all?"

Behind the drapes Phra Lo draws close to hear.   487
On catching this, he knows the pair are truly young.
He sits up close behind their ladyships, unseen,
while, unaware, the pair talk with the maids.

"We love this lord more than our hearts!   488
We've never ached so muc has this.
We want to know, but truly that is hard!
We beg you two to show us what to do."

At this, the maids turn, smile, and laugh.   489
"Who'd dare to teach you, mistresses?
From day one on, you loved, you yearned for him.
Who taught you both to moan and sob and pine?"

"If you won't teach us, please don't mock us more.   490
You have no care for us at all, it seems.
You've known moon, sun, day, night before we did.
We don't know so we ask. We wouldn't if we knew."

"O mistresses, what could we say?   491
You'll know full well when with the lord
in just a moment's time—don't fret—
a trice, you'll know the arts yourselves."

Phra Lo cannot contain himself. He laughs.   492
The ladies jump in shock and fear.
Both laugh with face a-gape like lotuses in bloom.
He draws the silken drape, reveals himself to them.

The pair now see the figure of the king,   493
as handsome as the sun, the heavens' disk,
forget their shyness, lose themselves, lock eyes,
unblinking view his beauty, "O! Is this a god?"

They still their hearts, and shyly bow their heads.   494
They both prostrate and *wai* to pay respect.
Their beauty charms his eyes and cheers his heart.
He gazes at them both. Himself he has forgot.

"Is this a golden lotus plucked from water straight?   495
Is this a star descended from the sky?
Or else the moon from heaven come to me?
The more I see their faces, more my heart's enthralled."

They gaze at him. They don't avert their eyes.   496
He gazes on the faces of the princesses,
his laughing eyes not straying from the pair.
They *wai* and *wai* and *wai* his lotus feet.

Now Roi and Ruen, hands clasped, regard the king,   497
then view the beauties who attend on him.
Eyes on the pair, the maids forget the king;
eyes on the king, they then forget the pair.

For them the sight of him is like the sun;   498
the sight of them, the sky-illuming moon.
"With sights that slake the heart like this,
how dare the moon display its shining face?

O Roi, my friend, please help me look.   499
We think our ladyships the best of all.
But, with this king, their beauty is enriched.
All gods all-knowing made these royal three!"

"Once this is seen, one can't avert one's eyes!   500
In all three worlds can such be found?
Our merit must be great, dear Ruen,
for us to view these worthy royal three.

Two men, where have you gone? Come see!   501
Admire the faces of their highnesses—
the very best, the glory of the world.
A king and sisters, three in beauty matched."

The maids gaze on and on.   502
As for two men, who have experience,
they enter on all fours, heads bowed,
sit far away and pay respect
to royals three
with hands clasped high,

prostrate in reverence.
They view the beauty of all three,
their eyes and hearts enthralled:
"In all the lands beneath the sky,   /10
we see alone the lord of worlds
and sisters two, these three.

Such shining beauty did the gods create?   503
These looks leave all the world with tired eyes.
And matched so well, so very, very well.
More fresh than fresh, adorable, superb!"

Four servants *wai* the royal three,   504
invite his highness jeweled lotus feet:
"Proceed inside the blessed bedroom, sire,
perhaps you're tired, and sisters too, all three."
Phra Lo proceeds with grace. The earth and heavens shake.   505
Two princesses proceed. The three worlds quake.
Three royals, heads held high, arms swung with grace,
like moon and stars that rise to light both sky and earth.

Roi and Ruen now bathe the royal feet,   506
pat dry all three and raise them on their heads,
invite the king to mount the bed of bliss,
where, angel-like, two princesses attend.

The maids draw closed the drapes, and say,   507
"Let not your souls stray far apart,
the ladies' souls be vines that coil the lord,
the king's a golden tree the vines entwine."

The maids take leave, salute the lotus feet,   508
withdraw outside and close the doors,
once done, go straight to find their men,
but sit apart, though love burns them to ash.

Love's turmoil's hard to still,   509
and yet, through steadfast loyalty,
they quell their hearts.

"Aware of shame, it's truly hard!   510
If we were unaware,
'twould be so vastly easier!

This place, just made for joy,   511
invites misdoing—dance
and play—had we no shame.

Some folk will point behind our backs,   512
yet if we feign we haven't seen,
who then can do us harm?"

Though love and lust surge hotter still,   513
and flames in thousands burn to ash,
a royal lodge demands respect.
They can restrain their hearts through loyalty.

"We are from lines of loyal folk.   514
We shun a wrong a dust-speck small.
Suspect of wrongs a hair-strand slight, we'd die
than live for folk to point behind our backs."

All four approve these words.   515
Each pair talks back and forth
until the heat of passion cools.

---

512   **point behind our backs** ชี้กำด้น, *chi kamdan*. Pointing at the back of the neck.
514   **point behind our backs** See v. 512.

The tryst

Meanwhile the royals three 516
with arms entwined, recline,
flesh pressed to flesh in bliss.

Devouring kisses, they caress, 517
as thrilled as supping nectar,
feeling, fondling lovingly,

entwining arms with arms in tight embrace, 518
flesh pressed to flesh. O, flesh!
So soft and pleasing flesh.

Faces bright as new, 519
face pressed to face. O, face!
So young and fitting.

Breast pressed to tender breast, 520
belly pressed to belly. O!
Soft belly, lovely breast.

First time joined in love, 521
awash in tastes, in scents,
awash in lusts, in worldly cares.

A lotus blooms, unfolding like a smile, 522
a flower, a flower within a flower,
a flower hid within a sacred lake.

---

517 **devouring kisses** ปากป้อน, *pak pon.* A phrase for feeding a baby by hand. It becomes clear later that the first bout is with Phuean.

518 **O ...** โอ้, *oo*, perhaps โอ่อ่า, splendid, best conveyed by the exclamation.

521 **worldly cares** สงสาร, *songsan*, saṃsāra. The worldly cycle of births and deaths, but also meaning "care" or "concern" (e.g., v. 535, 552).

The bees caress in couples, 523
aroused in lotus hearts,
now coaxing cries back-forth.

A dip in heaven's lake won't match 524
this silk-skinned beauty's lake
where bathing sates the heart.

A thousand pleasures in her lake— 525
a fish frisks freshly, feels
a lotus flower that blooms.

The banks beside the lake, so beautiful, 526
so pristine, clean and clear,
that heaven's hillocks can't compare.

"Because of merit I could come 527
enjoy a princess's golden breasts."
"O please, enjoy once more!"

His tryst with Phuean now done, 528
Phra Lo caresses lovely
princess golden Phaeng.

Though many poses played, 529
he is not tired, he does not pause,
aroused for making love.

Alike a horse of senses five, 530
his power by passion multiplied,
he pounds a pace with no respite.

---

527 **enjoy once more** พี่เอ้ยวานชมหนึ่งรา, *phi oei wan chom nueng ra*. It is not clear who speaks
this line.
530 **senses five** See v. 338.

He's like a tusker mad in musth,   531
with thrusting tusks and clutching trunk,
clung close in clinch, caress.

He softly soothes the princesses: 532
"Beloved ones, for me
to have these tender flowers was hard.

Say nothing now, I beg.   533
Allow me first, lithe lissome loves,
to have my due reward."

"Your virtues are too great to count.   534
Be kind towards us maidens, sire.
We had no knowledge, not one drop.
Take care of us as partners, worthy lord."

"It's nothing, ladies. Have no fears.   535
I love you past the bounds of earth and sky.
I'll care for you more than for my own self.
One watch without a sight of you, I'll die."

His strength and his desire are not destroyed.   536
Though both the pair are weary, wistful, weak,
yet love is like a fresh celestial shower—
now fresh, now limp, then brisk and bright again.

Loud thunder blasts the heavens, shakes the skies.   537
Earth quakes, is almost wrecked; and bellies churn.
At sea, the roaring waves are whipped to foam.
What wonders here! Trees yaw and sway all ways.

---

533 **due reward** เอาบุญ(เอาคุณ), *ao bun (ao khun)*. To expect gratitude in return. A long
metaphor of *bun/khun*, virtue and reward, runs through these few verses.
535 **watch** ยาม, *yam*. A division of the day, three or sometimes four hours.

A lion-king is nuzzling snug his lioness.   538
A tusker jogs his mate to jig and play.
A golden deer strides spryly forth to sport,
while rabbits, squirrels gambol, couple, chase.

A lotus, struck by sunny rays,   539
stays closed, unblooming, wary of the bee,
the bee that, lotus bathed and bleary drunk,
probes pollen-perfumed petals out and in.

No inch apart, no moment's rest,   540
still bent on battle, no relief.
Have pity for the lotus flowers, no longer fresh,
closed tight, not blooming like the pine-tree's flower.

The sun has nearly crossed sky's rim.   541
Two maids call out,
"It's evening soon, mistress."

The golden lord draws back the drape   542
and calls their treasured staff,
all four, to go inside.

He's thought it through, and says,   543
"Conceal this intrigue well.
Let no one see our ruse."

They promptly *wai* the lord,   544
receive the royal words,
and place them on their heads.

---

538 **A lion king …** In a series on the poem, the distinguished illustrator Hem Vejakorn (1904–69) rendered the images in this verse as a writhing collage with an art deco feel (Plueang and Hem, *Phra lo phap vijit*).

540 **pine-tree** สัตบรรณ, *sattaban*, sattapaṇṇa, seven leaf. *Alstonia scholaris*, a large evergreen (not really a pine but sometimes called a milkwood pine); here seemingly referring to Phra Lo. Alternatively, this means the *sattabongkot* lotus; see v. 89.

139

Afterwards

They call the lord to bathe and ease the heat, 545
inside a single golden urn
together with two princesses.

His lotus pressed among the flowers 546
incites a little playfulness,
revives their strength again.

He leaves the bath, by jeweled bed 547
is dressed, adorned, and comes,
reclines with them pressed close.

The servants pay respect 548
and bring in trays of food,
prepared in readiness.

The princesses prostrate 549
and urge his majesty,
"Please eat, O lord of ours."

He chucks their pretty chins, 550
and begs their ladyships,
"Please dine along with me.

Celestial food cannot compare, 551
because two silk-skinned beauties
are nestled close beside me as I dine.

Beloved, the food you feed my mouth, 552
is tastier than food divine,
and stirs my love and care."

---

552 **feed my mouth** ปากป้อน, *pak pon*. See v. 517.

And once they've eaten happily,   553
two treasured maids
salute and give advice:

"The sun will slip below the sky.   554
Your majesty, do not delay.
Now is the time, O mistresses."

The fragrant pair have no desire to leave.   555
The king regards the two of them with grief.
All three inflamed, lovelorn, lovesick,
press cheek to cheek as tears flow down.

O pity two young lady loves,   556
bowed low in homage on his lap,
their faces bathed in flooding streams,
their sobbing, weeping, grieving without end.

"Your highness, lord of all the world,   557
since first we heard the news about you, sire,
we could not eat from pining with desire,
nor sleep from fever, waiting, wanting word.

We prayed to every god throughout the hills,   558
to sprites that live in woods and trees,
imploring them to bring you here to tryst—
this wish fulfilled, we'll honor all these gods

with heaps of gold and silver, crores of gems,   559
and mounts with golden tusks, and male white buffalo.
Our prayers had merit: you survived to come.
If we'd no tryst with you, we'd have no mate.

---

559 white buffalo ควายเผือก, *khwai phueak*. Using the same adjective as a white (albino) elephant.

You came to be our guest, restore our souls.   560
Less than a day of love, we're parted quick.
Like this, are we to separate? Like this?"
With arms around the lord, they weep and pine.

Lamenting leaves him listless with his loves.   561
He bows to hide his face and weeps
upon their lovely backs. "My golden lotuses!"
No will to raise his face and leave his best beloved.

"I've known the bliss of Amarin, my sweet.   562
When first I heard the news of you,
if I could fly, I would have flown,
but could not—caged inside a net of love.

A spacious city, tuskers, horse, I left.   563
I left a mother, left a wife, to come.
I left my pretty consorts, sweet as flower bouquets.
I came alone to be inside your net.

I meet you two for just a single watch,   564
spent like a rope of three tight-plaited braids.
How can you turn and leave so fast? Once gone,
I'll forsake love. I'll hold my breath and die.

Should you not love me, please now go.   565
But if you love, how can you leave?
I came, intent, in secret, from afar.
If you leave me I'm orphaned and alone."

On hearing him, their turmoil knows no bounds.   566
"O let us beat ourselves to death!
Why do you say we rush to part from you?
We wish to be apart not half a breadth of hair!"

---

562 Amarin อมรินทร์, Indra.

As princesses talk back and forth with him,   567
the sun is slipping surely down the sky.
The maids advise the pair, "Now dusk is nigh.
If dark, there'll be an issue, reprimands."

They quickly *wai* the royals three.   568
"You'll not be parted long.
At eventide, return to tryst again.

Your handsome highness, please,   569
do tell the lovely pair
now's time to go."

Though pining, yet he says: 570
"Your gentle ladyships,
please go ahead."

The ladies pay respect.   571
He lifts their faces,
kisses both farewell.

With faces love-burnt dark,   572
they *wai* his feet and pine,
and slowly walk away.

Then turning back, they pause and peer,   573
looking small and pitiful,
farewell their lord, who farewells back.

"Don't leave us long, O sire.   574
Your highness, please,
come find us soon."

"My pain is worse than words can say.   575
I wish to go along with you.
To leave you is to die."

The maids clasp hands to pay respect,   576
invite the pair to go.
They reach the mounting stage.
A golden palanquin receives them there,
and ladies of the court attend,
but Ruen astutely keeps
the matter tightly covered up.
Once all the doors are closed,
their ladyships have reached the gate,
she feigns, "I've left some things   /10
back in the jeweled chamber-room.
Come Roi and help me look.
Please leave the gate unclosed."
Within no time at all,
they reach the palace-lodge of joy,
unlock the door,
and Roi waits there on guard,
while Ruen escorts the lord,
two aides behind.
In evening's cloak, unseen,   /20
Phra Lo, world-lord,
goes with his aides, disguised.

They reach the palace gate,   577
approach the noble couple's residence,
escort the lord upstairs,
and hide him in Roi's room.

The maids, who brought the lord,   578
conceal his aides
so they're not seen.

When night obscures the sky,   579
they take the king, world-lord,
and sneak upstairs to join the pair.

The blessed flowers   580
come out, receive the king,
and take him back inside.

"Why did you come so slow?   581
Will you leave us
to die of gloom?"

With arms they pull the lord   582
to mount a bed divine.
Their ladyships are thrilled.

The handsome lord reclines   583
on mattress, cushions, covers that
the sisters have prepared.

Fine drapes of lustrous silk   584
are hung from hoops of gold and *nak*
with patterns worked in gold.

The scents of flowers water-steeped   585
suffuse a sweet perfume
throughout the sleeping room.

A canopy festooned with pretty gems   586
and glittering with gold
gives shelter to the royalty.

They bring him royal cloth as dear as gold,   587
anointments of *krajae* infusion, scents,

---

580 **blessed** ภัควดี, *phakhawadi*, bhagavati. The blessed one, an epithet of the Buddha.

584 ***nak*** นาก, tutenague. An alloy of gold, silver, and copper with an appearance similar to silver.

587 ***krajae*** กระแจะ. Fragrant water made by steeping the bark of the *krajae* tree, *Hesperethusa crenulata*, Thanaka, and used like eau de cologne. It might come as a powdered extract for dissolving, sometimes combined with sandal and other ingredients.

a betel-tray with dragons, gem-inlaid,
and foods—the princesses present to him.

The three taste food and then taste joy.   588
Now making fast the golden bedroom door,
the maids go tryst with their two men, his aides.
They laugh and play and fondle lovingly.

Massacre

Discovery

The pair conspire to keep him hid,   589
known only by the two, their maids,
till roughly half a month has passed
of pleasure, smiles, and tireless play.

Sometimes they act as if unwell,   590
sometimes as if in bliss.
Sometimes they bloom, they play.
Sometimes they hide away,
chit-chatting secretly.
The maids alone can enter there,
no others are allowed.
The palace ladies
nudge each other, chatter privately:
"Things now are truly strange.   /10
Our pair of ladyships
and maids have something up."

The smoke leaks out.   591
One person knows and nudges more
to look and see.

Some find it shameful, scandalous.   592
Some just don't want to know.
The rumor spreads to reach
the royal father of the pair.

He comes to watch his daughters secretly,   593
and rages like a burning fire,
like grassland set ablaze.

He peeps at Phra Lo too,   594
and seeing him so handsome, so superb,
his rage just disappears.

"Perhaps through merit made,   595
though they were far apart, so far,
they now are close, so close. Miraculous!"

These stolen glances comfort him.   596
"Phra Lo is totally
in my hand's palm!

To have this king is like   597
the sky and earth are placed
within my palm.

To have him as a son-in-law unasked,   598
when this is known, my fame
will be supreme, beyond belief."

The king decides to show himself.   599
His daughters *wai* his lotus feet.
Phra Lo enquires.

---

592   **the royal father** King Phichai Phitsanukon.

598   **unasked** เขยแขก, *koei khaek*, "guest son-in-law." One who came of his own accord, not by invitation of the woman's family.

599/2   **Phra Lo enquires** He asks the princesses who this is.

They speak their father's name.
The famous lord,
clasped hands held high,
prostrates with reverence
and fitly speaks, head bowed,
"Your majesty, world-lord,
I left my realm,   /10
relinquished all,
and journeyed here alone.
Allow me, father-king,
to trust my family-line
to join with yours,
become a single lineage
until this era ends."
The king, on hearing this,
his heart blooms lily-like,
his face glows clearer, brighter than   /20
a monarch great
because of gaining this
fine lord and king
to be his premier royal son
beside his daughters two.
"I'll have them find a fitting day and month
to hold the marriage rite."
With these few words,
he goes inside the royal hall.
The news spreads to the dowager,   /30
who comes to carp and plead:
"O sire, this king,
a son of that black-hearted foe,
who killed your father dead,
now slyly comes to show contempt,
to slight our progeny.

599/33 black-hearted foe King Maen Suang, who did not kill Phimphisakon with his own hand, but brought about his death in war. See v. 7–8.

I'll have him captured now,
not let this foe live on.
I'll have him slashed to bits.
I'll have him sliced and flayed   /40
to shreds till satisfied."
However much she pleads,
the king declines to hear.
Returning to her residence,
she calls a squad of troops,
retainers skilled and senior,
and says deceptively,
"The king has given us the task
of having them all killed
for acting with contempt.   /50
You keep our mission hid,
unknown to anyone.
Whoever leaks it out
will suffer stringent punishment,
his neck sword-chopped stone-dead
for failing to respect my words."
The troops receive the royal writ
and proudly take the task.
"Your highness, kindly wait
to see the means we use."   /60
Hush-hush they dress and arm themselves,
and then at dead of night
in circles three
surround the palace ground,
not letting anyone pass in or out.
But Kaeo and Khwan are told
and promptly tell their king
about the plot in full detail.
The lord just smiles and jokes.
"I have no fear." He acts as bold   /70
as would a lion-king,
and brandishes his weaponry.

Then Kaeo and Khwan
present their services to him:
"Your servants, of sound mind,
do beg to die before you, sire."
And their two ladyships
bow low their heads upon his feet.
The mighty lord
consoles the royal lotuses: /80
"O blessed pair, be not alarmed,
it's nothing much, your ladyships."
His words give heart.
They slowly smile and laugh,
both feeling cheered,
and soon are truly bold.
"We also are of royal birth.
We are not cowards fearing death.
We'll have no other man as mate.
We will not live for royals to demean.   /90
We will not live for servants to disdain.
And should the heavens take our liege,
we'll die to follow him.
Don't be concerned for us, my lord!"
They strip their breastcloths, bind them tight,
don supple lowercloths, grasp swords,
and stand beside the king.
At once both Roi and Ruen,
high-spirited and true, declare:
"Should heavens take the royals three,   /100
who could we serve?
They'd all be too afraid!
We beg to die to trail our lord and mistresses,
to join you in the world above,
and leave a name for people to admire."
The two pay homage to their highnesses,
disguise themselves as men,
don shirts, and swagger, swords in hand.

Now Ruen, just raring for a fight,
comes on the right with Kaeo, /110
and quickly Roi
comes on the left with Khwan,
all keeping close, not far apart.
Upon this wondrous sight, the king
assumes the central place,
princesses close on either side.
He kisses their two ladyships,
and both of them kiss him.
Two aides draw two maids close,
embrace together and caress. /120
But soon some troops arrive,
come through the palace gate.
Kaeo swings and slashes with his sword.
Khwan stabs his sword blade-deep.
The troops turn tail to flee,
but others beat them back to fight.
The king advances, slashing hard,
dead bodies fall in piles,
severed heads in stacks.
Their troops hurl rocks and stones, /130
come swarming forward in force
with trees to batter down the wall,
but his two aides
war-dance and strike in fierce defense
like tuskers mad in musth.

They turn, engage, attack, 600
dodge arrows, not impaled,
dodge lances, left unscathed.
The foe let fly more barbs,
and fling more lances hard.
To left they come on thick,
to right they come on fast,
crowding in all sides.

Two aides attack and slash with skill,
stripping charms and lopping heads.   /10
Yet arrows hail on down.
First Kaeo is hit and writhes,
then Khwan is felled on top of him.
Ruen attacks with slashing sword.
Roi makes cut and thrust,
and sticks her blade hilt-deep.
That these are women, no one knows.
The raiders shoot and hit them both.
They fall, each with her mate,
their bodies sprawled on their two men,   /20
and die together there, all four.
Their lord, on seeing this,
accords his men great praise:
"Their loyalty endears my heart.
I fear we cannot be the same."
The princesses call laughingly:
"Those four feared not their fall,
so why should we of royal birth fear death
and suffer shame eternally.
To lose our lives or to survive,   /30
let's not be parted from our love, our lord.

Your precious highness, have no doubt: 601
we'll die but we'll not part from you.
Have no concern, O lord, that we live on.
When else will we have time to die like this?

When dead, we'll be reborn together, all,   602
to taste the world of heaven in the skies.
Why should we live for men to mock?
To live not seeing our lord's face, we'd rather die.

600/10   **stripping charms** เครื่องพลัด, *khrueang phlat*. Removing amulets and other devices
worn for protection and invulnerability to weapons, perhaps by cutting the neck
strings.

So soon, those four have gone to death.   603
We two of royal line can't leave our lord.
We love ourselves yet fear atrocious shame.
We love our lord, will die with you. How could we live?"

He hears their ladyships, his best beloved,   604
then laughs with pride,
and smiles in happiness.

Two princesses, one lord of worlds   605
are bolder than the boldest heart,
and braver than the brave in fear of shame.

With not one hair-strand's fear of death,   606
with swords in hand,
they face the foe.

They slash, and flash, and thrust, and stab,   607
swing swords, lop heads, chop legs.
All three appear so grand,
as fine as lion-kings,
so bold with swords in hand,
exuding power, no trace of fear,
all smiles and laughs,
advancing, dancing, arms held high,
imperious and menacing.
The foe form up and circle round   /10
like bringing straw to stoke a fire,
but keep their distance still,
while loosing arrows at the royal three.
With sword, he bats the barbs away,
but more arrive than he can block,
and soon an arrow strikes the king.
The two princesses without fear
come out to take the arrows shot,
standing by their lord.

The foe shoot more with poisoned barbs. /20
The three are hit, are riddled, shot.
Their blood flows down in floods.
They lean together now all three,
their faces turned towards the foe,
appearing like a work of art,
and pass away as one,
still standing tall as if not dead.
The foe in fear stay far away.
The news is spread,
and reaches King Phitsanukon, /30
who comes at once
and sees his daughters, most beloved,
and famed Phra Lo,
their bodies wholly bathed in blood,
still standing seemingly undead.
He wipes away his streaming tears,
and calls his daughters, calls his son-in-law.
However much he calls, no answer comes.
However much he nudges, nothing moves.
They stand there leant together, stiff. /40
The king then clearly understands
the royal three have met their fate.
He feigns he has no rage,
and says, "The criminals have all been killed.
They died together. That is good.
Let all those men, the brave and strong,
who volunteered to finish them,
come forward to take rewards.
For each of these brave men,
the prize is more than ever known. /50
I'll give them rank as *khun*
or *muen* or *phan*."
Straightway, the men are found and come,

607/25 **work of art** นฤมิต, *naruemit*, S: nirmita. Created.

not one omitted, every one.
He has their necks tied round with rope,
their elbows bound with cord,
their legs impaled by lance,
their names all written down,
then has them slashed like slashing down banana plants
by sword until they writhe to death.   /60
As for the leaders of the squad,
he has them boiled or burned alive.
The dowager he has flayed.
As she is not the mother of the king,
he has her executed painfully
and has them drag the corpse.
He goes then to his daughters' side
and weeps without relief:
"My dear beloved daughters, O!

Both beautiful as crystal glass,   608
however hard a hardship was, to see
my precious children's faces made it fade.

O may I die along with you!   609
Such pain I've never felt.
How can I live hereon?

My heart has overturned   610
with pain so deep I've never known.
O my two gentle daughters dear!"

607/56 elbows … lance ปอสับรัดมัดศอก แล้วให้เอาหอกร้อยขา, *bo sap rat mat sok laeo hai ao hok roi kh.* The form of words used here is very close to a punishment for disloyalty to the king found in *Ongkan chaeng nam*, the early Ayutthaya chant for the water-oath of loyalty ("Lilit ongkan chaeng nam," 10, line 3).

607/64 not the mother She was a wife of King Phimphisakhon but not the mother of King Phichai Phitsanukon and not the grandmother of the princessses.

608 crystal glass See v. 460.

Darawadi's grief

When Queen Darawadi,   611
their mother, hears the news,
her heart pounds fast, she faints
and falls, deranged,
her heart convulsed.
Court ladies give her care.
She boards a palanquin,
her retinue behind in tears,
to reach her daughters' residence.
The queen is dazed and weak,   /10
as feeble as a fallen golden vine,
with tears cascading down.
The palanquin is carried up,
and at the jeweled dwelling's tier,
she sees the royal three, deceased,
collapses, beats her breast,
and writhes from side to side.
"Your mother's here, my gems.
Perhaps you're mad at me,
and so won't talk with me at all,   /20
or dress yourselves for me to see,
or do your hair for me to touch,
or raise your faces for my kiss,
or douse yourselves in floral scent,
or civet or *krajae.*
You won't taste rice and fish.
You two are traveling heavenward,
abandoning your mother all alone.
Take pity on me, please!

611/25   **civet** ชะมด, *chamot.* Common name for several species of *Viverridae* that produce
a musk used in scent.
611/25   *krajae* See v. 587.

What makes you gladly rush to death?   612
Do open mouths and speak with me
so I can understand.

Did I offend you two somehow,   613
and anger you so much,
both go as guests to heaven?

What sadness caused this sudden turn?   614
Please think no ill, you two,
of your own mother, precious ones.

O, darkness lightens into dawn.   615
Go clean your teeth,
your mother's best beloved.

Relieve yourselves, my gems,   616
and on return
both go to bathe.

Get dressed and do your face,   617
tie sashes around your waists,
and walk to see your mother.

Come, you two, arrange some flowers   618
and offer incense, candles gold
before the feet of the All-Knowing One.

Return from there   619
to take your meal
along with me, my best beloved.

618　**All-Knowing One** พระบาทสร้อยสรรเพชญ, *phrabat soi sanphet*. MR Sumonajati Svastikul
("Sopsuan rueang kan taeng phra lo") speculated that this is a references to the Phra
Si Sanphet Buddha image cast in 1503/4 CE and placed in Wat Phra Si Sanphet in the
palace at Ayutthaya (Cushman, *Royal Chronicles*, 19). However, the phrase may simply
refer to the Buddha and here mean any Buddha image.

Whate'er I say, no answer comes.   620
Where'er I touch, no body stirs.
You stand there leant together, stiff.
Phra Lo, the lord of elephants,
does he forbid you to reply?

His majesty the king,   621
your father's come to visit you,
yet you won't look at him,

or turn your face to him,   622
or speak a single word
with me, O most beloved.

What's done within this life has little fruit.   623
I count myself still living, yet seem mad.
If I don't see my daughters here with me, I cannot live.
I'll die to see their two dear faces soon."

The royal kinfolk gather, loudly weep.   624
Court ladies slump in tears for their mistress.
Not one among the palace staff or cityfolk
resists to writhe with grief down on the ground.

Sobs sound from every subject, every home.   625
The earth's own breast seems set to overturn.
Sun, moon, and stars unseen, dim darkness reigns.
Wherever looked is water—people's tears.

From palace ladies to the king,   626
all weep, eyes stung with pain,
blood flowing in their tears.

Reconciliation

Two cities' grief

Through wisdom true and clear,
their august highnesses
compose their minds.
627

The weeping of the king and queen abates,
and then this royal pair
forbids all others too.
628

Once sounds of weeping fade,
the royal pair acclaim the valiant hearts
of these three noble ones:
629

"They stand there dead, so beautiful to see,
we know their hearts are truly royalty;
no others can surpass.
630

His men, two aides,
and Ruen and Roi, the maids,
not even gods can match.
631

All brave in heart, they died before their liege,
allied in death, within each other's arms,
both couples lovable!"
632

All people in the world
sing out their praise
aloud in every city state.
633

The sound resounds across the earth,
as if the sky did sweetly sing
to call them heavenward.
634

The oceans wail out loud.
The capital is fevered, every ward.
His Majesty Phichai Phitsanukon
commands his gracious queen,
Darawadi, be taken
to her residence.
He has three royal corpses bathed,
arrayed in royal cloths,
correctly wrapped and bound,
and one great gilt casket made, /10
the royal three placed there.
Another coffin he has made
to place Khun Kaeo and Lady Ruen,
and one, Muen Khwan and Lady Roi,
all done by customs for the dead.
The king proceeds inside the palace ground,
has royal craftsmen brought,
and gives commands
to have a holy Meru built
by conscript men from every branch, /20
and make a mountain all directions eight,
adorned with parasols and balustrades,
umbrellas, banners, flags,

635/9 **correctly wrapped and bound** ตราสัง, *trasang*. The term for wrapping and binding a corpse in a prescribed fashion. Separate cloths are used to cover the head, clasped hands, and feet, then the whole body is wrapped in a sheet and bound with lengths of undyed white thread in a prescribed form. This may be the earliest known appearance of this term (Sathiankoset, *Kan tai*, 49–53).

635/13-14 **Khun ... Lady ... Muen** Khun and Muen are titles denoting rank. In late Ayutthaya, these titles were at the lower end of a deep hierarchy, but in early Ayutthaya the hierarchy was much shallower, and these titles were above the median. The two maids have the title นาง, *nang*, at that time denoting noble status.

635/19 **Meru** In Buddhist cosmology, the mountain at the center of the universe; here a site for the cremation pyre.

635/21 **mountain** พนม, *phanom*. Meaning a smaller Meru.

635/22 **balustrades** ราชวัติ, *ratchawat*. A boundary for a ritual space, here probably a low fence made with a lattice of wooden laths, tied with cord.

635/23 **umbrellas, banners, flags** กลิงกลด, *klingklot*. *Kling* is a Malay-derived word for an

and baldachins of many shapes:
golden bird, swan-lion, swan,
adorned in suitable designs,
some drawn by horse,
some drawn by dragons, glittering,
some drawn by chariots,
tricked up as elephants /30
and splendid *khochasi*,
with riders on the chariots,
weapons brandished in their hands,
war-dancing, stabbing, bold,
some riding tuskers, *khochasi*,
and eagles, striding lions.
All are linked and drawn by hand
by sundry demons, gods, and *garuda*,
by humans, *naga, gandhabba*,
a string of figures finely made. /40

umbrella, and *klot* a large fringed umbrella carried by nobles and ranking monks; ธวัช, *thawat*, S: dhvaja, flag; บรรฎาก, *bantak*, pātāka, a long vertical flag.

635/24   **baldachins** บุษบก, *busabok*. An open pavilion, often placed over a throne or Buddha image, here placed on the backs of models of mythical animals in a funeral procession (Niyada, *Jitakam phap sat himaphan*, 76–85).

635/25   **golden bird** กระหนกวิหค, *kranok wihok*, kanaka vihaga. Perhaps one of the bird-creatures which come at the head of such processions, such as นกเทษ, *nok thet*.

635/25   **swan lion** เหมหงส์, *hem hong*. Hem(arat), a mythical lion with the head of a swan. Alternatively, *hem* simply means gold, or *hemhong*, an expansion of *hong*, the mythical swan or goose. In a description of the procession at King Borommakot's cremation, *hem* and *hong* are clearly two different animals (Niyada, *Jitakam phap sat himaphan*, 79, 90, 173).

635/26   **suitable designs** จำเนียม, *jamniam*. Some manuscripts have ทำเนียม, perhaps an old version of เทียม, *thiam*, same, meaning "lifelike" (Bickner, personal communication).

635/26   **some drawn by horse** The text has "some mountains (พนม, *phanom*) drawn by horse," but this must be a mistake; the animal shapes are being drawn.

635/28   **dragons** มกร, *makon*, makara.

635/231   *khochasi* คชสีห์. A mythical animal with the body of a lion and head of an elephant.

635/36   **eagles** นนทรี, *nonsi*. Probably a miscopying of นกอินทรีย์, *nok insi*, eagle.

635/38   **demons, gods, and** *garuda* อสุราสุรครุฑ, *asura sura khrut*. Asura, "non-gods," demons; *sura*, gods; and *garuda*, the mythical bird, modeled on an eagle, the mount of Visnu.

635/39   *gandhabba* คนธรรพ์, *khonthan*, S: gandharva. Celestial beings, often musicians.

They set up stages now for mask-play and for dance,
make firework towers and candle stands,
revolving lanterns set with glass,
hanging lanterns, carved and cut,
and lines of lamps on posts,
short torches placed below the walls,
and lamps beside the balustrades
in honor of the royal corpses three.
The king then summons
envoys and their deputies   /50
who take a royal missive
along with tribute various
to offer at the royal feet
of Queen Bunluea,
the mother-queen of solar race.
The bless'd one hears the missive read
aloud in full with all details,
and feels she won't survive,
she can no longer live.
She lies collapsed on cushions,   /60
her face hid in her hands,
weeps for her son beloved,
repeating on and on,
"O treasured child of mine!

I feared that it would be like this.   636
Though I forbade you countless times,
you did not hear your mother's words.

I wished for you to die before my eyes,   637
to die of fever, be a spirit-ghost

635/42   **firework towers** ระทา, *ratha.* A tall structure for displaying fireworks.
635/43   **revolving lanterns** โคมเวียน, *khomwian.* A square lantern, made from paper painted on the four sides, that revolves from the heat of the flame.
637   **before my eyes** แก่แม่รา, *kae mae ra.* This phrase is repeated at the end of each line of this verse except the last.

in our own city, son,
where I could treat you lovingly.
But in their city you have gone to die,
be killed by lances, pike, and sword,
and arrows poison-dipped—like this!

From first conceived, I cared for you,   638
not once neglectful in the slightest way,
until you grew to rule as sovereign king.
I loved my son more than myself a hundredfold.

You were no ordinary monarch, son,   639
a crown of kings above all heads.
From cities hundred-one came lords
each day with tribute to your lotus foot.

You savored joy in palaces like heaven, son.   640
In audience you sat while kings paid court,
and city-lords, officials, soldiers, masters, men
attended on your lotus foot as on the lord of skies.

Your tusker looked a pair with Indra's own;   641
your horse alike the sun's from heaven dropped;
your troops o'erspread the earth. With wealth and joy,
the world-lord's city seemed like heaven high.

What karma drew the princesses   642
to love my royal son?"
She grieves and trembles, every limb,
as if she'd surely die.
In pity for the royal dam,
Laksanawadi, having heard the news,
comes quickly to her highness' side.

---

640   officials หมื่นขุนพัน, *muen khun phan.* Three ranks of officialdom.
640   **lord of skies** ท้าวเมืองแมน, *thao mueang maen,* "lord-city-sky," meaning Indra.

His consorts come as well,
the world-lord's friends in joy.
Without exception, everyone   /10
comes to the dam's abode,
sees her crying, and enquires:
"What matter makes you weep?"
Once known, they beat their breasts,
release their coiled hair,
throw their bodies on the ground,
with cries and loud laments
that echo through the city,
and sound to those who hear as if
the city's heart is crazed enough to overturn,   /20
its breast about to break,
as all throughout the realm
lament for love of their world-lord,
as if about to die.

They weep without a pause, without an end,   643
as if they too will pass away
with their own lord, each one.

Politics and compassion

A minister, a senior man,   644
then calms the king's men down:
"Don't weep. Weigh up this matter first.

The realm is overwhelmed, unsure.   645
Please give this matter weighty thought.
Don't treat it lightly, anyone."

They go to royal audience,   646
report in detail to the queen,
who lends her ear.

---

644 **minister** มนตรี, *montri*. A senior official or counselor.

"Times past, we harbored fears about the realm.   647
Your majesty, pray think on times ahead.
Our lord has met his fate.

An ill-thought move could wreck the realm.   648
The spirits could make bad things worse,
but only if we watch and wait.

Think carefully on wording the response.   649
Make no mistake, not even slight,
to have a good result."

He quickly pays respect: "Your majesty,   650
pray give some weighty thought
to build a future on this past."

On hearing this, she thanks the minister.   651
"I thought I'd go to see my dear son's pyre,
but fear some politics, some talk, contempt.
I'd rather die. Best not to show my face.

Seek out those men who know all matters well,   652
astute and eloquent, those good with words,
ten senior officers; and have them well-prepared
to take a hundred *chang* of silver, same of gold,

the ninefold gems, and sundry cloth and silk,   653
each gift in quantity, and quickly now!
Take elephants and horse and troops—all swift—
to grace the world-lord's rites in lieu of me.

---

647 **Times past** A reference to Song's attack on Suang. See v. 8–9.
648 **The spirits could make bad things worse** This line plays with a proverbial saying,
ผีซ้ำด้ำพลอย, *phi sam dam phloi*, meaning disasters tend to come in a series, not singly.
652 *chang* ชั่ง. A unit of weight equivalent to 80 baht or 1,200 grams.

Take tribute for the King of Song   654
and for the mother of the sisters two.
Inscribe the words on golden leaves. Go quick.
Act properly—let no bad news reach me.

And once his rites are done, request   655
some relics of the royal three and aides
to bring back here. Take leave with due respect
and polished words. Don't tarnish us."

She has the visitors appear   656
to take leave of her royal self,
bestows upon them recompense,
and, quickly after this is done,
has envoys from her side assigned
to follow after theirs, not far behind.
They set off soon and in no time,
arrive, present the missive, pay respect,
and offer goods to grace the corpse.
The king allows them placed   /10
in proper fashion, every piece.
And when the burning rites are done,
the king has put the flame,
a grand event is launched,
a major festival,
with music everywhere.
The beats of drum and gong
and strains of horn and conch
combine in one resounding sound,
that shakes the surface of the earth   /20
like bolts of thunder hitting ground,
like oceans' crashing roar.
The lamps and lanterns lit

---

654   **golden leaves** ลานทอง, *lan thong*. Where *lan* is the tree which has leaves used as paper;
      perhaps here meaning a sheet of gold, as used for important diplomatic missives.
656   **visitors** แขก, *khaek*. Meaning the Song envoys.

in quantities defying count
shed light so bright,
so beautiful, so brilliant,
that every detail, everything,
appears magnificent.
And once events are done,
his majesty the king supplies the means   /30
to fashion urns to hold the relics left.
The king then has divided up
the relics of the royal three,
half placed within the hall of royal kin,
half for the visitors to take.
He has the road bedecked
to be a splendid carriageway
with decorations to the frontier point,
and sends the relics in a cavalcade.
Her majesty the Queen Bunluea   /40
bedecks a carriageway likewise,
receives the relics splendidly,
and takes them to her jeweled capital,
to Suang great and fine.
She readies there a peak-topped tower
to lodge the relics of the royal three,
and close beside on left and right
two halls of fine design,
to right Khun Kaeo and Lady Ruen,
to left Muen Khwan and Lady Roi.   /50
With loving heart, the queen prepares
a grand and marvelous event,
with various articles arranged

656/34   **hall of royal kin** หอพระญาติ, *ho phra yat.*
656/37   **carriageway** รัถยา, *rathaya*, S: rathyā. A road for carriages; name of a street used
for processions in Ayutthaya.
656/45   **peak-topped tower** กุฎาคารปราสาท, *kudakhan prasat*, kuṭagāra. A building with a
pinnacle.

to offer to the Holy Triple Gem
to benefit his majesty the king.
The treasury is tapped for alms
received by all throughout the land.
She has them build and ornament
the relic stupas, beautiful,
a great one for the royal three,   /60
to left and right, for aides and maids,
as if to tell the world
and heavens high above.
King Phichai Phitsanukon
has matters done the same.
Then missives writ with love
pass back and forth without a break,
convey the royal rulings made
about which day the relics are installed.
Both monarchs stage festivities,   /70
both cities looking glorious
for great and fun-filled festivals
and gifts of alms throughout the land.
The people, each and every one,
are moved to make some merit, send it on.

All nobles, commoners, and overseers,   657
each man and woman, all the world,
make merit, send the merit to the king,
all loyally intent to see this merit made.

656/54 Holy Triple Gem พระรัตนตรัย, *phra rattanatrai*. The Buddha, the Dhamma, and the
   Sangha.

656/54–5 to offer ... to benefit These two lines have been transposed in the translation.

656/75 send it on To perform a meritorious act, such as feeding monks and listening to
   chanting, then praying for the beneficial fruit of this act be sent to the deceased to aid
   the transition to another life. Today, during this prayer, people pour out a flask of
   water to symbolize the act of sending the merit.

657 all loyally intent ... Several manuscripts have an alternative line: All loyally invite
   the king to view the heavens (Bickner, personal communication).

May blessings come to those who voice this verse   658
which, like a garland woven with great care,
embellishes the ear at any time,
and like *krajae*, a little lifts the heart.

Finale

Here ends the work a king composed   659
to celebrate Phra Lo, a man in truth unique,
and aides so brave they died before their lord.
Their fame, supreme this world, ascends to heavens high.

Here ends the work a king set down   660
to chronicle Phra Lo, the bravest man.
Whoever hears, entranced, will never tire
of first love's thrill, of passion's heat, of love that's true.

658 *krajae* See v. 587.

Finale These two verses are probably late additions to the text.

659 **king** Some manuscripts have มหาราช, *maharat*, and some พระราช, *phra rat*. Scholars have speculated that the former may mean Phra Maharatchakhru, the head of the brahman departments of government, whose incumbent was a famed poet during the Narai reign. Delouche ("Le Lilit Phra Lo," "Quelques réflexions," and "Une hypothèse d'attribution") proposes that the poem was adapted from a Lanna original, that *maharat* is a title used for the king of Lanna in the Luang Prasoet chronicle of Ayutthaya (*Phraratcha phongsawadan krung kao*, CS 837, 18; Cushman, *Royal Chronicles*, 17), while *yaowarat* is the title of a son of Trailokanat who made the adaptation.

660 **king** In the Ministry of Education text, the word here is เยาวราช, *yaowarat*, the junior king or prince. However, in several manuscripts which contain this verse, the word is มหาราช, *maharat*, great king (Chanthit, *Prachum wannakhadi*, 739; Bickner, personal communication).

Cast of Characters

Character	Role	Thai	Literal Meaning
Suang			
Maen Suang	king of Suang	แมนสรวง	god in heaven
Queen Bunluea	his wife, the "queen-mother" of Phra Lo, sometimes called "the (royal) dam."	บุญเหลือ	merit remaining/ exceeding
Phra Lo	their son	พระลอ	
Laksanawadi	wife of Phra Lo	ลักษณวดี	lady of (good) attributes
Kaeo	servant/page of Lo	แก้ว	jewel
Khwan	servant/page of Lo	ขวัญ	soul, auspiciousness
Song			
Phimphisakhon	king of Song	พิมพิสาคร	form of ocean
the dowager	a wife of Phimphisakhon	ย่า	paternal grandmother
Phichai Phitsanukon	son and successor of Phimphisakhon	พิไชยพิษณุกร	victorious arm of Vishnu
Darawadi	wife of Phichai Phitsanukon	ดาราวดี	star lady
Phuean	daughter of Phichai Phitsanukon and Darawadi	เพื่อน	friend
Phaeng	daughter of Phichai Phitsanukon and Darawadi	แพง	valuable
Ruen	maid to Phuean and Pheng	รื่น	joyful, fresh
Roi	maid to Phuean and Pheng	โรย	cheerful, outgoing

Other			
Old Lord Tiger Spirit*	an adept	ปู่เจ้าสมิงพราย	ปู่, *pu*, paternal grandfather; เจ้า, *jao*, lord; สมิง, *saming*, tiger or ruler; พราย, *phrai*, spirit of a dead person
Old Sage	adept who helps find Old Lord Tiger Sprit	ปู่หมอเฒ่า	paternal grandfather; doctor; old
Sitthichai	adept helping Bunluea	สิทธิไชย	victorious power

*   *Pu jao saming phrai* may simply mean "king of the spirits." *Saming* is the Thai transcription of a Mon word that may also mean a tiger. In *Ongkan chaeng nam*, the loyalty-oath chant believed to date to the beginning of the Ayutthaya era, *Pu saming phrai* appears in a long list of gods, spirits, and other powerful figures invoked to detect and punish any infringement of the oath. He appears in a verse (23) about spirits of the mountains in the company of the spirits of the black, white, great, and *klai* mountains, meaning Kalakuta, Krailasa/Kelasa, Meru, and Citrakuta ("Lilit ongkan chaeng nam," 9; Reynolds and Reynolds, *Three Worlds*, 292–94).

Pu jao saming phrai is also an ancestor spirit of the Mon, honored in spirit shrines in Mon communities, notably in Samut Prakan district, where the name has also been given to a municipality.

The title *pu jao* appears in two old Tai chronicles from Lanna. *Pujao luang kupkham* appears in *Tamnan mueang suwanna khomkham* and *Pujao lao jok* in *Tamnan singhanawati kuman*. Both these chronicles appear to record Tai groups moving along the Mekong into Lanna.

Pujao luang kupkham appears as the greatest of the spirits of the rivers and mountains at the time of the Buddha Kassapa (*Prachum phongsawadan*, pt. 83).

Pujao lao jok appears as an ancestor of Mengrai, a Lawa who barters his knowledge of metal with the Tai for rice and the right to settle in the valleys.

The princesses asleep by Hem Vejakorn (v. 374).

The death scene by Hem Vejakorn (v. 607).

Afterword

Lilit Phra Lo counts among the best-known works of classical Thai literature. It was anointed as part of the "national literature" in 1916, and has been studied in schools since the 1930s. Several editions have been published. Almost every luminary of Thai literary criticism has published a book or article about the poem. The contrast with *Twelve Months* is rather stark.

Until the 1970s, academic debate focused on the dating, authorship, and origins of the work, and the technical quality of the poetry. Somehow, the details of the plot were subject to little scrutiny. When students challenged Thailand's old order in the 1970s, *Lilit Phra Lo* became a lightning rod, criticized as feudal, decadent, indulgent, misogynistic, and prurient. The literary establishment mounted a defense on the grounds that the work is a repository of great poetry, and that the plot reflects Buddhist teaching on the working of karma. Amongst creative artists, there was a different and fascinating reaction. In the last quarter of the twentieth century, the Phra Lo story was reworked by novelists, film-makers, and dramatists more times than any other work from old Thai literature. These reworkings recast the story with little respect for the original, adapting the plot and the characterization to reflect present-day conceptions of love, heroism, and morality.

In this Afterword, we first briefly summarize the debate on the poem's origins and then review the modern history of the work. In the final part, we analyze the structure of the poem as a drama.

History of the Text

Dating and Authorship

The dating, authorship, and origins of the work remain uncertain. Virtually every scholar of old Thai literature over the past seventy years has contributed to a debate on these issues, but without a clear result.

Estimates for the dating of the work have ranged from pre-Ayutthaya times to the early Bangkok era. There is only one piece of information external to the text: an excerpt from the poem is cited as an example of good composition in *Jindamani*, a treatise on language and literature from the Narai reign (1656–88).[1] However, the language and meter clearly come from the early Ayutthaya era. The poem has several words and phrases that are not in use today, but can be found in other early literary works, especially *Mahachat Khamluang* and *Yuan Phai*, or in inscriptions from Sukhothai in the thirteenth and fourteenth centuries. The metrical forms were designed for a system of three tones that had disappeared by the seventeenth century (see Note on Translation above). Today, there is a scholarly consensus that the work originated around 1500.

Several attempts have been made to date the poem more exactly from information in the text. The opening invocation celebrates an Ayutthaya victory over Lanna, and this event has been identified with various historical battles. However, there were around twenty clashes

---

1.   Fine Arts Department, *Jindamani*, 32.

between Ayutthaya and Lanna between the 1430s and 1540s,[2] and there is nothing in the reference in *Lilit Phra Lo* to identify any particular one. Besides, this opening invocation may have been added to the poem at a later date. Verse 618 mentions making offerings at the feet of *soi sanphet*, which several scholars, beginning with MR Sumonajati Svastikul in 1945, have identified with the Buddha image named *phraphutthajao phra si sanphet* in the chronicles, cast by King Ramathibodi II in CS 865 [1503/4 CE] and placed in Wat Phra Si Sanphet in the Ayutthaya palace.[3] However, as *sanphet* (all-knowing) is a common epithet of the Buddha, the identification is likely but not conclusive. The last two verses both begin, "Here ends the work of a king," and various attempts have been made to identify what king is meant. Moreover, since these verses were probably added to the poem later, and since the words for "king" differ across the manuscripts and printed editions, this pursuit has not born fruit.[4]

The form of the text itself is evidence on its origins. The storytelling is linear and rather fast-paced, unfolding through time, with no leaps forward or back. Much of the story is told through dialog among the characters. The narrator is invisible. There is no commentary on the events, and no moralizing. There is a lot of repetition of phrases and rhymes. These are characteristics of storytelling in oral tradition all over the world. The prolog attests that the work was performed: "… here's told in verse of excellent Phra Lo …. The sound when sung, none can compare. Just hear its music—rivals none are known" (3–4).

2. See Baker and Pasuk, *Yuan Phai*, 5, fn 10; Niyada, "Lilit phra lo."
3. Sumonajati, "Sopsuan rueang kan taeng phra lo."
4. Delouche ("Le Lilit Phra Lo," "Quelques réflexions," and "Une hypothèse d'attribution") suggests that both *Lilit Phra Lo* and *Twelve Months* were composed by an unnamed son of Trailokanat who, according to *Yuan Phai*, was sent to Sri Lanka to fetch monks when his father entered the monkhood in Phitsanulok around 1465.

In the manuscripts, the text is continuous. There are no breaks into sections or chapters, and no headings. In the passages of dialog, there is no indication of who is speaking to whom. Some transitions between scenes seems a little abrupt, as if something is missing. In places, two adjacent verses seem to be alternative drafts. These characteristics suggest that this text was either transcribed from a performance or, more likely, was a record kept by a reciter. In performance, the reciter would have distinguished the characters in dialog by differences of voice; marked breaks in the action by pauses; and embroidered the story in the course of the recitation.

Such works designed for performance and passed down in oral tradition may accumulate over many years with several people contributing. The language and meter found in the texts suggest the original was written around 1500 CE, but the story may have existed in oral form before then, and has probably been amended during recopying in subsequent years. The attempt to identify a date and author is unlikely to succeed.

Texts and Editions

The Thailand National Library holds fifty-four volumes in the form of *samut thai* or *samut khoi* accordion books, including two complete sets. One volume carries a date of 1860. All are in the orthography of the middle to late nineteenth century and appear to stem from a single source as the variations are minor.[5]

According to the Fine Arts Department, King Chulalongkorn had his half-brother Prince Aksonsat Sophon (1826–1903) arrange a first printing at the royal press, of unknown date but perhaps 1902, and

---

5. Bickner, *An Introduction*, 62.

now not found in any library.[6] This same text was reprinted by Tai Press in 1915, by the National (then Wachirayan/Vajirañāṇa) Library in 1926, and by the Fine Arts Department many times since with only minor modifications.[7] In 1934, the Ministry of Education published an edition prepared by Phra Worawet Phisit, using the National Library text and adding verse numbers and some glosses.[8] In 1954, Chanthit Krasaesin edited a version showing variations found in the various manuscripts and providing renderings in modern Thai of verses he considered difficult to understand.[9] Phra Worawet published an annotated text with a version in modern Thai in 1961, and Plueang na Nakhon (under the name Nai Tamra na Mueang Tai) published a similar work in 1994.[10] In 2001, Cholada Ruengruglikit published an annotated edition based on the National Library text.[11] Robert J. Bickner compiled an unpublished version based on the manuscripts rather than the printed versions.

In 1937, Prem Chaya (Prince Prem Purachatra) authored what he called "a rather freely adapted version" of the poem in English

6. See the introduction to *Wannakam samai ayutthaya lem 1* (11). Chanthit (*Prachum wannakhadi*, 18) states that *Lilit Phra Lo* was first printed in 1875 by Nai Thep, who had a press on a raft at Pak Khlong Talat, but the Matichon history of Thai printing estimates that Nai Thep only began printing in 1890, and does not mention *Lilit Phra Lo* amongst his output (Matichon, *Sayam phimphakan*, 22–24).

7. *Lilit Phra Lo* (1915); Wachirayan Library, *Lilit Phra Lo* (1926), often reprinted as *Lilit phra lo khong krom sinlapakon*; the latest version appears in *Wannakam samai ayutthaya lem 1*, 385–494.

8. *Phra Lo Lilit* (1934), reprinted under the title *Nangsue an kawi niphon rueang lilit phra lo khong krasuang sueksathikan* (Ministry of Education edition of the poem Lilit Phra Lo). Phra Worawet Phisit was a monk and professor of Thai language and literature at Chulalongkorn University.

9. Chanthit, *Prachum wannakhadi thai*.

10. Worawet, *Khumue lilit phra lo*; Nai Tamra, *Lilit phra lo*.

11. Cholada, *An lilit phra lo*.

broadcast as a radio play by the BBC.[12] In 1999, a translation by Pairote Gesmankit, Rajda Isarasena, and Sudchit Bhinyoying was published as part of a project to promote ASEAN literature in translation.[13] In 1960, Ousa Sheanakul Weys and Walter Robinson made a translation that was never published.[14] In 2013, Pei Xiaorui and Xiong Ran published a Chinese translation in verse.[15]

The Modern Drama of *Lilit Phra Lo*

Origins

In 1932, Prince Damrong Rajanubhab wrote that the Phra Lo story was "a folktale (*nithan*) from the Lanna kingdom that seems to have been written down by a king before he ascended the throne."[16] Scholars have since been hunting for this original tale.

In the old Thai-Lao epic, *Thao hung rue jung*, there is a place called Kalong, the name of a river in *Lilit Phra Lo*, and the hero has a posthumous battle in the heavens with the god known as Thaen Lo. In several old works, including the chronicle of Lanxang, Lo is the son of the founder-god, Khun Borom/Bulom.[17] However, there is no similarity in any of these works with the tale of Phra Lo. In the Shan region, there are several versions of a story with a hero named Jao Sam Lo. In the version in the Tai Koen language, Jao Sam Lo's merchant

---

12. Prem Chaya, *Magic Lotus*. Prince Prem relieved Phra Lo of having a wife to cheat on, toned down the sex and magic, and ended with a fine flourish: "Together in one funeral pyre shall these lovers be cremated, and with their ashes we shall sow in both our countries' fields the seeds of perpetual peace."

13. Pairote, Rajda, and Sudchit, "Lilit Phra Lo."

14. Ousa and Robinson, "Phra Law Lilit."

15. Pei and Xiong, 帕罗赋>翻译与研究.

16. In the *Nangsue bantuek samakhom wannakhadi* [Annals of the Literary Society] 1, 5, quoted in *Wannakam samai ayutthaya lem 1* (8).

17. Sumonajati, "Sopsuan rueang kan taeng phra lo."

parents refuse him permission to marry his sweetheart, after which she gives birth to their child in the forest, the baby dies, she dies soon after, and Jao Sam Lo commits suicide.[18] Other than the name "Lo" and a tragic ending, there are no parallels between the Shan tales and *Lilit Phra Lo*. Prince Damrong's folktale remains elusive.

The two rival cities in *Lilit Phra Lo* are named Song and Suang. Song is also the name of a district town in Phrae Province. In 1945, MR Sumonajati Svastikul proposed that Song in Phrae is the city in the poem.[19] In 1951, the local authorities in Song renovated a stupa called That Hin Som (sour stone reliquary), renamed it Phrathat Phra Lo (holy reliquary of Phra Lo), and claimed it is the stupa mentioned in the closing part of the poem. In 1989, the temple published a chronicle of the stupa claiming it was built by the father of Phra Lo's beloved princesses in 1539 CE.[20] The name of the surrounding village was changed from Ban Klang (middle village) to Ban Phrathat Phra Lo (Phra Lo reliquary village). Two shrines were also built for Old Lord Tiger Spirit, the magical adept from the poem, who then rapidly emerged as the guardian spirit of the locality. In 1978, a statue depicting the death of Phra Lo and the two princesses was constructed close to the stupa with an inscription dating the incident to 2042 BE (1499 CE). The statue was modeled on a famous illustration for *Lilit Phra Lo* by Hem Vejakorn, but with the dress changed to Northern Thai style. A *wihan* (preaching hall) was added, and a Buddha image installed and named Phra Si Sanphet following a verse in the poem (see v. 618). In 2008, the local authorities constructed Lilit Phra Lo Park on the outskirts of the town, with another statue of the death scene, a representation of Old Lord Tiger Spirit's cave, and other depictions of

---

18. Soison, "Thai Literary Transformation," 65–67.
19. Sumonajati, "Sopsuan rueang kan taeng phra lo."
20. Soison, "Thai Literary Transformation," 78–79.

the story. The park now offers visitors the opportunity to repeat Phra Lo's divination at the Kalong River; to be photographed framed by a heart of flowers; to buy "Phra Lo packets of spiced rice," supposedly based on a recipe that a wet-nurse made for Phra Lo on his departure from Suang; to acquire a protective amulet with the Si Sanphet Buddha on the front and Phra Lo chasing the cock on the back; and to worship on a "Phra Lo day" in the Thai calendar's fifth month.[21] The province of Phrae promotes itself to tourists as the "love land of Phra Lo."[22] In 1990, Wat Luang in the provincial capital built a "Khum Phra Lo" (Phra Lo's residence) on the occasion of a visit by Princess Mahachakri Sirindhorn.

Song city and Phrae Province have been very successful in exploiting an association with the poem, but there is no strong evidence for this association. Sites for the other town, Suang, have been claimed in Phayao, Chiang Rai, Lampang, and Roi-Et provinces.

Status and Controversy

Lilit Phra Lo is recognized as a masterpiece of early Thai literature. In 1916, it was among eight works selected as excellent examples of their genre by the Literary Society (*Samoson wannakhadi*) created by King Rama VI to promote Thai literature.[23] Prince Damrong explained that *Lilit Phra Lo* was preferred over two other superb examples of *lilit* (*Yuan Phai* and *Talaeng Phai*) because the other two "were based on history, which was a constraint, while the *Phra Lo* story was only a folktale which gave the author more room to narrate in a captivating

21. Cholada, "Lilit phra lo dai ma jak tamnan rak."
22. For a tour of these sites courtesy of the Phrae provincial tourist office, see www.youtube.com/watch?v=ZT6mq3QkN3k.
23. Thanapol, "Royal Society of Literature," 48.

way."[24] From 1934, the poem was used for teaching in secondary schools.[25] The exotic setting and dramatic plot of the poem attracted the attention of artists. Hem Vejakorn, the most prolific and celebrated Thai illustrator of the mid-twentieth century, produced his longest sequence on *Lilit Phra Lo*.[26] Chakrabhand Posyakrit, a national artist, rendered several scenes in oils.[27]

Yet, there was some difficulty in accommodating such a work in the canon of a national literature that was supposed to be a repository of good moral values. The plot is about a romance between a man and two rather young ladies. The story includes a lot of love magic, climaxes in an erotic scene, and ends in a bloody massacre. The literary world engaged in debates on the dating, authorship, and correctness of the poem's use of metrical forms, but somewhat ignored the plot and its interpretation.

In 1950, the celebrated left-wing poet Atsani Pholajan wrote an article under the pen-name Indrayuth in the magazine *Aksonsat* criticizing *Lilit Phra Lo* as "feudal literature," written "to serve the king" and still promoted by the "feudal-bourgeois ruling class" which

muddles together art and immorality, claiming they are inseparable … pursues its own pleasure to the utmost, losing humanity, becoming shameless, and descending into bestiality … composes works that confuse art with obscenity to satisfy their own bestial lust … and uses these works to lull and mislead the people into not

---

24. Damrong, "Kham winitchai." On the *lilit* form, see Note on Translation above.
25. Wibha, "Thatsana," 119.
26. Plueang and Hem, *Phra lo phap vijit*.
27. Some examples are posted on www.chakrabhand.org.

thinking about freeing themselves from exploitation by the ruling class.[28]

In other articles in the column entitled "Reflections on Literature," Atsani-Indrayudh urged people to read literature which was relevant to their own lives and to the struggles for democracy and equality.[29] The impact of this critique was immediate but short-lived, because all free expression was suppressed by military dictators, sending Atsani into hiding and his publisher into jail. In the 1970s, when a rebellious student movement attacked Thailand's old order, including its literature, Atsani's articles were rediscovered, republished several times, and hotly debated. Atsani was heralded as "the first socialist critic" of Thai literature, and several other critics condemned Lilit Phra Lo as feudal, prurient, and meretricious.[30] The literary establishment mounted a defense based on the grounds that the quality of the work's poetry was outstanding, and its plot dramatized the Buddhist theory of karma.[31] From the left, Cholthira Kladyu (Satyawadhana) dissented, arguing that Lilit Phra Lo is "a real gem with so many faces sparkling so brightly that some people can see only a few of these faces,"[32] and offering a more subtle defence:

The 'truth' that is the core of Lilit Phra Lo is that humans have desires, have sensual needs, and try to satisfy those desires, but sometimes people obstruct those efforts. Such can happen to anybody, not only

28. Indrayuth, "Lilit phra lo," 82–84.
29. See especially Indrayuth, "Niyai phuenban pen kaen samkhan ying nai chiwit sangkhom khong pracharat."
30. See the introduction by Ida Arunwong in the 2016 reprinting by Aan; and Cholthira, "Sunthariyaphap," 73–75.
31. Sumali, Withi thai nai lilit phra lo; Suphon, "Phra lo"; Wibha, Phra Lo.
32. Cholthira, "Sunthariyaphap," 79.

kings and nobles .... The author decided to show that the behavior
of the characters, allowing desire to dominate reason, responsibility,
and custom, was not virtuous and thus was punished by painful
death ... but the author also understood that the reason behind such
behavior is the 'truth' that humans find difficult to avoid because it
arises from human nature, namely love, anger, lust, and illusion (but
may be suppressed).[33]

Atsani's attack may have helped inspire another, more subtle and
fascinating response. Over the last quarter of the twentieth century,
Lilit Phra Lo was adapted into several novels, short stories, stage
dramas, and films—many more times than any other old literary work
in this era. Strikingly, these adaptations borrowed the characters'
names and some plot elements from the original, but drastically
changed the plot, the characterizations, and especially the ending.[34]
The leading film-maker, Cherd Songsri, with the help of the leading
actor of the era, Sorapong Chatree, and a short story by the leading
writer, Yakhob, transposed the main characters into a modern rural
setting and a completely different plot in which the hero has an affair
with his wife's sister and commits suicide after the wife dies in
childbirth.[35] The leading popular novelist, Thommayanti (Wimon
Jiamjaroen), retained the framework of the original plot but recast the
princesses as exemplary modern women, and completely omitted the
erotic climax.[36] Patravadi Sitrairat, a leading actress and theatrical
producer, adapted Thommayanti's novel for the stage with the accent

---

33. Cholthira, "Sunthariyaphap," 87, 89.
34. These adaptations are brilliantly analyzed in Soison, "Thai Literary Transformation."
35. The short story had first appeared in 1933, and the film title *Phuean-Phaeng*
appeared in 1970 (Soison, "Thai Literary Transformation," 146–49).
36. Thommayanti, *Rak thi tong montra.*

on a theme of revenge. Another novel transformed Phra Lo's wife, a minor character in the original, into the heroine in a plot where Phra Lo is lured to Song wholly by magic, shows no interest in the princesses, and is killed by the dowager.[37] Another film transformed Phra Lo into a heroic king, omitted the erotic climax, and replaced the final scene of reconciliation between the two cities with a revenge-fueled war resulting in one city being burnt to the ground.[38] In 2019, Patravadi (Sitrairat) Mejudhon directed the story as a musical variety show, with a dramatic scene of the dowager's lust for vengeance, and an ending of Buddhist moralizing, neither of which appears in the original.[39]

It is usual for Thai authors and film directors to adapt old works with the aim of pleasing the modern audience, yet the violence done to the original in this case—by leading artists of the time—went beyond the usual intensity. These adaptations aimed to make the plot and the characters conform to contemporary conceptions of modernity and morality. Kings had to be suitably heroic, women strong and admirable, villains properly villainous. The erotic climax disappeared.

Phra Lo as Drama

The original text of *Lilit Phra Lo* is a drama, though a drama delivered by a reciter rather than a cast. Unsurprisingly, the tale has been repeatedly adapted to contemporary styles of stage performance. The Front Palace King, Mahasak Phonlasep, adapted the story into a traditional dance-play during the Third Reign (1824–51). Chaophraya

---

37. Nittaya, *Rak thi thuk moen.*

38. *Phra Lo* by Thangai Suwannathat (1968) (Soison, "Thai Literary Transformation," 125).

39. Patravadi, "Lilit Phra Lo 2019." Other additions included a violinist on a skateboard.

Thewet (MR Lan Kunchon) staged another version in the Fifth Reign (1872–1910).[40] In the 1900s, Prince Narathip Praphanphong, a son of King Mongkut and a distinguished poet, adapted the story as *lakhon rong*, a fusion of the traditional dance-drama with Western elements such as dialog and costuming. King Chulalongkorn attended and appreciated the play and the singing.[41] Prince Naris (Narisara Nuwattiwong), another son of King Mongkut, famed as a musician and designer, put the episode of the cock to music as part of a dramatic presentation of scenes from the Thai classics.[42] Prince Prem Purachatra's English-language play was performed on BBC radio in 1937, and an adaptation staged in Malaysia in 1981. A local play version from Phetchaburi was published in 1982.[43] Patravadi Sitrairat Mejudhon staged a spoken Thai version in 1986, and a musical version in 2019.[44] Modern troupes have updated the dance-drama type of presentation with a mix of Thai and Western styles of modern music and dramatic staging.[45]

In keeping with the work's evident dramatic character, we here analyze the plot as a drama. The story can be divided into seven sections or "acts" which differ in setting, mood, and style.

40. Fine Arts Department, *Chumnum rueang phra lo*.

41. Mattani, *Dance, Drama, and Theatre*, 119–24, 138–47.

42. Mattani, *Dance, Drama, and Theatre*, 129–31.

43. Lom, *Bot lakhon*. We have not seen this. It appears in WorldCat in the Library of Congresss and elsewhere, but not in any Thai library.

44. Patravadi, "Lilit Phra Lo 2019."

45. See, for example, the "Song in Praise of Phra Lo" performed by Ten Phichaya and Lin Walanrat in the series of *Khonsoet kan kuson luk thung khu thai*, www.youtube.com/watch?time_continue=597&v=t8fLLLQEhSk.

1. Introduction (1–48)

The first act sets up the plot by establishing two frames. The first frame is the politics underlying the eventual tragedy. This political situation is described by the reciter in a narrative like an opening chorus. The poem is set in a time of warring. The chorus celebrates Ayutthaya extending its power by "attacking forcefully, destroying cities great, dispatching Lao and Kao, heads lopped by sword and writhing bodies strewn around" (1). One city-state attacks another and causes the death of its ruler. The desire for revenge is passed down to following generations. This political framing reflects Siam and neighboring territories in the thirteenth to sixteenth centuries when several city-states established by warrior dynasties were vying for power.[46] Phra Lo's fate is thus not only the fruit of his own karma but arises from the politics of revenge in a warrior-dominated society.

The second framing is the romance between Phra Lo and the two princesses. This frame is established mostly by dialog in scenes that shift back and forth between the two city-states. The three fall in love without meeting, solely on the basis of third-hand reports of their beauty. This framing resembles another old story, *Samutthakhot* (Pali: Samuddaghosa), which comes from the same era, or earlier. *Samutthakhot* became the leading story in the collections of *jātaka* (stories of the Buddha's previous births) that originated in Southeast Asia and are now found in Thailand, Burma, and Cambodia. These collections are conventionally called the *Fifty Jātaka*.[47] Samutthakhot is a prince (and bodhisatta) of exceptional beauty. A princess of a neighboring city hears of his beauty, falls in love, and makes prayers at a shrine to gain him as a husband. A group of brahmans travel from

---

46. Baker and Pasuk, *A History of Ayutthaya*, ch. 3.
47. Baker and Pasuk, *From the Fifty Jātaka*.

there to Samutthakhot's city and tell him of her beauty. He promptly plans to travel to see her. His parents forbid him and propose instead to send envoys to ask for her hand, but he begs until they agree. On seeing Samutthakhot's beauty, the father of the princess agrees to the marriage instantly.

The rest of the two stories is very different. The resemblance in this framing may be a result of adaptation, but could reflect merely that the two stories derive from a similar milieu of creating and narrating tales.

2. Old Lord Tiger Spirit (49–155)

The second act is wholly about using supernatural power to draw Phra Lo to Song against the resistance of his entourage. The scenes shift between the two cities and the wild mountains. The telling has a high proportion of dialog. The pace is fast, and the action is often dramatic.

To draw Phra Lo to Song, the princesses tap the wild power that exists in nature and can only be mobilized by adepts. The search for an adept proceeds upward through three levels of the profession's hierarchy before Old Lord Tiger Spirit is identified, stressing that he has exceptional powers. His name (*pu jao saming phrai*) can be translated simply as old-lord-king-of-spirits, but the Mon word *saming* can mean both king and tiger, and this touch makes his title distinctively wild. He has the status of a king or god. The text refers to him with pronouns and verbs reserved for royalty and deity. The princesses receive him like a king or god, abasing themselves. His self-description places him outside civilization and outside time:

> I am a lord divine of mountain peaks.
> The title they have given me, 'Old Lord,'

does mark the mass of merit I have made.
I'll live this world a million years until the era ends.(109)

Modern images, for example, in book illustrations, cartoons, and
the historical park in Song, present him as a classic rishi from Indian
legend—aged, with a long beard and coiled hair, always seated cross-
legged. But the text does not endorse this imagery. Rather, it stresses
the total plasticity of his physical appearance. He appears and
disappears in a flash. He transforms himself from tiger to human, from
young man to old.

He lives deep in the wild mountains, far from the civilized city. The
journey to his home by the princesses' maids crosses forests and
foothills before ascending his mountain, allowing the poet to showcase
his expertise in intricate wordplay around the names of flora and
fauna. Such passages are found in old Indian poetry and became
conventional in Thai verse, where this may be the oldest surviving
example. The passage also emphasizes the physical and civilizational
distance between the city and Phra Lo's world by describing travel
through several eco-systems. The sights and sounds of plants, animals,
and birds along the way are engineered by Old Lord Tiger Spirit to
make the maids nervous on the inward route and joyful on their
return.

In old Siam, the use of love magic appears to have been common
enough to be expressly forbidden by law.[48] The conjuring of Phra Lo

---

48. In the Miscellaneous Laws in the Three Seals Code, there is a section on magic and
spirits. Clause 169 subjects anyone found using love magic (ยาแฝด, *ya faet*) to punishments
of forty lashes, public shaming, and execution. However, the previous clause states that,
should someone die as a result of love magic, the adept cannot be prosecuted because "it
was the karma of that person who died; even the gods pass [from the heavens to the human
world, when their karma so determines] so how could a human live on" (*Kotmai tra sam
duang*, III, 179–80).

requires three rounds, again stressing the range and excellence of Old Lord Tiger Spirit's skill. In the first two rounds, he uses yantra (*yan*), graphical devices incorporating various powerful images, including magical numbers, excerpts of prayers in sacred languages, gods and powerful animals both real and imaginary, and symbols of the Buddha. These devices must be made by an adept and activated by ritual. They can be tattooed on the skin, printed on cloth to be worn, written on paper rolled and inserted in an amulet, or burnt to ash and inserted in a ring or other portable receptacle. Today, there are still booklets with selections of designs for various uses. Mostly now they are carried for protection, but can also be put to aggressive use. In the text, they are placed together with a drawing depicting the desired result, namely Phra Lo lying with the princesses. The imagery in the yantra is sadly not described. In the first round, the images are drawn on a ball, and in the second on a kind of flag that is flown by armies and ritual processions. The drama of these first two scenes is heightened by the delivery device, a massive tree used as a catapult, another touch of wild power.

Phra Lo's entourage successfully repels both these attempts. In the first case, they simply try everything, from spirit adepts to "foreign cures," and something works. In the second case, these measures fail, a powerful adept is found, and Phra Lo is placed inside a mandala, a ritually defined space, with various forms of spirit arrayed around and above to ward off Old Lord Tiger Spirit's powers. In the third round, Old Lord Tiger Spirit changes strategy. He recruits an army of the spirits that reside in every aspect of nature. The recruits include some famous spirits who also appear in a Sukhothai inscription and an old oath of loyalty to the monarch. The spirits ride on various wild animals, transform themselves into hybrid beasts, hurl rocks and trees, and trample forests flat. This is a bravura display of wild power.

For defense, Song has the spirits of the city who reside in shrines for the city pillar, and the personal protective spirits of the king who reside on the ceremonial royal umbrellas. In this confrontation, these are no match for the wild horde.

Once these defenses are shattered, Old Lord Tiger Spirit sends the love magic loaded into a "flying betelnut," rather like a drone. Betel or areca was universally chewed as a mild stimulant, and also figured in the politics of courtesy. Betel was offered in ceremonies of welcome and of invitation, such as a marriage proposal. The use of betelnut in this scene is a fantastical exaggeration of its everyday ritual role.

At the end of this act, Old Lord Tiger Spirit disappears from the plot except for a short scene when the princesses grow impatient for Phra Lo's arrival, and Old Lord Tiger Spirit uses a cock to lure Phra Lo at a speedier pace. Colorful cocks have long been bred in Asia for their beauty and for cockfighting.[49] Perhaps the combination of their striking appearance and their aggression has given them some sacred reputation. On the basis of a story about cockfighting in his youth, images of fighting cocks have become associated with the great warrior king Naresuan, and appear as attendants and offering at his statues and shrines. This practice has spread to other shrines.

In the poem, a beautiful cock becomes the last flourish in the display of wild power. Although the scene of the cock luring Phra Lo is short (350 words) and deceptively simple, it is one of the best remembered scenes from the poem, often depicted by artists and illustrators and rendered in a famous dance, *Phra lo tam kai*, "Phra Lo follows the cock," set to Prince Naris's music.[50]

---

49. The original strain in Thailand is probably the native red junglefowl (*Gallus gallus*), but has been hybridized over centuries, most recently using Japanese shamo birds.
50. See www.youtube.com/watch?v=Gv9prFVcOaA.

3. Departure (156–230)

After the travel, open spaces, massed characters, and dramatic events of the second act, the third is intimate and personal, mostly conveyed through dialog. Phra Lo is leaving his city. He says farewell to his wife, his consorts or "friends in joy," and his ministers. All express their grief at his departure, but are resigned to the fact. The exception is his mother, Queen Bunluea.

The relationship of mother and son is very special. In many Thai stories, including several in the *Fifty Jātaka*, the hero is constantly interrupted in the middle of a quest or romance because he thinks of his mother, feels guilty about abandoning her, drops everything, and sets out to find her. Often this impulse is explained as gratitude for the virtue or goodness (คุณ, *khun*) of the mother in giving birth and raising the child.

To dissuade Phra Lo from leaving, Queen Bunluea first deploys reason. She suggests they send envoys to ask for the princesses' hand in the conventional way. She warns him of the danger given the history between the two cities, and the violence they have shown in the recent spirit battle. When Phra Lo remains adamant on leaving, she plays the maternal card:

> Ten months my belly held your excellence,
> with care to not forget myself one mite.
> And after birth, O lord of all three worlds,
> I bathed you, fed you, held you, took good care.
> . . .
> Since you were small I raised you, cared,
> and taught you all until you'd grown,
> become a king, the ruler of the realm.
> Now will you leave me here to die of grief? (185, 188)

From there she turns immediately to the son's duty to the mother at death:

> While I'm alive I'd hoped to bank on you,
> and planned on death to trust you with my corpse,
> but hearing you'll desert your mother's breast,
> when dead who can I trust to tend my pyre? (189)

Finally, and most extraordinarily, her maternal love gives way to a simpler passion:

> I praise your cheeks, your forehead, hairline, hair,
> admire your mouth, your pretty eyes,
> your moon-like face that charms the eye.
> O handsome king, I kiss your cheek, caress your ear.
>
> I kiss your nose, beloved—your scent's unmatched.
> I kiss your chin, and neck—my heart capsized.
> I kiss your skin, your breast—in bliss, my son—
> your shoulder, back, your breast again, your side, your arm."
> (192–93)

Phra Lo is clearly taken aback. He chides his mother for this unseemly behaviour. Bunluea concedes, and gives him her blessings and advice. The subject of this advice is the attributes of a good ruler, somewhat inappropriate in the circumstances where Phra Lo is abandoning his rulership, but such advice is another borrowing from ancient Indian literature which became a convention in Thai verse.

The remainder of the act is taken up with the logistics of the departure, in particular an account of Phra Lo dressing, and a description of the army that will accompany him—both conventional scenes.

4. Journey (231–387)

As Phra Lo leaves his city, intimacy gives way to action again, and the telling becomes mostly narrative, interrupted by passages of dialog. The journey between the cities resembles the heroic quests found in several *jātaka* tales.

On the journey, Phra Lo is in between cities, in the less secure and less familiar space of the forest and rural countryside. This is emphasized by conventional passages describing the forest along the way, but also by sojourns in villages which Phra Lo and his entourage find strange and pitiful:

> "These houses, see, aren't like our city ones.
> The rabble's dwellings seem so badly shaped,
> not good to look at, not one bit ... "

> "O sire, to cool they bathe in cloudy streams.
> So poor, they chew on smelly salty fish.
> Sometimes for lust a wench's a must when lacking else.
> Not eating when you crave, how can you live?" (245–46)

Phra Lo is not only out of place but becomes out of character. Over the course of the journey, he gradually loses his kingliness. He starts out with an army that is "magnificent" and "massive." Along the way, batches of troops are successively sent home so the number dwindles to three hundred, thirty, fifteen, and finally only his two personal aides. At the border, he exchanges his kingly clothes for disguise as a local chief. On reaching the princesses' city, he pretends to be a brahman on a visit from India, losing even his origin. Ultimately, he is left all alone in an empty house in an abandoned garden—the total antithesis of a king at the center of his family, polity, and world. On hearing of this, the princesses' maids are reduced to tears: "How could

he stay like that? It's pitiful. / He's never suffered so. I'm mortified."
(437)

In this uncertain and insecure region between cities, his mind
wavers. He repeatedly debates with himself whether to go onwards or
turn back. He is torn between memories of his wife, mother, and
consorts, and the lure of the princesses:

> "I would turn back, but think of those ahead.
> To go, or not to go, that is the nub.
> This thinking desolates—I fear ahead, I miss behind." (233)

His troops and aides urge him to turn back, but he continues on,
eventually reaching the Kalong River, which is deep and fast-flowing
enough for them to make a raft for the crossing. This is his Rubicon,
a symbolic boundary, a crucial moment in the plot. After the crossing,
he asks the river for an omen. This is a common device in such stories.
The Thai term, เสี่ยงทาย, *siang thai*, means to "risk a prediction."

In the previous two acts, the audience has been briefly reminded of
the fate hanging over the story. Old Lord Tiger Spirit peered into the
future and saw "the fruit of karma from the past ... what's to come
cannot be stopped—the end is quick, the death is quick" (83). During
the departure, Bunluea reminded Phra Lo, "We killed their grandfather,
cut off his head. / They harbor hate and scheme revenge. / Will you
go there to stew in their hand's palm?" (180). Phra Lo now brings this
issue to the foreground by asking the river, "If I'm to go and not return
alive, / may now the waters swirl—or else flow straight" (296). The
result is bad: the waters not only swirl but turn red, the universal color
of blood and danger. Phra Lo understands the meaning but is past the
point of return: "I cannot turn. / I've stepped on foreign land / with
both my feet" (304). He fears being branded as a coward if he turns
back. As Duangmon (Paripunna) Jitjamnong observes, he is drawn

ahead "not only by sexual desire but also by the love of his own status, which partly is a result of his training in the values required to maintain the institution of kingship."[51]

The tragedy is now certain. The remainder of this act is taken up with scenes to delay the ending and allow the suspense to build. Phra Lo and his aides negotiate their way across the border; sojourn in villages; reconnoitre the way ahead; enjoy the forest; and comment on local color. The splendid cock makes his appearance. Phra Lo, his two aides, the two princesses, and their maids all have dreams which predict that their tryst will take place, but look no further into the future.

To cross the border and to gain entry to the royal park at Song, Phra Lo and his aides make liberal use of bribery. The prominent roles of bribery, magic, and subterfuge create a morally ambiguous setting for the tryst.

Phra Lo arrives at his destination un-kinged, uncertain, and fated.

5. The Park (388–588)

At the end of the journey, the setting, mood, and pace change again. Dialog dominates. The romantic climax takes place in a park or garden reserved for royal use outside the princesses' city. Whether such gardens existed in reality is doubtful, but they appear in several tales. Here the garden represents a space apart, a storybook reality, a site of suspended belief. The birds and plants make Phra Lo welcome, and create an amorous atmosphere. Phra Lo's two aides and the princesses' two maids meet in the garden, not through any prior arrangement but through the inevitability of the plot. The site for their meeting

---

51. Duangmon, *Bot wikhro*, 33.

happens to be a pond of lotuses, a concentration of erotic symbols—
water, flowers, buds, seeds, bees, fish.

Here the tale's romantic climax begins with an arousing prolog.
Earlier in the tale there have been hints of the lusty character of the
two maids (e.g., 67–68). They now take the lead in quickly pairing off
in the pond with Phra Lo's two aides. One maid tells the other:

> "O Roi, for love, please don't be dim.
> Pray take our guest and go that side
> to pick and eat whate'er he wants,
> and help make sure he's satisfied." (413)

The two couples make love in the pond, on the bank, and in the
pavilion, after which

> the maids lean forward and ask their lovers' names.
> "Where are you from? How are you called? Pray tell.
> So we may know your names and city home." (422)

More delaying devices now appear to build more suspense. Phra Lo
is fetched. The maids return to inform the princesses. The princesses
visit the dowager. They travel to the park in a great entourage of
palace women. The maids shoo this flock out of the way, and deliver
the three lovers to the "bed of bliss."

In much later Thai poetry, trysts are described in the form of *bot
atsajan*, "wondrous scenes," using metaphors of ships, storms, fish, and
horses. Here the portrayal is more complex. Some is formal and
ritualistic. Some is less mannered and more human. Immediately
before meeting Phra Lo, the princesses suddenly succumb to nerves,
shyness, and a realization they have no idea what to do, leading to a
humorous and human exchange with their maids.

"O please, since we were born, were small,
we have no knowledge, not one bit.
To go in, just like that? Please help!
I'm shy and getting shier out of fear."

"You're not a child, your highness, now.
Some things not done you have to do to know." (485–86)

Phra Lo reveals himself and the scene takes on a ritual touch. The three royals gaze at each other's beauty in a mute tableau. The four attendants join in, extending the scene. "Such shining beauty did the gods create? / These looks leave all the world with tired eyes" (503). At the attendants' invitation, the three proceed into the bedchamber with great drama.

Phra Lo proceeds with grace. The earth and heavens shake.
Two princesses proceed. The three worlds quake.
Three royals, heads held high, arms swung with grace,
like moon and stars that rise to light both sky and earth. (505)

In Phra Lo's encounter with the first of the pair, the narration seems to begin inside his head, conveying his exultation, then transitions into a rather realistic, non-metaphorical description: "Breast pressed to tender breast, belly pressed to belly" (520). Though the telling then resorts to flowers, fish, bees, horses, and storms, the mood remains lyrical, and the description is rather detailed: "A lotus, struck by sunny rays, / stays closed, unblooming, wary of the bee" (539). In another human touch, the two pairs of servants sit outside, struggling to keep their hands off one another "though love burns them to ash" (508).

The tryst is a great success. Afterwards, the trio bathe, eat, confess mutual love, and part in tears. The maids smuggle Phra Lo and his aides into the palace so the joy can continue.

6. Massacre (589–626)

The scene, pace, and mood change again. The setting is now inside the Song palace. Phra Lo is in the jaws of the tiger. The pace accelerates. The telling is again mainly narrative with short passages of dialog.

The love of the previous act is rapidly replaced by savage violence. Phra Lo is soon discovered. The father of the princesses is initially enraged, but then sees the opportunity to gain a splendid son-in-law, and begins to plan a marriage. The dowager, widow of the slaughtered king, however, is bent on revenge. She organizes a murder squad. All seven—Phra Lo, the two princesses, their four servants—are killed, riddled with arrows in a dramatic tableau "like a work of art" that has inevitably been rendered in painting and sculpture. The father of the princesses is appalled. He has the members of the murder squad "slashed like slashing down banana plants," the squad's leaders "boiled or burned alive," and the dowager "flayed ... executed painfully and has them drag the corpse" (607). In little more than a page, the stage has been strewn with more bodies than is standard for a Shakespearean tragedy.

7. Reconciliation (627–660)

After the deaths of Juliet and Romeo, the Duke of Verona demands his city's warring clans seek reconciliation. After a tragedy similarly contrived by conflict between love and politics, the response is the same but more elaborate. Shakespeare ends his play within a page, but here there is a full final act on a theme of Buddhist-inspired reconciliation. The telling is mostly narrative, similar to the chorus in the opening act. The pace is rather fast, while the mood is somber but purposeful.

After the massacre, the city of Song is overcome with grief. The king has the three lovers placed in one coffin, and does the same with the two couples of their servants. He then sends news to Queen Bunluea, Phra Lo's doting mother. This is a delicate moment, deciding whether the cycle of revenge will continue. A minister advises Bunluea: "Your Majesty, pray think on times ahead ... . An ill-thought move could wreck the realm ... pray give some weighty thought / to build a future on this past" (647–50).

Bunluea accepts the offer of peace. She decides not to attend the cremation herself for fear it may provoke an incident. Instead, she sends an envoy with gifts and instructions to request a portion of the cremated remains. The division of the relics then becomes the focus of a drama of reconciliation. The bodies are cremated and a great festival is held. The relics are divided and half are sent to Bunluea. "Then missives writ with love / pass back and forth without a break" (656) to arrange for the relics to be simultaneously interred in a triple stupa in each city, along with great festivity and merit-making.

The Finale in Historical Context

This final act is remarkable. In contrast to the resolution of *Romeo and Juliet* in the Duke's short speech, this act is over two thousand words. The modern critics who sprang to the defence of *Lilit Phra Lo* argued that the ending portrays the working of karma, retribution for Song's unprovoked attack on Suang, and maybe also for the inappropriate behavior of Phra Lo and the princesses—basically, they got what they deserved. There is no trace of such moralizing in the work itself. Instead, the text describes a process of reconciliation. This may have a historical context.

The period from around the 1430s to 1600s was an age of warfare in mainland Southeast Asia, driven by the ambitions of rulers and new military technologies—greater use of elephants, gunpowder, and foreign mercenaries. Society became militarized. The death rate probably increased, both from deaths on the battlefield and from the famines and epidemics created by dragging massive armies across the landscape. Then, in the early 1600s, the fighting lessened, partly because people resisted. In Burma, there were revolts against recruitment. In Siam, people hid in the forests, took the robe, or bribed the recruiting agents to avoid the draft. The size of armies dwindled. Campaigns failed.[52]

Lilit Phra Lo was written during this age of warfare and reflects its ethos. The celebration of Ayutthaya's military success in the opening lines, and the description of the army at Phra Lo's departure, closely resemble passages from *Yuan Phai*, the military poem of the era.[53] The savagery of the punishments in the finale resemble punishments found in law codes of the time. But the final act of reconciliation perhaps reflects the revulsion against warfare that brought the fighting to an end and ushered in an era of peace and prosperity in the seventeenth century. King Ekathotsarot (r. 1605–11) legendarily broke an oath sworn to his brother (Naresuan) to continue the fighting. King Songtham (r. 1620–28) began to develop a model of kingship based on Buddhist values. Perhaps the last act of *Lilit Phra Lo* reflects the mentality that lay behind this momentous shift in the history of Siam in the early seventeenth century.

Tailpiece

Setting out the poem as a drama highlights several aspects.

The overarching theme is about the clash of love and politics, the private and the public. This is established from the start by the prolog,

---

52. Baker and Pasuk, *A History of Ayutthaya*, ch. 3.
53. Baker and Pasuk, *Yuan Phai*.

which draws two frames for the work, one about love, the other about politics, particularly about the politics of rivalry and revenge, very similar to the framing of *Romeo and Juliet*. There is no hint here or in the finale about the moral implications of the story. Of course, readers and critics are free to draw such implications. The emphasis on this aspect in modern debate on *Lilit Phra Lo* grows from the modern conception of the didactic role of Thai literature, not from the text.

The tryst in the royal park is the axis of the plot. From the first scene after the prolog onwards, everything is leading towards this point, while everything after the tryst is its consequence.

The poem is clearly about passion, but a rather unusual example. The passion is sparked without any direct contact, purely by information conveyed by intermediaries, and is fanned by a whole act of love magic. The two parties are strangely contrastive. The two princesses seem to represent a naïve sexual and emotional awakening. As characters, they remain amorphous, unformed. Their two-ness seems unnecessary, without consequence. We learn nothing about them, not even which (if either) is the elder. By contrast, Phra Lo is a man of experience, connections, and complexities. He has a wife, consorts, doting mother, and the responsibilities of kingship. He is the focus of both his family and his polity, so his actions have multiple consequences.

As long as both parties remain in their cities, Phra Lo and the princesses are more role than character, more representative than human. This changes with Phra Lo's journey from Suang to Song. The territory between the cities, including the royal park outside Song, is a space in between where things become looser and more ambiguous. Phra Lo gradually sheds his kingly role and later also his personal identity. The trickery, bribery, and subterfuge used to penetrate foreign territory creates a morally ambiguous atmosphere. Phra Lo's desperate need to seek out the princesses melts into dithering indecision. The scene with the cock shows him weak and easily deceived. As the fixed roles and certainties fall away, Phra Lo becomes more human, more character than role. He relates to the beauties of nature, and observes rural society along the way. He becomes more intimate with his aides, who serve as his eyes and arms in the unfolding intrigue.

The journey of the princesses from the palace in Song to the park is much shorter but similar in theme. They deceive the dowager and the palace ladies who accompany them to the park. They become more dependent on their maids and more intimate with them. With their lapse into shyness on the eve of the tryst, they become more human, a trend that continues through the tryst and its aftermath to their show of bravery in the massacre.

The tryst scene is remarkable for its length, detail, richness of imagery, range of emotions, and gentle humanity. The prolog with the aides and maids lengthens and deepens the scene. The princesses' attack of shyness and Phra Lo's failure to stifle a laugh bring in humor, humanity, and realism. The scene employs the usual symbolism of such "wondrous scenes," but interleaves passages of dialog and description that provide a counterbalancing realism. The vignette of the aides and maids sitting outside while "love burns them to ash" adds an extra dimension. The aftermath of bathing, eating, confessing love, and reluctantly parting further extends the scene and its nuances. The author(s) clearly intended this scene to be the climax of the poem.

In the massacre, the two frames of the story, love and politics, private and public, collide, most strikingly in the handful of consecutive lines where the princesses' father plans the marriage and the dowager plots the killing. The principal characters now become fully flesh and blood rather than role, emphasized with irony by the scene where the mother addresses the slaughtered princesses as if they were still alive.[54]

The final act resolves this clash of public and private, while also returning from a world of ambiguity to one of order and certainty. The violence of the massacre is unwound by a clear and lengthy sequence—outpourings of grief; negotiation to end the cycle of revenge; synchronized installation of the relics in both cities; and, finally, a mass celebration and merit-making.

In retrospect, the ease with which *Lilit Phra Lo* was embraced as part of Siam's "national literature" is rather surprising in view of the erotic theme at the heart of the work, the prominent role of magic, and the violence of the massacre. In the first sixty years after *Lilit Phra Lo* was anointed as part of the national literature, academic study focused on the dating, authorship, and origins of the story, and on controversies over the quality of the poetry, with little attention to the plot and its possible meanings. After the attack by Atsani and the 1970s' left, the literary establishment argued in defense that the work displays the Buddhist morality of karma, and thus fulfills the purpose of literature to teach morality. Creative artists recomposed the story to reflect their idea of what its morality should have been. In all these critiques and rewrites, the tryst scene, the axis of the original plot, was demoted in importance or disappeared completely. The final act of reconciliation suffered a similar fate, perhaps because its theme is compassion rather than moral judgment.

Lilit Phra Lo is a drama of love and death, passion and politics, private and public, about the intimacy of all humanity.

---

54. A scene with affinities to Ophelia's final soliloquy: "There's fennel for you, and columbines: there's rue for you; and here's some for me: we may call it herb-grace o' Sundays: O you must wear your rue with a difference. There's a daisy … " *Hamlet*, act 4, scene 6.

Twelve Months

Fig. 1. Images of reclining Visnu with triple lotus thrones: **a.** and **b.** found at Thaton, Burma, possibly ninth to tenth century CE, photographed in the 1890s, destroyed in World War II (Temple, *Notes on Antiquities*, pl. XIV, XIVa); **c.** Bagan Archaeological Museum (*Trongjai, Upathawathotsamat*, 106); **d.** from Kawgon Cave (courtesy of U Thein Lwin).

Invocation of the gods and king

Felicitations! O lotus-throned lord in heaven high   1
blithe-born from navel, shining bright
three crowning gems on blooming lotus-thrones
sprung from a sweetly flowing flower spray

O discus-holder Krisna, crowning emperor   2
who savors worldly joys, anointed and exalted

1   **Felicitations** ศรีสวัสดิ, *si sawat*. Be of good fortune. A conventional opening.
1   **lotus-throned** กมลาศ, *kamalat*, kamala āsana. An epithet of the god Brahma (see next but one note). These three opening verses honor Brahma, Visnu, and Siva respectively.
1   **blithe-born** The verb "born" has been moved from the third line.
1   **three crowning gems** ... In the Vaisnava Puranas, as Visnu lies on a sea of milk or on the serpent Ananta, a lotus sprouts from his navel in which appears the god Brahma, seated in lotus position, who then creates the world. At Thaton, two stone reliefs were found showing a recumbent Visnu with a lotus rising from his navel and branching to three thrones bearing Brahma, Visnu, and Siva; see fig 1a, 1b. Both were shattered by Japanese bombing in World War II and survive only as photographs from the 1890s (Luce, *Phases*, 170–71, pl. 89, 90; Oertel, *Note on a Tour*, 22, pl. 11; Temple, *Notes on Antiquities*, 31–33, pl. XIV, XIVa; Thein Lwin and U Min Han, "Images of Brahma"). There are similar images on display in the Bagan Archaeological Museum (Trongjai, *Upathawathotsamat*, 106, see fig. 1c), and the Hmaw Zar Museum from Sri Ksetra (Samerchai Poolsuwan, personal communication, July 2019). Another survives from Kawgon Cave (U Thein Lwin, personal communication, July 2019); see fig. 1d. At Preah Khan, Angkor, the lotus rising from Visnu's navel also divides into three but the branches end in flowers, not thrones (Roveda, *Images of the Gods*, pl. 4.1.20). Winai (see Samoe, "Thawathotsamat wipak," 23) suggests the third line refers to such an image, but none is known outside Burma. Alternatively, the three gems (ไตรรัตน, *trai ratana*) are the Triple Gem of Buddhism—Buddha, Dhamma, and Sangha—and the line reads, "the Triple Gem atop the lotus-throne crown." Perhaps the ambiguity and double meaning is intentional.
1   **blooming** The word has been moved from the fourth line.
2   **discus-holder** จักรกรี, *jakrakari*, S: cakra-kari.
2   **Krisna** This verse invokes Visnu, focusing on his worldly incarnation as Krisna, famed for his romantic exploits.
2   **worldly** สงสาร, *songsan*, saṃsāra. The cycle of birth and death in worldly existence.
2   **anointed** (อภิ)เษก, *(aphi)sek*, abhiseka. Anointment, for instance at the installation of a king.

delights in Kama-Rati's treasure-gems
the pleasure arts, the noose-snares of desire

O god supreme of gods both great and small   3
who savors bliss in thrills at watch-beat times
with winning winsome raindrop maidens
the joy of trysting tender lissome flower-girls

great king, the refuge of the universe   4
who rules the realm and keeps the land in peace—
lords offer fulsome praise and golden flowers
and bow their jewel-crowned heads as offerings

the king, created beautiful as by design   5
upholds ten virtues pure, strives for the realm

2   **Kama-Rati** Kamadeva, the Hindu god of love, a creation or offspring of Brahma, and his consort Rati, daughter of Daksa.

2   **noose-snares** คล้องห่วง, *khlong huang.*

3   **god of gods** เทวินทร, *thewinthon,* deva indra. Meaning Siva.

3   **watch-beat times** ย่ำยาม, *yam yam,* "beat time." *Yam* is a three-hour time period, punctuated by a drumbeat from a tower in the center of Ayutthaya. The phrase *yam yam* can mean "repetitively" or "all the time." The term combines allusions to evening and rhythm as a metaphor for lovemaking.

3   **raindrop** พินทุ, *phinthu,* bindu. A raindrop, a maiden descended from heaven.

4   **refuge of the universe** จักรวาฬภูวนาถ, *jakkawan phuwanat,* cakkavāla bhūvanātha.

4   **fulsome praise** วนนัต, *wananat,* S: varṇa nāda. Loudly praised. Alternatively, vana (forest) + ana (breath) + tva (being), "the breath of the forest."

4   **golden flowers** กมุทมาศ, *kamutamat,* kumuda māsa, golden lotus. Assumed to be a poetic reference to the "gold and silver flowers" (*bungai mas*) offered as symbolic tribute to an overlord.

4   **bow ... heads** เกือบเคียร, *gueap sian,* "almost head." Tentative; one manuscript has เกลือก เคียร, "rolling heads," which is perhaps better.

5   **created beautiful ...** รังสฤษฏ์รังเรข, *rang sarit rang rek.* The line may merely mean that the king has been properly installed, but alternatively reflects the idea that a king is supreme in all ways, including physical beauty, as fine as if it were crafted.

5   **ten virtues** ทศธรรมวิมล, *thotsatham,* more usually ทศพิธราชธรรม, *thotsaphit ratchatham,* dasabidharājadhammā. The Ten Royal Virtues, an old code of rulers based on Buddhist principles: munificence, moral living, sacrifice, honesty, gentleness, self-restraint or austerity, non-hatred, non-violence or not causing harm, patience or tolerance, and non-oppressiveness. Chanthit (*Thawathotsamat Khlongdan,* 64) argues there are several lists of ten that could be meant here, and prefers ทศบารมี, *thotsabarami,* dasa pāramī,

rules over sixteen places great and world-renowned—
pray heaven's blessings for the new-come king

Love remembered

my sole young heart-partner, surpassing words   6
best budding bloom I tend-touched care-caressed
embraced your body's beauty, supped the finest taste
and never left you lone past half a watch

I loved you, jewel gem, and you alone   7
your fivefold charms inspired desire, lit lust
I succored sacred flowers, circled my beloved
lest sudden breezes brushed and bruised your breasts

I succored body beautiful and flesh so fair   8
were ever our two noses far apart?

---

the ten perfections, qualities to be perfected in order to become a Buddha: generosity, virtue, renunciation, insight, diligence, tolerance, truthfulness, determination, loving-kindness, and equanimity.

5 **sixteen places** สุโสฬศ, *su salot*, su (good) + soḷasa (sixteen). Meaning sixteen great places (มหาชนบท, *mahachonabot*, mahā janapada) in northern India visited by the Buddha during the forty-five years of teaching following his enlightenment, as listed in early Buddhist texts. Chanthit (*Thawathotsamat Khlongdan*, 65) suggests this means sixteen cities under Ayutthaya. Maneepin ("Khlong thawathotsamat," 116) suggests the king was born from the sixteen Brahma levels of the heavens.

5 **new-come king** ใหม่ศรี, *mai si*. Possibly Boromracha, who became king in Ayutthaya when Trailokanat moved to Phitsanulok in 1463. He may have remained king after Trailokanat died in 1488, and have died himself in 1491, but the dates and sequence of succession are very confused in this part of the chronicles. Alternatively, this is Intharacha, who was installed around 1482. See Afterword.

6 **taste** รส, *rot*, rasa. In ancient Indian aesthetics, "rasa" meant all forms of sense-experience, and possibly that is the meaning here. In everyday Thai, the word means "taste." Here and elsewhere in the poem, "of love" has to be assumed in this phrase.

7 **jewel gem** รัตนเรข, *rattana rek*. Perhaps a reference to the "gem woman," one of the seven gem attributes of the *cakkavatin* wheel-rolling world emperor: wheel, elephant, horse, gem, woman, treasurer, son (see Reynolds and Reynolds, *Three Worlds*, 136–70).

7 **fivefold charms** เบญจฤดี, *benjaruedi*, pañcarati. Five loves or five ways to inspire love: form, taste, scent, sound, touch.

I cherished you upon a bed divine
were ever our two bodies parted half a span?

pressed close, my breast, your breast, as one   9
why were you parted from my side so far so fast?
I miss my perfect golden lotus flower
long left without joy's taste my sorrow swells

I miss our making love, knowing pleasure's taste   10
our faces joined, my heart inthrust in you alone
I miss those times, the fragrance of your face
was there a watch I failed to fondle you?

I miss your special soft sin-sensuous tongue   11
that fired my heart and roused my lust
I miss your scent, your dulcet voice divine
flesh pressed on tender flesh to seem as one

I miss the times of roving like a *naga* lord   12
my arms embracing, circling, coiling round
the beauty of all beauties—passion's taste
deep loving, sliding, winding, folding tight

I miss caressing golden lotus, holy lake   13
dipping down past lily bud, parting petals wide
I miss my cherishing the perfect flower's crown
and prying 'part the flower whorl below Meru's mount

8   **half a span** กึ่งกร, *kueng kon*. Half an arm.

12   ***naga* lord** ภุชเคนทร, *phuchakhenthon*, S: bhujaga indra. Snake-lord.

13   **dipping ... bud** พลิต, *phlit*. An old Khmer word for plunge, but echoes *phlit* from Sanskrit *valiṣa*, clitoris.

13   **flower's crown** มิ่งมาลีไลย, *ming malilai*. Peak flower.

13   **whorl** เกลียว, *kliao*. Now the spiral on a screw or light bulb; in Pallegoix (*Dictionarium linguae thai*, 336), twisted, as of string.

13   **Meru** เมรุ. In Buddhist cosmology, Mount Meru or Sineru is the center of the universe, above which rise the heavens, the abodes of the gods. Samoe ("Thawathotsamat wipak," 31) suggests Meru is also a term for the vagina, and ต่ำ, *tam*, below, is also a

I miss the times, as lord young-king, we met alone 14
I pressed my cheek on your sweet peerless cheek
I miss the stream where *naga* played in lotus gold
sated supping passion's joys a-blooming yet again

I miss the lovely lily, gem of lotus flowers 15
petals duly parting wide at watch-beat times
for bees to sup the taste and dip the golden lake
to slip inside and bathe in fragrant streams

your flower's crown and fair fine skin 16
the dark-hued bees caressing constantly
sounds spilling from your face, your shining face
upon the bed divine with you, not once alone

the days my arms entwined your bosom tight 17
two touching shins that rose and fell till wet
the days I fused the elixir and cream
a-lying happy, wrapped together, lapping love

to bathe in Tāvatiṃsa, lake of gods, is good 18
yet equals not your crystal lake at watch-beat time
in heaven's lake the nectar tastes sublime
but bathing in your lake eclipses all three worlds

your face the finest, fragrance fair 19
dark sapphire eyes that shine, and lashes lush

---

verb for describing repetitive back-forth movements in weaving or laundry. The syllable เลีย, *lia*, lick can be found buried in words in this verse and the previous one.

14 **young-king** เยาวราช, *yaowarat*, yuvarāja. Young or junior king. See Afterword.

16 **flower's crown** มาลัยโมลิศ, *malai molit*, "flower peak-most."

17 **elixir and cream** ถนำทึก, *thanam thuek*, a Khmer term for medicine, perhaps here meaning an aphrodisiac or vaginal lubrication; and นพนิต, *nopanit*, navanīta, butter.

18 **Tāvatiṃsa** ไตรตรึงษ, *traitrueng*. The heaven of thirty-three gods, where Indra presides.

19 **dark sapphire** นิลารัตน, *nilarattana*. Nila or nin can mean black, dark blue, or dark green. It is used for elephants with a bluish tinge in their hide. Below (v. 62), he compares her eyes to a striking dark-blue flower.

faultless brows that curve like Kama's bow
a maiden's precious breasts—firm, fine, and proud

O, lissome, lovely lady, fair-eyed, young   20
though parted, heart and soul I stay with you
in every detail perfect, golden lotus mine
am I lack-love, lithe lovely darling bud?

Literary comparisons

one time, the son of Dasaratha, city-lord   21
was parted from his Sita, traveled lone.
though she returned to join the prince, as wished
have you, my maiden, gone away so far?

Sri Aniruddha, parted from his love   22
Sri Usa, pried away so very far
as gods and humans made them separate
yet gained his maiden back, possessed again

19 Kama See v. 2.

20 lack-love นิรารส, *nirarot*. The Pali-Sanskrit nī (without) rasa (taste, sense), which originally meant "inspid," had been adapted in Thai as นิราศ, *nirat*, to mean without sensual experience, without love, and hence "parting," and a genre of poetry about parting and loss. See Afterword. Here the word seems to have been extended by doubling rasa for emphasis, which perhaps gives an echo of นิโรธ, *nirot*, nirodha, destroy, destruction. This word is not known today. It appears five times in the poem, always as the second word in the final line of the verse (see v. 53, 67, 76, 190). The form "lack-love" appears in Shakespeare's *A Midsummer Night's Dream* and in Allen Ginsberg's "Kaddish." See Afterword.

21 Dasaratha ทศรถ, *thotsarot*, "ten-(direction)-chariot." The father of Rama in the Ramayana.

21 prince ยุพราช, *yupharat*, yuvarāja. Young-king. See Afterword.

22 Sri Aniruddha ... Usa A Puranic tale, long popular in Siam. Princess Usa dreams of Aniruddha, grandson of Krisna, and has him magically abducted to her room. Her father separates them and imprisons Aniruddha, but Krisna comes to his rescue. All are reconciled and the couple are married (Cholada, "The Thai Tale of *Aniruddha*"). The poem here uses the Indian honorific, Sri (Maneepin, "Thawathotsamat: nirat rue tamra").

Samuddaghosa, parted long 23
from Vindumatī, struggled in pursuit
his body sick, he pined, he sped ahead
and brought the maiden back to lie beside

Sudhana, handsome as a portrait drawn 24
was parted from Manoharā and pined
but battled through the forests, joined his love
I fear that you've donned wings and flown away

Pācitta lost his tender Arabimba 25
had even passed away and quit this life
yet lived again to join his gem and share love's taste
some karma's parted us—let your good karma cure

Lord Sudhanu, the master of the bow 26
was parted from his shining moon princess
young Cirappa, his lovely lady love
yet strove till he possessed her once again

23 Samuddaghosa ... Vindumatī A *jātaka* tale in which Prince Samuddaghosa, a bodhisatta, is separated from his wife Vindumatī after a log they are riding on the sea breaks apart in a storm. They are eventually reunited with help from Indra (Baker and Pasuk, *From the Fifty Jātaka*, 75–86).

24 Sudhana ... Manoharā An old story, made into a *jātaka* tale, in which Manoharā, a *kinnari*, is married to Prince Sudhana but is then forced to flee back to her home at Mount Kailash, from where Sudhana retrieves her after an epic quest (Baker and Pasuk, *From the Fifty Jātaka*, 1–26). For the meaning of *kinnari*, see fn 188, v. 156.

24 donned wings คล้อง, *khlong*, put on (round neck). The wings are assumed from the Sudhana story where Manoharā dons her *kinnari* wings and flies away to escape execution.

25 Pācitta ... Arabimba An old story made into a *jātaka* tale, in which Prince Pācitta twice has to rescue his beautiful wife Arabimba from abduction, and is shot dead by a hunter but revived with medicine provided by Sakka/Indra (Baker and Pasuk, *From the Fifty Jātaka*, 87–98).

25 karma's parted ... An obscure line, perhaps meaning that his (bad) karma has caused their parting so he calls on her to use her (good) karma to rectify the situation.

26 Sudhanu ... Cirappa In this *jātaka* tale, Prince Sudhanu gains the hand of Cirappa in an archery contest, is then separated from her in a shipwreck, and has adventures in the ogre realm before they are reunited (Baker and Pasuk, *From the Fifty Jātaka*, 331).

must this, my only breast where rested once your flesh   27
now hurt as we're apart, and must my heart collapse?
O, jewel, fount of fortune, lotus flower of mine
I heap your gold and gems on this bruised breast

Month Five: Citra (March–April)

the month of Citra's here—my heart is hot   28
each watch-beat time your body's scent speeds here
I seek and search for you, lovely lady lost
but Indra, Brahma, Yama hamper your return

the sun ascends and stirs the sky alive   29
sun's rays flood forth and fill the firmament
the moon, blaze-battered, begs for life, and yet
its pain is less than pain that parting brings

on high beyond the skies in heaven's halls   30
the gods both great and small waft on the air
the water-wanting earth, though desert-like
is not as hot as I left waiting long

the seven oceans great are parched by heat   31
and waterways in thousands desert-dry

27 **fount of fortune** วลีภาคย, *waliphak*. This may mean "my beauty," but more likely is the same as วานิภาคย, *waniphak*, S: vaṇi bhāgya, desire/wish + fate/happiness, an appellation that he uses throughout, meaning like "the best thing that ever happened to me."

28 **Citra** เจตร, *jet*. In the original, where month names appear, they are in a Thai version of the Pali-Sanskrit but are rendered in the Pali form in the translation. See table in Afterword.

28 **watch-beat time** See v. 3.

28 **scent speeds here** Alternatively, "my body wafts to you."

28 **Yama** ยม, *yom*. The god of death.

31 **seven oceans** เจ็ดสินธุ์สาคเรศ, *jet sinthu sakhare*. In the Three Worlds geography, there are seven "large bodies of water"—Anotatta, Kaṇṇamuṇḍa, Rathakāra, Chaddanta, Kināla, Mandākinī, and Sīhapapāta lakes—and probably this is what is meant here (Reynolds and Reynolds, *Three Worlds*, 292). Alternatively, it could refer to the seven rivers of ancient north India: Ganga, Yamunā, Sarabhū, Sindhu, Aciravatī, Sarassatī, and Mahī.

the pain that sears my breast from missing you, lost love
a hundred times this drought would not compare

the earth, the breast of Dharaṇi, is cracked apart   32
the waterworld below there seethes and quakes
the pain from parting fragrant love of mine
O, perish earth and sky, this pain won't pass

the sun that courses 'cross a limpid sky   33
is parching streams and rivers desert-dry
our parting brought my breast relentless pain
more heat than all the suns till era's end

a thousand suns' bright-shining rays   34
that scorch three worlds and torch all things
destroy the triple spheres in flaring flames
yet equal not the heat from parting you, princess

the heat that sears three worlds and ages four   35
and makes the world of men a molten mass

---

32 **Dharaṇi** (แม่)ธรณี, *thorani*. The goddess of the earth.

32 **waterworld** (บา)ดาล, *badan*, *pātāla*. The watery world in the earth's core, inhabited by *naga*.

34 **torch all things** The image of the era-destroying fire appears throughout the poem. At the end of a Buddhist era (*kalpa*), seven suns rise in succession, creating a fire that incinerates the world, the Himavanta, Mount Meru, the heavens of the gods up to the first six levels of the *brahma* worlds, and down through all the hells. After a very long time, rain falls, first in drops the size of dust, becoming bigger until the drops are 100,000 *yojana* across, causing floods to rise from the world up through the realms of the gods to the first three *brahma* levels. Eventually, four winds start to blow and, when the water has dried, the *brahma* who took refuge in the upper levels untouched by fire and flood come down to be born as humans in the world (Reynolds and Reynolds, *Three Worlds*, ch. 10).

34 **princess** น้องไท้, *nong thai. Thai*, "great," indicates royalty. This is the first of several indications that she is royal in some way. "Princess" is used here as English lacks a term for non-specific female royalty.

35 **three worlds and ages four** ไตรยุคทั้งสี่, *trai yuk thang si*. Alternatively, the fire that burns three of the four ages. In each *kalpa* (era), there are four *yuga* (age). At the end of these, the world is destroyed by fire and the cycle restarts (see v. 34).

the heat I hide inside's a hundred thousand more
as three fires burn and boil and burst my breast

the earth and every land is parched, the heavens dried   36
the withered leaves, the flowers that wilt and droop
the vines that twine round trunks now burnished gold
the shriveled creepers hanging limp—all deepen gloom

the sky seems scorching as the sun itself   37
I'm lovesick for the world's crest-crown
I fret and flail, a million miseries felt
a million Merus burnt sky-high would not compare

all herds of deer in hills and caves   38
can find no food nor place to play
the pangs of hunger prick their eyes with tears
no joy, no place to prance—all deepen grief

on plants in thousands leaves have yellowed, dropped   39
and even twigs and flowers have turned to dust
on mountainsides the trees are lifeless, sad
O, times for joy are burnt and gone—help me

the picture-pretty birds all like to sing aloud   40
but nothing now is heard—I'm husk-hoarse, hurt
my love has left, has flown, has fled, unseen
O, birds sing loud and strong to make this end!

fens, ponds, and streams are dried to puddles   41
in Tāvatiṃsa, *nāga* lords must squirm to swim

---

35 **three fires** ไตรกำเดา, *trai kamdao*. Perhaps shorthand for the "fire that burns the three worlds" (or eras) in the first line of the verse. Chanthit (*Thawathotsamat Khlongdan*, 93) suggests lust, craving, and delusion.

37 **world's crest-crown** จอมจิ่มหล้า, *jom jim la*. Peak of the world.

37 **million** The number is แสน, *saen*, hundred(s) of thousands, meaning "very many."

38 **deer** See v. 103.

41 **nāga** Given as พาสุกรี, Phasukri/Wasukri, the lord of the *nāga*.

in Rathakāra Lake the fearsome dragons
must flog themselves to flail ahead

thousands of creatures in thousands of streams   42
suffer in sorrow as if stoked with fire
the day of your parting, fairest of face
millions of Merus went reeling to ruin

O, gem lady supreme, fair-skinned and beautiful   43
I'm lone, ablaze, bereft of joy, my world upturned
may royal Hari, three-eyed guardian-god
please purge the grief that grips and gripes my heart

the Citra month's gone by with clear, bright light   44
all regions of the earth now chop and change
this season-shift upsets, unsettles, and unnerves
O Indra, king of gods, come tend this torment new!

I miss the taste of love, your body's every part   45
the pause before possessing you, on fire
O gem princess, my fount of fortune, O
please share your body, part place in my heart

41   **Rathakāra Lake** กรรารก, *kararot*, usually รถการะ, chariot-maker. One of seven lakes in the Himavanta (Reynolds and Reynolds, *Three Worlds*, 292). In the *Three Worlds* and other sources, the lake is named but not described, and has no association with dragons (Samerchai Poolsuwan, personal communication, February 2019).

41   **dragons** มังกร, *mangkon*. This may mean crocodile or *makara*, a sea-monster.

42   **Merus** สุเมรุ, *sumeru*. See v. 13. Meru is sometimes used in poetry to mean a mountain.

43   **gem lady** รัตนนารีศ, *rattana narit*. See v. 7.

43   **Hari ...** ตรีในยสุรารักษหริราช, *trinai surarak harirat*. Possibly three-eyed is Siva, guardian-god is Brahma, and Hari is Visnu, or the line refers to Harihara, a combination of Siva and Visnu.

44   **the seasons ... unnerves** Alternatively, reading ฤดี as *rati*, love: this season love upsets, unnerves, unsettles me.

45   **gem princess** แก้วสมเด็จกลาง, *kaeo somdet klang*. "Gem" is the epithet for the seven possessions of a world-rolling emperor (see v. 7); *somdet* is a Khmer-derived form of address to someone of very high rank; *somdet klang*, middle majesty, was perhaps the title of an official consort (and is now the name of a prized amulet).

45   **fount of fortune** วานิภาคย, *waniphak*. See v. 27.

you slip-slid from my side, and gave great grief 46
apart, afar, I cry myself husk-hoarse
O young, full-blooming jewel, elegant of limb
I'm left bereft of joy and quick for love

I yearn for you, heart hot, head spinning round 47
at times my blurry eyes see things flash-flash
I seem to see soft tender you there watching me
then lust and longing roil and wreck my heart

a-missing you, my eyes roam round the sky 48
they see the moon vie with the sun to shine
the moon is tender you, my queen supreme
at times I supped your cheeks' soft subtle scent

a month arrives apace anew—tears fall 49
and streaming rains enshroud the stormy sky
for pity, press upon my breast, O love of mine
month's end—your face, where have you gone to hide?

Month Six: Vesākha (April–May)

the month Vesākha roars, the heavens pour 50
I miss the flowers, garlands, places of yours
this season's love, your belly, utmost joy
my belly hot and hurt against your navel's bud

the restive sky's loud cries, like my laments for love 51
send sudden pains to pierce my heart—I fall
this month proclaims the time to plow has come
my heart's drought-dry but waters drench my eyes

46 **full-blooming** เพ็ญ, *phen*. Full, used especially of the moon.
46 **elegant of limb** ภุชภาคย, *phuchaphak*, S: bhuja bhāgya.
48 **queen** ฉายา, *chaiya*, S: chāya. Shadow, and the name of the wife of the sun god Surya, hence a wife, especially of royalty.
50 **navel's bud** ขวั้นสะดือ, *khwan sadue*. Where *khwan* is the joint between a fruit and its stalk.

since I was parted from you far and long   52
the grumbling sky declaims its doleful gloom
the breezes blow, bring flowing, flooding rains
the heavens' restless rage compounds my grief

I'm parted far apart my lady love   53
the sun and rabbit-moon can live alone
but wandering this wilderness, this world
I must lack love, my heart forced far apart

I see the smiling moon as you alluring me   54
why does the moon look like my darling bud?
I ache without my fount of fortune fine
who quicked my lust, aroused, enraptured me

the drought in all three worlds is past   55
but karma's caused a block—I fall apart
at night I miss the state of utmost bliss
and weary, hungry, worn, I roar aloud in pain

through this sixth month, I've wailed and wept no end   56
this season countryfolk all plow the earth
atop a plow's upcurving shaft, a flag there flaps
I think your hand is beck'ning me and race behind

I reach the flag and it's not you—I fall   57
unsettled, hot, love-hungry, wracked by fear

53 **rabbit-moon** ศศิ, *sasi*. The pattern on the moon is seen as a rabbit (Pali *sasa*), and the
moon is sometimes called the ศศิธร, *sasithon*, sasidhara, "rabbit-holder," here abbrevi-
ated to *sasi*.

53 **lack love** นิราศ, *nirarot*. See v. 20.

54 **darling bud** หน่อเหน้า, *no nao*. Young shoot (of a plant).

54 **fount of fortune** See v. 27.

55 **karma ...** This is the first time in the year that he broaches the idea that his situation
is the result of some action in the past—a theme that will develop through the poem.
Bad deeds in the past create karma that can suddenly create an obstruction or
blockage (here ทำกั้ง, *kam kang*), meaning difficulties of various kinds.

57 **wracked by fear** พรั่นกว้า, *phran kwa*. This is the first appearance of a phrase that appears

the flapping plowshaft flag as seen afar
is not your hand, your face, but just a plow!

Month Seven: Jeṭṭha (May–June)

the month of Jeṭṭha's here, the sky roars loud   58
Varuna's golden streams spread through the sky
Vesākha long I slept alone and moped
the more I mope, my haggard face droops down

alone, my skin and hair are dry and red   59
my breast is hot and withered, back a board
as heaven's greenish belly growls and groans
dream-dazed I wail and weep in welling streams

famed Akaniṭṭhā in the sixteenth realm   60
or Indra's jeweled seat, the Paṇḍukambala

or golden Meru, shining all directions ten
can they relieve my pain and lift my gloom?

---

six times, always at the end of the second line of a verse (see v. 109, 121, 177, 183, 224).

58   **Varuna** พรุณ, *pharun*. The god of rain.

60   **hair** โมลิศ, *molit*, from Pali, moli, hair bun. Duangmon ("Khwam ngam," 38–40) and Chanthit (*Thawathotsamat Khlongdan*, 116) read this word as meaning "earth," and "breast" in the next line as "surface," so the two lines are about nature, not him: the earth is dry and very red / the surface hot and harsh.

60   **Akaniṭṭhā** อักขนิษฐ, *akkhanit*, "none inferior in rank." A class of deities in the sixteenth and highest of the Pure Abodes (Suddhāvāsa), worlds with only a remnant of material factors. Reynolds and Reynolds (*Three Worlds*, 358) call this the "Realm of *brahma* who are supreme."

60   **Paṇḍukambala** บัณฑุกัมพล, "pale yellow woolen stone." Indra's throne in the Tāvatiṃsa heaven. In the Three Worlds, "Under this [Pāricchattaka] tree there is a dais of gem stone, which is called Paṇḍukambala and is 480,000 *wa* [fathoms] long.... The color is deep red like that of the flower called *sa-eng*, and it is soft as a cloth cushion or the comb of a royal golden swan. Whenever Indra sits on this stone slab, it is soft and he sinks down to his navel; but when Indra gets up and leaves the stone, the stone fills in just as it had been before" (Reynolds and Reynolds, *Three Worlds*, 233).

this month the rain clouds flood the skies 61
and paint the peaks of forests green again
on fire with lust, I crave the bud of foreign gold
and, glimpsing you in flashes, thrill all through

the forest's daubed with eye-like blue pea-flowers 62
as pretty as your made-up painted eyes
love-lotuses glow-gleam like gold and gems
I cherish blooms like cheeks both full and fair

Lord Varuna bestrews the skies with rain 63
spurs hearts of countryfolk throughout the world
to start their labors, speeding out to plow
apart from little you, I wait, in vain

you wove some petals, love, recall the day 64
wind swirled them up and strew them 'cross the sky
your fingernails up high like nine-gems glittering
I see each nail, my jewel, paint-patterned gold

did sky or earth slink up and swallow you 65
conceal you far away to break my heart?
where do they slyly spy my golden lotus love?
in pain I pray and beg for your return

---

61   **bud of foreign gold** จาวทองเทศ, *jao thong thet*, "bud-gold-foreign." *Thet* (from desa, place, country) usually refers to something foreign from the west—India, Persia, Arabia. Is this another indication of her exotic origins?

62   **blue pea-flowers** อัญชัน, *anchan*, añjana. *Clitoria ternatea*, blue or butterfly pea-flower, a creeper with striking deep blue flowers.

62   **love-lotuses** บัวกาม, *bua kam*. A metaphor rather than a genus.

63   **Varuna** See v. 58.

64   **up ... glittering** โชรช่อ, *chor cho*. *Chor* is unknown, possibly from a Khmer word meaning "raised." *Cho*, meaning a bunch, could refer to the leaves or her fingers, or (as here) mean shine or glint.

64   **nine-gems** เนาวรัตน, *naowarat*, nava ratana. Usually diamond, ruby, emerald, topaz, garnet, sapphire, moonstone, zircon, and cat's eye. Often a metaphor for riches or luxury.

I pine for you so far apart, my jewel   66
from grief and bitterness, disgorge my gut
get up, deep-longing, seek my fragrant love
in fear you may be sick, I ask and wait for news

the seventh month's slipped past with stormy skies   67
apart from you, heart chafes and stomach churns
at dead of night I lie without a sound
I am lack-love, forsaken and forlorn

Month Eight: Āsālha (June–July)

at night I prick my ears to hear the watch   68
curled up, I wait with bruised and burning breast
breath stifled, lying still, no sneeze, no sound
eighth month has come—where have you gone to hide?

I count the days, the months I wait, O sleek-of-skin   69
nights, days, and months do pass and pass again
I fear this body seems to pass away
I pine for little you but pine in vain

I fear the gods both great and small   70
are grieved that I should drown so deep in you
perhaps the king of gods has made us part
and left me sad—sad, sorrowful, and sore

---

67 **lack-love** นิราศ, *nirarot*. See v. 20.

67 **forsaken and forlorn** โตรดตรอม, *trot trom*. Another repeated phrase, appearing in total five times (see v. 190, 227, 234, 236), always at the end of a line, and all but once in the fourth line of the verse.

68 **watch** ยาม, *yam*. See v. 3.

70 **king of gods** สุราเชนทร ทิพราช, *surachenthon thipparat*, sura jana indra dibba raja, "great-being-Indra-divine-king." Meaning Indra.

71 **sad—sad** Starting with this verse, the last line of several verses has a doubled word. Wherever possible, this is reflected in the translation, usually with an em-dash to mark the intervening cesura.

in rains-retreat, sky-lotuses spew streams   71
drums thunder through the heavens, tell the world
the Lord Omniscient's teachings, great insight
and all rejoice in starting dhamma deeds

I bow before the bodhi tree in hope   72
recall Omniscient's virtue, pray and pray
when listening to the dhamma, still I pine for you
but you don't care so what's the point of prayer?

hands clasped at Lord Si Sakya's golden feet   73
while bowed, my eyes are flooded, dripping blood
I take some time to offer flowers, in hope
the hope I'll see the sight I've craved months long

perhaps your eyes or else your body, love   74
possess me, thus oppress me, churn my gut

71 **rains-retreat** พรรษา, *phansa*. A three-month period, usually July to October, when itinerant monks stay in a *wat* during the rains. For the laity, it is a time of abstinence, like Lent.

71 **sky-lotuses** สโรชฟ้า, *sarot fa*; saroja, "lake-born," meaning a lotus. Sky-lotuses are clouds.

71 **Omniscient** สรรเพชญ, *sanphet*, S: sarvajña, P: sabbaññu. All-knowing, an epithet of the Buddha.

71 **dhamma deeds** ทำธรรม, *tham tham*. Keeping the precepts, attending sermons at the *wat*, etc.

72 **bodhi tree** โพธิ, *pho(thi)*, *Ficus religiosa*, pipal. A tree under which the Buddha gained enlightenment, often planted in *wat*.

73 **Lord Si Sakya** ธาศรี ศากย, *ta si sakya*, Sakyamuni. Sage of the Sakya clan, an epithet of the Buddha; here a Buddha image. The image may be the Sihing Buddha in Wat Phra Si Sanphet and the occasion may be the ceremony named *asat* (อาสาธ, a Thai version of the month's name, Āsāḷha) when a number of novices equal to the king's age were ordained. This image was honored for three days and three nights, and candles held by the king in the ceremony were then sent to *wat* in the capital and provincial cities (*Khamhaikan chao krung kao*, 249; *Khamhaikan khun luang ha wat*, 104). This ceremony appears in the late-Ayutthaya record, but is not mentioned in the Ayutthaya Palace Law, King Chulalongkorn's account, or Wales's study (Baker and Pasuk, *Palace Law of Ayutthaya*; Chulachomklao, *Phraratchaphith*; Wales, *Siamese State Ceremonies*).

75 **gut** ไส้, *sai*, intestine. In the thinking of the time, the stomach and related organs were the seat of the emotions.

I grieve in need of you, of you alone
month eight—eight watches long I wail and weep

in what direction do you stay, my love   75
the sky, the water world, or lands beyond?
O stream-crown bearing god, four elements creator
please seek the maiden, let me hear the news

past life, did we divide a pair of birds or deer   76
or seize the goods of someone thrown in jail?
and, as rebound, my heartstring's slipped away
made me lack-love, so far apart, alone

O gods who made her disappear, show mercy once   77
I offer you a hundred thousand maidens, lords
for her, the single, perfect, treasured bloom of mine
I bow to offer you these fragrant gems divine

this month has come, are little you asleep?   78
or has the thousand-armed one dragged you off
has Surya of sacred power smuggled you away?
O moon, destroy the sun so I see her again!

---

75   **water world** See v. 32.

75   **stream-crown bearing god** ชฎาธารเทพ, *chada thara thep*, "crown-stream-deity." Siva
     has Ganga, goddess of the waters, in his hair.

75   **four elements** สฤษฎิ ศรีสี่, *saritdisi si*. The elements are earth, water, wind, and fire.
     Winai (in Trongjai, *Upathawathotsamat Khlongdan*, 181) suggests this means four faces
     rather than four elements.

76   **a pair ... to part** This is a common motif found in *jātaka* tales and elsewhere, explaining
     some misfortune experienced in the present as the result of a comparable misfortune
     inflicted on others in a previous life, here the separation of couples.

76   **seize the goods** ริบราช(บาตร), *rip rat(chabat)*. Seize on royal order, a common punishment.
     The "goods" might include wife and children.

76   **as rebound** มาทัน, "it's arrived." The karma of the past action has come into play.

76   **lack-love** นิราศ, *nirarot*. See v. 20.

78   **thousand-armed one** พันกร, *phan kon*, thousand arms. Surya, god of the sun.

78   **Surya** สุริย. God of the sun.

78   **destroy the sun** The sun (or sunlight) has to be assumed in this line. Chanthit

I hail the holy words that subdued demons once   79
the tongue whose taste and scent are savored close
I hail the dulcet, sweet, sublime discourse
the words a young and lovely princess spoke

perhaps your karma made us part—mine too   80
times past, I relished, reveled in your flesh
upon a bed bedecked in brilliant hues
the sweet taste lingers still, the scent will never fade

eighth month has come and flown away   81
my breast is choked, my withered heart still waits
a new month's come, the ninth, my lady love
but still your face—your face I do not see

Month Nine: Sāvana (July–August)

O loveliest lady, maiden like the moon   82
will one more month go past with me this way
breast burning, heart unhinged from parting still?
the words I send each day, have you not seen?

ninth month, should I still wait for you, my love?   83
just now an evil omen came to pass
my bones and sinews twitched, my body yawned
whoever cries at this is marked to die

this month has brought on tears like floods of rain   84
apart, apart from you so far, so very far
the rain beats loud, the town and country cool
apart from lovely you—for you alone I pine

(*Thawathotsamat Khlongdan*, 135) suggests he is calling on the moon to destroy the
darkness.

79 **subdued demons** เกลาสูร, *klao sun*. *Asura* are a class of deities who have become low
and malevolent. This line perhaps refers to those that assaulted the Buddha as he
approached enlightenment.

heart aches, I long to hold your form divine   85
my body's wasted, skin is dry and rough
because you slipped, slid, hid so far away
this month my eyes rain floods—where have you gone to hide?

this month, most graceful lady, bids me ponder why   86
why am I parted far, far-flung away
ninth month, is there some block, some bar
parts me from little you—for little you I yearn

the sky looms dark, rain-laden clouds drift by   87
and splashing downpours soak and swamp the land
the flooded streams and rivers surge and gush
I weep and wail and wait, no sight of you

at night the thunder rumbles round the sky   88
Vayu envelops Varuna with clouds
the lord, intent on seizing you, swoops down
inside the clouds that darken—darken all around

perhaps he's flipped, head over heels, my love   89
he's failed to catch you, take you off this time
the lord is hiding there in Vayu's clouds
were it my mind, I would have swept you off

to be apart so long, young gem, inspires desire   90
to share the taste with you, to lie clasped tight
alone, I'm love-drunk, dopey, fit to die
without love's arts, how do you trap me now?

it's strange how passion lodges, lingers in the breast   91
I know I'm floating empty-hearted, 'rapt by you

86 **most graceful** กลนิศ, *kolanit*, from S: kalana, behavior.
88 **Vayu** วายุ, *wayu*. God of the wind.
89 **the lord** ซีสา, *chisa*. A respectful form of address from Khmer. In this and the next verse, it appears to refer to Varuna.

I peer into a void bestrewn with moon and stars
and know the moon is my young lover's face

does not your fine complexion match the moon?   92
though bodies human, heavenly are not the same
the moonlight is so bright, so glorious
I thus thought up all this—this simile

who drew a rabbit, placed it on the moon?   93
the face is boring, hang it elsewhere, please
your pretty face, where has it vanished to?
the moon is always there—where are you always hid?

the brightly colored garland round your neck   94
until was worn, lay on a jeweled seat
although you left alike the setting moon
you crossed sky's rim and failed to rise again

Month Ten: Bhadda (August–September)

now Bhadda's here, the far skies roar   95
the waters damp my eyes and swamp the banks
your husband rages from the power of lust
tears flood my face, flow down to fill the streams

you flash-flash 'fore my swimming eyes   96
my breast burns badly, little lotus lost
again, again I glimpse leaves fluttering
as if my fragrant lissome love had come

---

92 **bodies human, heavenly** กรรกับกร, *kan kap kon*. Literally, "body and light."
92 **simile** ประเหล *phrahen*. From a Khmer word meaning "same" or S: praheli, riddle, enigma.
93 **rabbit** See v. 53.

in Bhadda month now Sārada comes round   97
let fathers, mothers gather one and all
make offerings to the holy lotus-foot
I search but see you not—where have you gone?

I hurt as if my heart's on fire, O Hari Lord   98
please treat my turmoil, yearning, deathly gloom
I offer prayers to Hari's consort royal
to wash these ten long months full clean away

did Hari, lord and king, create you, lady love   99
intent my heart would fix on you alone?
among the finest angels in three worlds
have any matched the dust of your young feet?

soft-skinned beloved was made to gild the earth   100
but karma clove you from my breast, far, far away

whose forehead do you brighten now, beloved?
I'm badly bruised, my gem—my gem, tenth month is here

---

97 **Sārada** สารท, *sat.* A festival falling on the 15th waning of the 10th month, usually in September, near the equinox. According to King Chulalongkorn, in ancient India, Sharada was the season following the rains, and the festival marked the harvesting of the earliest rice, made into an offering to brahmans. In Siam, this was converted into offering a special sweet, *krayasat*, made from new rice, sugar, peanut, and sesame, to the monks. Some believe the dead return to the human world on this day, thus merit made for them is especially effective (Chulachomklao, *Phrarachaphithi*, 419–42; Wales, *Siamese State Ceremonies*, 231–36). However, this may be a different form of the festival. In India today, roughly at this time of year, Sharada Navaratri is a nine-day festival celebrating various forms of the old mother goddesses who have been integrated into Hinduism as consorts of Siva and Visnu, especially Durga, Saraswati, and Parvati. V. 98 below suggests that something of this brahmanical form is being practiced here, but had vanished before the accounts by Chulalongkorn (Chulachomklao) and Wales.

96 **Hari Lord** See v. 43.

98 **Hari's consort** Probably Visnu's consort, Laksmi.

100 **forehead do you brighten** เอาเจิมไปแจ่ม, *ao joem pai jaem. Joem* is to make an auspicious mark with powder on the forehead (perhaps the image is prompted by the brahmanical Sharada festival, see v. 97), and *jaem* means brighten.

tenth month has truly come, I'm losing heart   101
as months pass by and seize, snatch you away
I sob and sorrow, sad with heart destroyed
I'm left alone to swim in pain and grief

in rains-retreat, the Lord Omniscient's bathed   102
I went with you to hear a sermon told
O, have you spurned my heart, gone off alone
and left your husband here to howl till hoarse?

this month the deer migrate, did you dance after them   103
as deer called out to deer to cross the streams?
Kattika month approaches, waterways will flood
did you leave me—leave with the youthful deer?

my merit's all been shared with gods supreme   104
these gods should not behold my sorry state
a breast that burns and aches, my breath near gone
a heart that boils and seethes, a hundred mountains hot

e'en if the sun, a god supreme, should die   105
or Holy Meru lean so far it falls
or all three worlds decay and mankind die
the hurt won't match your vanishing, your loss

my heart's caved in, collapsed, my love   106
from being far apart from you this long

101 **rains-retreat** See v. 71.
101 **Lord Omniscient** See v. 71.
101 **bathed** ภิเษก, *phisek*, abhiseka. Ritual bathing, in this case of a Buddha image.
103 **deer migrate** The forests of Siam once teemed with deer of several species, hunted
      for their meat and skins. In the rainy season in the late sixteenth century, according
      to Diego de Couto, "all the wild animals of the forest—deer, antelopes, wild cattle and
      other animals—take shelter in the high places, and the Siamese go there with many
      boats for hunting" (quoted in Breazeale, "Portuguese Impressions of Ayutthaya," 54).
104 **hundred mountains hot** เดือดดาลร้อนร้อยส่วนเสล, *dueat dan ron roi suan sen*. Perhaps
      meaning as hot as a hundred mountains are big, or hotter than a hundred heated rocks
      (Chanthit, *Thawathotsamat Khlongdan*, 160; Maneepin, "Khlong thawathotsamat," 131).

the waters splash, a boat goes racing by
snakes down the stream, is hailed as champion

my heart is bruised and burnt—I yearn   107
survive by drinking tears that flood my eyes
alone, abandoned, far apart from you
not granted mercy, not one strand of hair

with hands I raise a lotus, honor heaven's power   108
O gods both great and small throughout the skies
I beg to tryst the little dancer, ever her alone
but all the gods in Meru's heavens mercy have they none!

your noble words, great lover, still, still stay   109
deep in my navel down I'm wracked with fear
was it the gods that kidnapped you away
left me long lonely longing, craving your caress?

Month Eleven: Assayuja (September–October)

the moon shines softly bright as it should be   110
Assayuja's here, a month I held you close
why am I still without my best gem queen?
I meet but rowdy crowds who cram the waterways

this month is picturesque, the waters flood   111
on riverbanks I'm missing you, my gem

---

106   **is hailed as champion** ถวายเลิศ, *thawai loet*. Presented (to the king) as champion (in a boat race).

107   **strand of hair** Meaning not even mercy as little as a strand of hair; a common simile.

108   **little dancer** นุชนาฏ, *nutchanat*, S: nuja nāṭa. Probably an endearment and appreciation (as pretty as a dancer), not a description.

109   **your noble words** ชงครา, *chongkhra*, compressed from ราชโองการ, *rachongkan*. Royal utterance.

109   **deep in my navel down** ในรลุงนาภิ, *nai ralung naphi*, "in-deep-navel." Meaning similar to "the pit of the stomach." See v. 75.

110   **gem queen** รัตนชาเยศ, *ratana chayet*. See v. 7, 78.

as splendid royal barges race in rivalry
O gentle lady, parted far from me!

the Lion's Visage, decked in gold, looks brilliant 112
and Glorious Victory's like a craft divine
the golden paddles glint and glitter bright
the rowers, backs tattooed, drive on with spirits high

the paddlers part the waters, fly downstream 113
they cant their oars then plunge and pull with power
I ache afar from you with flooding eyes
think back, recall the time of our first tryst

Lion's Visage dashes past, oars canted, flying fast 114
I think of how my gaze ne'er left the Victory Throne
I see wild sugar tufts a-blowing in the wind
a slender boat, with paddles dancing, heads in open air

111　**barges race** Assayuja/Atsayut is the name of the month and also its major ceremony, a ritual boat race between barges of the king and the primary queen. If the king's barge loses, "there will be overflowing joy and happiness," but if it wins there will be a time of hardship (Baker and Pasuk, *Palace Law of Ayutthaya*, 120, clause 180; *Khamhaikan chao krung kao*, 249–50; *Khamhaikan khun luang ha wat*, 105).

112　**Lion's Visage** (ไกร)สรมุข, *(krai)son muk*, kesara mukha. The barge of the primary queen.

112　**Glorious Victory** ศรีสมรรถไช, *si samanthachai*, S: śrī samanta jaya, "glorious-entire-victory." The barge of the king.

112　**spirits high** ฮึดฮือ, *hoet hoe*. Duangmon ("Khwam ngam," 159) suggests there is the sound of huffing and puffing in the words.

113　**cant their oars** ฉายฉาก, *chai chak*. Pausing with the oar raised slightly above horizontal.

114　**Victory Throne** พิมานไชย, *phiman chai*, vimāna jaya. The name of the queen's covered seat on the Lion's Visage barge, described in the "Boat Songs" by Prince Thammathibet (mid-eighteenth century): "Lion's Visage has faces on four sides / a covered throne that reaches the clouds / golden curtains beautifully embroidered / roof as red as a dragon" (Thammathibet, "Bot he ruea," 201).

114　**wild sugar** เลา, *lao*. Saccharum spontaneum, a tall, tufted grass, placed on the bow of the queen's boat.

the Noble Swan, as splendid as your slender craft   115
is built so frail I fear will overturn
but, softly swaying, glides in graceful harmony
the boat knows the water, the water serves the boat

I watch a trooper hoist a flag and sweep it down   116
that moment shows who won, who lost right there
alike the love and pain my little dancer's caused
halfway at Bang Thamo the rowers raise their oars

my eyes are set on watching for your boat   117
I scan the banks, see nothing, see not you
just river waters flowing stirred to foam
the hearts of earth and sky cry out for you

the foamy waters froth and my tears fall   118
I hide upon the whirlpool's banks, my heart afire
O, you live in my heart, and yet your body's gone
the hearts of earth and sky weep floods of rain

all seven rivers joined, the seven streams as one   119
would equal not my tears of lust and loss
I weep from lust for you, and wonder why
I ache to taste the flower inside a flower soon

115　**Noble Swan** วรหงส, *wara hong*, vara hamsa. Probably the Suphannahong, golden swan (Chanthit, *Thawathotsamat Khlongdan*, 173; Cushman, *Royal Chronicles*, 25, 48; *Phraratcha phongsawadan chabap phraratchahatthalekha*, I, 69, 99).

116　**alike the love** ... The meaning of the line is hard to fathom. Perhaps he is comparing the contrast of winning and losing to the contrasting love and pain that she is causing him. Alternatively, despite the race, all he is thinking of is the love and pain.

116　**Bang Thamo** บางถมอ. Rock village near Bang Kaja at the southeast corner of Ayutthaya.

118　**whirlpool** เกลียว, *kliao*, spiral. Meaning the disturbed water where two rivers meet at the southeast corner of Ayutthaya.

119　**seven rivers** See v. 31.

119　**wonder why** These two words have been moved from the fourth line.

the world's at play but I look on unmoved   120
and weep, my heart destroyed by fires of love
I grieve and yearn, breast empty, missing you
I ache alone, afar—hurting, hungry, hoarse

the festive month has come, I scan the roads   121
my heart feels hot, aflutter, wracked by fear
the season's come for sport, but you have gone elsewhere
abandoned, anxious, hot, I wait without relief

our parting pains my heart, the heavens pour and pour   122
Aggi and Vāyu join, the lightning strikes with rain
Lord Varuna has drenched me thoroughly, and yet
my eyes stream more by many thousand times

in Assayuja month, the waters flood the sky   123
I beat and bang my breast to break apart
the sky is damp and dismal like my bitter heart
yet cannot match my flooding, flowing tears

the thunder echoes eerily and winds whirl round   124
all continents and lands in thousands burn
the era-ending fires annihilate three worlds
but O, my breast is hotter, many thousand times

did you escape the world to hide, a-rivaling the moon?   125
or was the moon my rival, jealous over you?
I look all round and see the moon has slipped away
the shining moon's a torch, yet you're unseen this world below

---

122 **Aggi and Vāyu** อัคนี, *akhani* and (พระ)พาย, *(phra)phai*. Gods of fire and wind.
123 **era-ending fires** See v. 34.
125 **or was the moon** ... A line open to many interpretations. Possibly: I'll block this
rivalry from my concern for you.

Month Twelve: Kattika (October–November)

in Kattika the golden moon shines specially bright 126
mid wisps of cloud against a limpid sky
the heavens' heart glows light and bright as clouds dispel
yet my abandoned heart knows only scorching heat

the sky's as bright as if the sun did shine 127
my heart is torrid, dark, and drunk on you
perhaps the festivals have made me sick and sad
I hurt because I love you, cry for you

the waterways are full and flowing, swirling fast 128
boats big and small are paddled on the stream
right down to Bang Khadan, the whirling navel-pool
the season's come to make the floods recede

the boats that chased the waters reach their docks 129
the weary paddlers slowly row, half-bowed
my oarsmen, drained and dizzy, huff and heave
because they rowed with bodies bobbing powerfully

---

127 **festival** พิธี, *phithi*. It may mean *vidhi*, destiny or fate, but more likely refers to his missing her during the Assayuja ceremonies.

128 **Bang Khadan** บางขดาน (กระดาน). Flat village near Bang Kaja, the southeast corner of the city, where two rivers meet and swirl.

128 **whirling navel-pool** ดินสดือแม่, *din sadue mae*, "river's navel." See v. 118.

128 **floods recede** ไล่ชล, *lai chon*, "chasing the water." In the Palace Law, called ไล่เรือ, *lai ruea*, "chasing the boat," a ceremony to make the water level fall after the rains in time for the harvest (Baker and Pasuk, *Palace Law of Ayutthaya* 121, clause 182). Writing about the late sixteenth century, Diego da Couto described the event: "When they want this river to switch to draining away ... the king goes out of the city with all of his great lords, in [a procession of] many vessels grandly gilded and adorned, with many festivities and playing of musical instruments of all sorts. It is said that the king goes to expel the water out of the kingdom. Among all of his festive occasions, this is the main one." The highlight of the event was a boat race "with voluminous shouting, frequent screams and much clamour" (quoted in Breazeale, "Portuguese Impressions of Ayutthaya," 54).

129 **chased the waters** ไล่ชล, *lai chon*. See v. 128. The line means that the ceremony is over.

month Kattika's for making lantern offerings   130
all men and women find a place to play
with singing, making music—fiddle, flute, and *khaen*
fingers picking strings, ding-ding, and dancing round

inside gilt jeweled lanterns candles shine   131
my breast is like a golden lantern lit
flames heat and raze my heart and fire desire
my breast is burning up and churning round

I'm grieved my fount of fortune's disappeared   132
the joys of watch-beat time are barred, denied
I think of how my princess played the joys of love
those flames aren't hot—I'm hotter still by far

on posts the lanterns raised hang high as offerings   133
my heart hangs too—O may your soul not die!

the fires of lust are scorching me to writhe alone
and you don't stay to share with me the heat

month Kattika is here and waters whelm the world   134
the watery floods spread slowly far and wide

130 **making lantern offerings** The festival of ตรองเปรียง, *trong* later *jong priang*, "raising
fat", a brahman lantern ceremony, probably derived from Dipavali, to honor Siva,
Brahma, and Visnu on the full moon of the twelfth month. In the version based on an
Indian original, recorded in later manuals and practiced in the early Bangkok era, the
lanterns are hoisted on posts for fifteen days, and on the first day the king anoints the
three main posts with cow fat. In the version from the Borommakot reign, lanterns
are hung all round the palaces and the city wall for fifteen days leading up to the full
moon (Baker and Pasuk, *Palace Law of Ayutthaya*, 120, clause 181; Chulachomklao,
Phrarachaphithi, 6–10; *Khamhaikan chao krung kao*, 250; *Khamhaikan khun luang ha wat*,
105; *Tamra phraratchaphithi kao*, 9; Wales, *Siamese State Ceremonies*, 288–89).
130 **fiddle, flute, and *khaen*** ซอปี่แคน, *so*, generic term for fiddles; *pi*, generic term for
blown woodwind reed instruments; *khaen*, the Lao multi-pipe reed mouth organ.
130 **fount of fortune** See v. 27.
132 **princess** สมเด็จ, *somdet*. A royal prefix.
133 **O may ...** This can be read many ways: May *I* not die; may you not be dead, etc.

submerging roads and filling banks of rivers full
and thinking back I'm swamped in tears none see

I watch the waters swell and splash just like my eyes   135
delirious, distressed, a madman like
not seeing you return, I rage inside
hopes unfulfilled, I lay me down sprawled flat

the waters of your love and of my lust once fused   136
why have the waters of your kindness dried?
the northern waters flow to join the greater stream
waters meeting waters thus—thus should matters be

I share the merit made, intent there should be fruit   137
I offer holy oil, the merit shared with you
the golden lantern shines, a rival to the moon
I beg to send the merit made by these good works

great boats go snaking down the waterways   138
they cover streams and rivers through the land
I offer trays of food as alms to monks
and pray to tryst with lithe young lissome you

the strings of lanterns dangle down in rows   139
the pulleys groan like windmills turned by breeze
when raised, the lanterns spin, my heart sinks missing you
the pulleys' groans of passion leave me lonely, low

136　**the waters … ** ชลกาม … เกลศชล, *chon kam … klet chon*, S: jala kāma … jala kleśa. This verse
　　　has an elaborate wordplay on different meanings of water. See the next two notes.

136　**waters … kindness** ฤไทชล, *ruethai chon*, S: hṛdaya jala = น้ำใจ *nam jai*, "heart-water,"
　　　meaning kindness, love.

136　**northern waters** ชลเหนือ, *chon nuea*. Meaning the upstream tributaries of the Chao
　　　Phraya system.

136　**greater stream** ชลใหญ่, *chon yai*. Meaning the Chao Phraya River or the sea.

137　**holy oil** พระเปรียง, *phra priang*. Animal fat, especially cow fat, which gives the name
　　　of the festival (see v. 130). The word comes from Khmer.

138　**alms to monks** บินทบาต, *pinthabat*, piṇḍapāta. Food placed in the alms bowl of a monk.

the pulleys' groans of passion stir my yen for you   140
now pulled by strings, the lanterns reach the tops
the garlands blow away and flowers float up high
the groans are like your moans to raise the heat

Month One: Māgasira (November–December)

the deer have come to dance, I dwell on lanterns still   141
on play times, love plays, plays of give and take
on plays with you pressed close to passion's peak
on plays now missed whose memory metes me pain

I think of love—the first month has arrived, beloved   142
the rains have left the sky, yet I still fret and yearn
my heart is dry, I raise my eyes to emptiness above
I see the fields and streams, floods gone and waters low

the body of water has left the earth's crust   143
grass wilts and withers, dying, stunted, sad
like me so far apart the little dancer beautiful
my body hugging pillows, hearing silence still

choked, heavy-hearted, hungry, low   144
this season chafes my heart and churns my gut
my breast flip-flops like fish when water's gone
while eager egrets foraging still find the food they want

I'm dismal, lonely, widowed, lone   145
breast shakes with hope—a hope that's unfulfilled

---

141 **deer** The month is called มฤคเศียร, *maruekhasian*, S: mṛga śira, deer's head, after a
constellation, the fifth lunar mansion, part of Orion. See also v. 103.

143 **body** อก, *ok*. Breast. In this and the last line, the word translated as "body" means
breast or chest, and can be used to describe a surface such as sea or land.

144 **my breast ...** Alternatively, this line reads: the fish have disappeared, making my
breast fearful.

145 **widowed** หม้าย, *mai*.

a wading pelican can peck lank-fish, as dreamed
an eagle cries eek-eek—I echo cries of pain

a stork swoops down on herons here 146
they leave their nests and clumsily fly off
this season, water's gone, the sand is bare
just tiddlers—sweetlip, mistfish, minnow, scissortail

the mistfish spines if touched will burn like catfish do 147
when swallowing in curry, watch for bones
I think of you, my lovely lotus parted far from me
you know, my noble friend, I still feel stabbed

the fields are full of ripening paddy's yellow ears 148
alone I'm left to waste away, O fair-of-skin
the country people come and go in crowds
my breast still burns, I weep in deeper gloom

145   **pelican** (กระ)ทุงทอง, *(kra)thung thong. Pelecanus philippensis*, spot-billed pelican.

145   **lank-fish** ปลาทอง, *pla thong*. Today meaning the ornamental goldfish *Carassius auratus*, but here a river fish, unidentified, with a name invented here to mimic the wordplay.

145   **eagle cries eek-eek** ออกอุก, *ook uk*. Ook could be *Haliaeetus leucogaster*, white-bellied sea eagle. Alternatively, it could mean "out," part of the calling verb. The calls of many eagles are whistles and squeaks.

146   **stork** กระสา, *krasa. Ciconia* (various).

146   **herons** กระสัง, *krasang*. Appears often in literature, but identification has been lost. Called herons here because *krasa* and *krasang* are often paired in this way, and *krasa* is used loosely for waders like herons and storks.

146   **mistfish** ... สร้อย *soi, Dangila leptocheila*, sweetlip; สิ้, *si*, usually ซิว, *siu, Rasbora trilineata*, etc., scissortail; ซ่า, *sa, Labiobarbus* (various), species of carp and minnow; แขยง, *khayaeng*, various small river fish including *Pseudomystus siamensis* and *Mystus mysticetus* (hence "mistfish," invented here).

147   **catfish** ดุก, *duk. Clarias* (various), the common name for catfish in general.

this month's for watching kites float in the sky   149
I see a mewing kite that's coaxed to climb
the kite string spins, and my heart's spinning too
I see a stuck kite jerked to climb, and my heart squirms

the kites careening, keening make me glum   150
the sounds of squeaking, creaking churn my guts
alone I soar up fast to seek my only love
with breast afire from missing you, I scan the skies

O wind, please blow her news as well, O wind!   151
make haste to fetch my soulmate, fly back fast
I love and I still yearn although my heart's destroyed
O kites, send news and beg her to return

the kites now take the tidings, fly up high   152
the winds propel the kite strings soaring up
I wait for news, concerned how you may be
kites bring no news, pains sting my listless heart

this season sees folk play at festivals   153
all over, men and women gather with their friends
their accents hail from almost all the world
they tour the city having so much fun!

149   **kites ... mewing** In the list of royal festivals from the Borommakot reign: "In the first month, there is the festival of *khlaeng* for flying 'mewing' kites to summon the seasonal wind" (*Khamhaikan chao krung kao*, 250; *Khamhaikan khun luang ha wat*, 105). The mewing (หง่า, *ngao*) is the cry of a tomcat for a mate. This obscure verb appears in the second line of this verse, but spelled with the consonants transposed, possibly a copying error. La Loubère wrote: "That [the kite] of the King of *Siam* is in the air every Night for the two Winter-months, and some *Mandarins* are nominated to ease one another in holding the String" (*New Historical Relation*, 49). Gerini wrote that in this month during the Ayutthaya period "large paper kites were flown with the object of calling up the seasonal wind by the fluttering noise they made" (quoted in Wales, *Siamese State Ceremonies*, 221).

150   **guts** See v. 75.

153   **accents ... all the world** Ayutthaya was famed as a city of "forty languages" in the seventeenth and eighteenth centuries, but this line confirms that its cosmopolitan character was established earlier.

this deer's head month, the full moon's bright   154
the moving limpid moon illumes an open sky
Trīyampawāi, friends go along in groups
'O, has this devotee appeared alone this time?'

the twice-born start to hang the plaques   155
plaques smooth alike your navel-belly flower
when swung, the coupled ropes cry out
and O, they make me think of you still more

154   deer's-head See v. 141. This line can be read as the deer's head constellation is shining brightly.

154   Trīyampawāi ตรียามพวาย, *triyamphawai.* A brahman festival, adapted from a Tamil original in which Siva is invited to earth, propitiated for ten days, and then sent back to the heavens. Today, the event is twinned with a similar rite for Visnu as Trīyampawāi-Trīppawāi, but this twinning occurred much later, possibly in early Bangkok (McGovern, "Balancing"). Often called the Swinging Festival. See v. 155.

154   devotee ดนัย, *danai,* tanaya. A son, but here meaning a devotee of Siva, a worshipper at this festival. The line seems to report a brahman addressing the author.

155   twice-born ทวิช, *thawit,* dvija. Meaning brahmans.

155   plaques The best-known feature of the Trīyampawāi festival is a swinging contest between teams of young brahmans. This event, held in Bangkok at the Great Swing by Wat Suthat, was abolished in 1934. At the time of this work, however, the only things swung may have been wooden plaques inscribed with images of deities, as still happens in the version of the ceremony held in Nakhon Si Thammarat. According to Van Vliet, the custom of people swinging came from India in the reign of Ramathibodi II (1491–1529), that is, after the likely date of this poem. There is no sign of people swinging in the description here. Today, the festival features three นางกระดาน, *nang kradan,* wooden panels carved with images of Nang Thorani (Wales: "the usual female figure represented as wringing out water from her long hair"); Ganga; and the sun together with the moon. In the record from late Ayutthaya, after the swinging the plaques were placed in holes in the ground. In the ceremony as described by Wales, these images were brought out to observe the swinging. Nowadays, they are brought out at night, inserted in three holes, left there for three days, and then taken back inside the temple. This procedure is said to ensure cooler weather. The plaques are kept in the Devasathan (โบสถ์พราหมณ์ *bot phram*) near Wat Suthat (Baker *et al, Van Vliet's Siam,* 212; *Khamhaikan chao krung kao,* 251; *Khamhaikan khun luang ha wat,* 106; Nathan McGovern, personal communication; Siriphot, "Lo chingcha" and "Triyamphawai-tripawai"; Wales, *Siamese State Ceremonies,* 250–51; Wright, "Phraratchaphithi triyampawai").

155   navel-belly flower ขดานดวงดือดอกไม้, *khadan duang due dok mai,* "board-navel-flower."

I watch arms posed, a votive dance   156
they're like a pair of splendid *kinnari* divine
their golden horns all glitter prettily
I see their faces, not like yours—this month's a bore

the five begin to offer up the plaques   157
the lady of the earth looks like my young princess
the chief of robes brings water for the royal feet
I watch the rites as love burns up my heart

the goddess of the earth is like you—beautiful   158
I see the likeness, thus I stay alive
she's like but she's not like my golden flower
a thousand sorrows stir me sadder still

deer's head is over, done and gone   159
you've disappeared, not seen throughout the world
the first month's passed, the second's here, I brood
and still no sight, I long lament the lady lost

---

156   **kinnari** กินริน, *kinarin*, kinnarī. A fabulous female being with a human head and upper body on the lower body of a bird. A paragon of beauty.

156   **golden horns** เสนงทอง, *sa-neng thong*. Part of the festival is a dance by people probably representing *nāga*, a feature found in other festivals and thus probably a local addition to the India-derived ceremony (Wright, "Phraratchaphithi triyampawai," 164). In photos in Wright's article, the dancers are men wearing a helmet with a crest like the head of a *nāga*. Here the dancers appear to be women.

157   **the five** Probably the head brahmans.

157   **lady of the earth** นาริศธรณี, *narit thorani*. Mae/Nang Thorani, goddess of the earth.

157   **chief of robes** ภูษาธิก, *phusathik*, bhūsā adhika. In the Ayutthaya Palace Law, Trīyampawai is described as a bathing ceremony (Baker and Pasuk, *Palace Law of Ayutthaya*, 123).

158   **I see ...** Alternative: I see the likeness, cannot tear my eyes away.

159   **deer's head** See v. 154.

Month Two: Phussa (December–January)

the Flower-Anointment, praise and blessings!　　　　160
the gem-princess alone is nestled in my heart
but I don't see my only lissome lady love
I hark the earth and sky, but lonely silence reigns

the chief and other twice-born enter now　　　　161
to offer blessings, chants of 'Om,' and eulogies
to offer conch-borne water to the king
presenting prayers of praise in rhythmic chants

the ministers of ranks illustrious　　　　162
and overseers, the *muen* and *khun*, all bow

160　**Flower-Anointment** บุษยาภิเษก, *butsayaphisek*, S: phuṣya abhiṣeka. *Butsaya* is the fifth constellation, Prasepe in Cancer, a circle of five stars, seen as flowers, often lotuses. *Aphisek*/abhiseka is anointment. This ceremony (*puṣyābhiṣekaḥ*) is found in a mid-tenth century Angkor inscription (K.806, v. 66) in which the king was "reconsecrated to his office annually by the royal chaplain and the royal astrologer" through "a stream of nectar poured from one hundred golden vases." The nectar was melted butter and the king sheltered under a blanket (Sanderson, "Śaiva Religion among the Khmers," 382). At Ayutthaya, the ceremony appears to have been an annual re-enactment of the anointment for installing a king, perhaps to replenish the divinity invested in the king by the gods. Wales (*Siamese State Ceremonies*, 121) wrote, "The object of the ceremony is said to have been the maintenance of the welfare of the kingdom, presumably by means of the reinforcement of the king's divine powers." According to the description in the Palace Law, the king proceeded to a throne hall, was anointed by the brahmans, and presented with elements of the realm (the military, the civilians, etc.) by officials—the same procedure as at installation. There was then a feast (Baker and Pasuk, *Palace Law of Ayutthaya*, 121–22, clause 183). In the version from the Borommakot reign, the king sits on a throne of seven flowers and has his fingernails trimmed before lustration by the brahmans (*Khamhaikan chao krung kao*, 250; *Khamhaikan khun luang ha wat*, 106). The ceremony lapsed after the fall of Ayutthaya in 1767 (Chulachomklao, *Phraratchaphithi*, 69).

161　**the chief and other twice-born** ... In the description of this ceremony in the Palace Law, "Phra Ratchapurohit and Phra Khruphiram offer conch water. Phra Mahethon and Phra Phichet offer *klot* water." These four are the two chiefs of the brahman department and their respective deputies (Baker and Pasuk, *Palace Law of Ayutthaya*, 121–22; *Kotmai tra sam duang*, I, 265).

161　**offer blessings** These words have been moved from the previous line.

162　**overseers, the *muen* and *khun*** มื่นขุนมูลนาย, *muen khun munnai. Munnai*, nobles in

attending on his majesty, young-king sublime
O, I care for you—where have you gone to hide?

you once attended all these goings-on   163
and sat beside, not leaving till the business done
because of karma past, you slipped, slid, hid away
alone I grieve and yearn—yearn with streaming eyes

an eerie sky proclaims that we must be apart   164
month two is almost past, I swallow my desire
the head-anointment rite, some singing is performed
I watch a dance to wish long life much multiplied

to foster joy the city's decked like heaven   165
as fine as Kosiya's glorious city dropped to earth
gate-guards patrol the gold-embellished Trimuk Hall
high on a pediment, Garuda looks superb

---

charge of manpower, who had titles of *muen* and *khun*, at that time titles of officials
below ministerial rank.

162   **his majesty, young-king sublime** สมเดสปิ่นเสาวคต ยุพราช, *somdet pin saowakhot
yupharat*, sugata yuvarāja, "well-faring young-king" (see Afterword). This line could
refer to one person or two (the king and young-king).

164   **head-anointment rite** มูรธาภิษิต, *murathaphisit*, S: mūrdha abhiṣeka. A rite of
purification, part of the long Flower-Anointment ceremony (*Khamhaikan chao krung
kao*, 250). See v. 160.

164   **wish ... multiplied** บนหมั้นหมื่นทวี, *bon man muen thawi*. Literally, pray for security
increased ten thousand times (for the king).

165   **Kosiya** โกสีย, either "owl" or "belonging to the Kusika family," meaning Indra.

165   **Trimuk** ตรีมุข, three-portico. Name of a building in the early Ayutthaya palace,
location unknown, burnt down in 1426/27 (Cushman, *Royal Chronicles*, 15; Kreangkrai,
"Sathapatyakam," 300), or another building of this shape.

165   **Garuda** ครุฑ, *khrut*. A mythical animal with the upper body of a human and the head
and nether body of a bird, based on an eagle. The mount of Visnu and thus a symbol
of kingship.

the Surya Vairocana shimmers shining bright   166
the Candra Vimāna seems like a jeweled sky
with colored gems aglitter on a gold facade
I think of being parted—parted, 'sotted over you

the royal hall is beautifully adorned   167
there lords in thousands bow their heads and raise their hands
with garlands helmet-hung a-swaying to and fro
on horse, they grip their polo sticks and scramble for the ball

I watch the jeweled chariot glide across the sky   168
in haste to hide alone beyond sky's rim
perhaps Lord Surya has led my love away
your leaving me has slashed my heart to shreds

---

166 **Surya Vairocana** สุริยไพโรจน์, *suriya phairot*, "glorious sun [god]." A palace building, possibly the Benjarat Mahaprasat throne hall, called เบญจรัตนมหาปราสาทสุริโยภาษวรา, *benjarat mahaprasat suriyophatwara*, when King Trailokanat legislated part of the Law on Revolt and Warfare in 1476 (*Kotmai tra sam duang*, IV, 132).

166 **Candra Vimāna** จันทรพิมาน, *janthara phiman*. Palace of the moon, an unidentified building in the palace.

166 **colored gem** จำรูญรัตน, *jamrun-ratana*. Possibly the name of another (unknown) building rather than a description.

167 **royal hall** พระพลานไชย, *phra phlanchai*. Probably the main audience hall.

167 **lords** กษัตริย, *kasatriya*, S: kṣatriya. Presumably subordinate rulers, using a term normally meaning a king. This verse suggests such subordinate rulers were summoned to the capital for this ceremony, as they would be for a coronation, and played polo as part of the celebration.

167 **grip their polo sticks** กรกอดคลี, *kon kot khli*. A rare reference to playing polo at Ayutthaya. The Palace Law refers to the parade ground as the "polo ground" and has clauses on procedures when the king plays (Baker and Pasuk, *Palace Law of Ayutthaya*, 83, 89). In some *jātaka* tales composed in Southeast Asia, a bodhisatta plays polo in the sky with Indra (Baker and Pasuk, *From the Fifty Jātaka*, 44–46, 348, 352). Polo emerged from nomadic tribes in Central Asia, was adopted as a game of kings in Persia, and had spread to China by the seventh century CE, Japan by the eighth, and India by the eleventh (Chehabi and Guttmann, "From Iran to All of Asia"). It thus may have reached Siam from either east or west. The terminology used in Siam does not help to identify the origin.

168 **jeweled chariot** เกวียนแก้ว, *kwian kaeo*. The sun.

the dancers strive to show their charms   169
like *apsara* in heavens in the skies
this festival won't soothe my ruined heart
O, not to see your face—my face is gashed with grief

you hide your beauty, do you, queen of queens?   170
I beat the breast you left behind, I weep
I search but find no trace of best beloved of mine
the maid divine has hid in her own room

the special Golden-Candles launch like heaven's lights   171
arrayed in strings of gold and sprays of gems
on seeing these at once a million sorrows burn
with blazing heat that's blasted me so long

the Elements-Divine look grand on firework towers   172
they brighten up the world with swirling sprays
O, since my jeweled lotus lover danced away
I wilt in suffering hundred times their fire

now pitter-patter-splash my tears   173
fall like a lotus half-split from its stalk

---

169   **apsara** อัปสร, *apson*. Celestial maidens, paragons of beauty.
170   **queen of queens** นารินทรนาริศ, *narintharatharit*, S: nārī indra nārīsa, "lady-great-lady-great."
170   **maid divine** สุรางค, *surangk(ana)*, S: suraṅga.
171   **Golden-Candles** เทียนทอง, *thian thong*. A type of firework, like "roman candles." None of the fireworks mentioned here can be identified, except generics like rockets, crackers, and pin-wheels. Probably this display is the finale of the Flower-Anointment *butsayaphisek* cermony. Most of the fireworks are named after flowers. Chanthit (*Thawathotsamat Khlongdan*, 256) claims the device mentioned in v. 181 was used at this ceremony, but he does not cite a source. La Loubère wrote: "I saw no Fire-works, in which nevertheless, the *Chineses* of Siam do excel, and made some very curious during our residence at *Siam* and *Louvo*" (*New Historical Relation*, 48).
172   **Elements-Divine** ทิพยธาตุ, *thip that*, S: dibya dhatu. Either a firework or a reference to their ingredients.
172   **firework towers** รันทา, *rantha* (or *ratha*). A tall frame for displaying fireworks.
173   **half-split from its stalk** The image of a flower broken from its stalk but still attached

the more I watch, the more I'm scorched and scared
and even worse than fire, my heart feels slashed apart

though nobles big and small all give me heart   174
no use—O, seeing them I sorrow more
my nine-gem dazzling garland, best beloved
must I bear hardship heavier than stone?

sweet sprays of Blue Pea-Flowers like sapphire gems   175
seem like your pure and deep blue eyes, my love
but when I think of them, my heart is choked with heat
and flies to find celestial streams within your room

the Flowers-of-Flowers fall like nymphs divine   176
descending decked in garlands from the skies
the sight excites the triple humors three
but they avert their faces so you shine alone

the sight of dazzling Fire-Bouquets embroils my heart   177
our parting hurts—crash bang—I'm wracked by fear

---

by a strand of fiber is a simile for a relationship that is not irrevocably broken.

174   **nobles** มนตรี, *montri*, S: mantri. A minister, official, or royal courtier.

174   **give me heart** มนทาน, *monthan*. Alternatively, this means scholars at court, and the line reads: though nobles, big and small, and scholars are all here.

174   **nine-gem** แก้วเก้า, *kaeo kao*. See v. 64. Here perhaps another firework.

175   **Blue Pea-Flowers** See v. 62. Here probably the name of another firework.

175   **deep blue eyes** นัยนิล, *nai nin*. Nin can mean dark blue, dark green, or black. Southeast Asian eyes are almost invariably black, but this verse and verse 62 make a point of comparing her eyes to the striking blue of the blue-pea flower.

176   **Flowers-of-Flowers** กณิกากริเกศ, *kannika kanniket*, S: kaṇikārikeśa. A firework.

176   **triple humors three** ตรีไตรธาตุ, *tri trai that*, ti dhātu, possibly S: tridosha. The three energies or principles governing the body in ayurvedic medicine, namely air, fire, and water; or the three happinesses, รติ, *rati*, love; ตัณหา, *tanha*, craving; and ราคะ, *rakha*, lust.

177   **Fire-Bouquets** เพลิงเพียย, *phloeng pheyiya*, where *pheyiya* comes from Khmer for a flower garland. A firework. Where a very similar word, เพีย/เพียะ, appears in a firework display in *Khlong Nirat Hariphunchai* (166), Prasert interprets it as the sound of a firework exploding.

pin-wheels spin up, then fall and fade, like love
again my face is flooded wet with tears

I pine for you and weep until I'm hoarse 178
the passion burns my breast and churns my gut
exploding crackers palpitate my heart
sky-piercing rockets, please beg her to come!

Fire-Lilies thunder in the sky 179
the sound of fireworks spreads across the earth
the rockets rise with sparkling colors, sizzling sounds
or is this noise my breast on fire, my heart ablaze?

the Purple-Gems fall singly like my falling tears 180
I watch the Pearly-Sprays cascading sparks
like dark and glossy eyes that sink into my heart
I look again, it's not your face, I'm pierced by pain

I watch Celestial-Garlands like those flowers 181
that once adorned your ears and lovely hair
O, garlands in the sky are not my best beloved's!
when love is strong, but lover's gone, tears flow

the pin-wheels fly up high and spin in sky above 182
my heart is hot alike these firework towers
young lady of desire, you've parted from my heart
more pain as fires of passion break my breast apart

---

177 **pin-wheels** กังหัน *kanghan*. A rocket-powered wheel that spins up into the air from the ground or water.
179 **Fire-Lilies** อัคนีสาโรจ, *akhani sarot*, S: agnī sāroja (lake-born, a term for lily or lotus). A firework.
180 **Purple-Gems** สวายเพชร, *sawai phet*. A firework.
180 **Pearly-Sprays** มณีมุคพวง, *mani muk phuang*. A firework.
181 **Celestial-Garlands** เพยียทิพย, *pheyiya thip*. A firework.
182 **lady of desire** มารศรี, *marasi*, S: mārasrī, "desire-lady."

Red-Lotus, Orange-Gem, Night-Jasmine weave a wreath   183
as bright as candles mountains-high—I'm wracked by fear
a Diamond-Garland scorches, shakes my heart
I sicken, breast burnt-broken, soul far-flown

I watch Celestial Lanterns float above   184
with flags, pipe-flags that flutter in the sky
they're like the lulling-lamp at times of making love
of supping passion's super senses hundred five

the rockets rise in ranks with raucous sound—
    the world careens   185
they scintillate like bees at watch-beat time, and cascade down
light up the surface of the world so wonderfully
I think of when we walked with little you wrapped tight

describing everything, the lovely skin   186
of this pure lotus lady love, the only one
each single thing, each limb that shines
in you, young lady, I am branded, trapped

of you I miss each single thing, of you   187
and seethe and sob with no relief
your perfect body's every part still flays my heart
should all three worlds expire, this feeling would not fade

183   **Red-Lotus** จงกล, *chongkon*, chongkolani. A red lotus, here a firework.
183   **Orange Gem** แก้ว, *kaeo*. *Murraya paniculata*, a type of jasmine. Orange gem is an invention, here a firework.
183   **Night-Jasmine** กรรณิเกศ, *kanniket (kannika)*. *Nyctanthes arbor-tristis*, hursinghar, night jasmine, here a firework.
183   **Diamond-Garland** เพียรเพชร, *pheyiya phet*. A firework.
184   **pipe-flags** เทียว, *thiao*. A flag in the form of a tube.
184   **lulling-lamp** โคมจำเรียง, *khom jamriang*. Perhaps a lamp that emitted soothing sounds. A bedside lamp is a recurring image in Sanskrit love poetry (Parthasarathy, *Erotic Poems*, 69, 81, 114).
184   **super senses** สุรส, *surot*, su rasa. Good tastes/senses, of which there are five: form, taste, scent, sound, touch. The "hundred" has perhaps been added as hyperbole.
186   **branded** ตรา, *tra*. To stamp or seal, perhaps shortened from ตราตรึง, *tra trueng*, tight.

Month Three: Māgha (January–February)

third month has come, the moon revolves 188
I think of you lone-lonely moon that lights the sky
I battle with a heart that seethes with discontent
breast bruised burnt-baked in gloom anew, again

O, gem outshining every shining gem 189
may this new month bring me a clear bright heart
both night and day, yoked pair of times
will now the sound of my appeals bear fruit?

I fret about my best beloved fragrant flower 190
to be apart is sorrow, sadness, strife
O fair-coiffed lady, why make me like this?
sick, lack-love, and hot, forsaken and forlorn

O heart divine, my crown of princesses 191
can I exist now lonely and alone?
were great Lord Indra's *apsara* to journey here
my breast would still be burnt—do you have mercy none?

my heart, my fount of fortune, finest flower 192
when nestled close beside my jasmine spray
the soft scent billowed, blessings absolute!
I spilled my heart and gave it full away

the moons have come and gone without the taste of love 193
your face is like the moon dipped down to earth

---

190 **fair-coiffed** โมลีวิไล, *moli wilai*, beautiful hair-bun/topknot.
190 **lack-love** นิราศ, *nirarot*. See v. 20.
191 **crown** โมลิศเกล้า, *molit klao*, hair-bun + great + head; highest.
191 **princesses** นารินทร, *narinthon*, S: nāri indra, lady + great/royal.
192 **fount of fortune** See v. 45.
192 **blessings absolute** อุดมภาคย, *uttama phak*, uttama bhāgya. Supreme fortune.

prime mistress of my heart, you've mesmerized my mind
so when the moon arrives anew, I just won't look

the sun shines bright, the moon shines bright   194
that means: the moon and sun pass by, pass by
I muse that you have come, my ladyship divine
my eyes are streaming tears, my heart is thrilled

O lovely lady, is my heart enrapt by you   195
to pine and grieve and crave, burnt black by love?
inside my mind I see a golden lotus flower
and miss the little dancer—must I lie and weep?

full moon's as beautiful as lotuses at Sārada   196
apart from you, I blunder blindly, fall down flat
O, lady in your prime of prettiness, of fairest face
now vanished utterly, unseen, my breast is stung

third month, my gem, you'd start to show your skills   197
of weaving flowers in garlands beautiful
on Triple Veda night, auspicious time
you once would place a spray of pretty flowers

---

194   **the sun ...** In this line สุมามาลย, *sumaman*, S: sumāmālya can be read as flowers or moon-flower, so this line could mean that the sun is shining on flowers, but the following verse suggest this couplet is about the sun and moon.

196   **full moon ...** Alternatively: on the full moon the lotuses are as beautiful as at Sārada.

196   **Sārada** See v. 97.

197   **Triple Veda** ไตรเพท, *trai phet*. Three Vedas. This is Sivaratri, Siva's night, a ritual washing of the lingam, celebrated overnight on the full moon (see previous verse) in the third month. This festival appears in Chulalongkorn's study of the annual cycle but not in the Palace Law or the Borommakot-era list. He noted, "there is no royal offering at this ceremony; it's something the brahmans do themselves" (Chulachomklao, *Phrarachaphithi*, 840). Wales called it "a ceremony performed by the Brahmans for their own benefit" (*Siamese State Ceremonies*, 297). But here she appears to make and offer a garland.

197   **auspicious** ยามโยค, *yam yok*. Joined times, conjunction.

third month, my lotus lady, only you   198
my breast is burning, eyes are dripping streams
this month I'd hoped you'd speed to me, but no
the more the months race by, the farther you're away

I count the months, my little lissome lady love   199
say you will come or speed the months on by
beloved, lovely flower, where have you disappeared?
the more the months arrive, the longer you're unseen

the bees drink deep from pretty blooms   200
they bathe in scents and revel in perfume
I'm pained because our parting was abrupt
it plucked my life and hacked my heart adrift

at eventide the longing's worse, my lady love   201
the rabbit moon shines bright to vie your smile
I mope and miss your body's lovely parts
the captivating fragrance of your cheeks

the white orb circles through the sky—is that your face?   202
the rabbit mark's a blemish, it's not you
your beauty's pure, surpassing artistry
as limpid-light as lotuses, sublime beyond the moon

I wonder where the winsome maiden went   203
I tear the karma from my breast and tip it on a fire

200 **hacked** ... Literally, severed my heart's stalk.
201 **rabbit moon** See v. 53.
202 **rabbit** See v. 53.
203 **I tear** ... The line is difficult to complete. It could be past tense (I have torn), or a
     prayer (let me tear), or connected to the third line (Phaisop has come to burn).
     Chanthit (*Thawathotsamat Khlongdan*, 285) notes that one manuscript reads, "I must
     tear the karma," which makes clearer sense but is outweighed by the consistent
     wording in all the other sources.

the time for sending Phra Phaisop is here
but still not seeing noble you, I cry alone

the brahmans start by making hills with ears of rice   204
and end by offering scents and flowers

---

203   **Phra Phaisop** พระไพสพราช, *phra phaisop-rat*. This is the rice deity, usually known in Thai as Mae Phosop. As Terwiel has shown ("Rice Legends," esp. 30–31), the name probably comes from Sanskrit *vrai* (rice) + *srava* (wealth), which became *peisrap* in Khmer and then Phaisop or Phosop in Thai. Because of the similar sound, the name is sometimes confused with Vaisravana (Vesavanna), the Sanskrit god of wealth, also known as Kubera/Kuvera. In the Ayutthaya chronicle's account of the installation of King Ekathotsarot in 1605 CE, Vaisravana appears as พระไพสพ, the same spelling in Thai as the *phaisop* version of the rice deity (as used here). Indeed, it is possible that the two deities are fused or confused here. In this line, the name has the suffix -*rat*, meaning king or god. V. 208 seems to cast Phaisop in a male role, and nowhere in this passage is Phaisop clearly female (Cushman, *Royal Chronicles*, 199; *Phraratcha phongsawadan chabap phraratchahatthalekha*, 180; *Phraratcha phongsawadan ... mo bratle*, 212).

204   **the brahmans** ... This passage refers to ธานยเทาะห์, *thanyatho*, S: dhānya daha, meaning "burning rice," a ceremony held to mark the start of the rice harvest and threshing. In La Loubère's description (*New Historical Relation*, 20) from the 1680s: "Amongst other things, the *Oc-ya-Kaou* [lord of rice] offers them [spirits] a Sacrifice, in the open field, of a heap of Rice-sheaves, whereunto he sets fire with his own hand." According to the description from the Borommakot reign (*Khamhaikan khun luang ha wat*, 106), "the king went to burn rice at the ricefields of Wat Photharam [slightly east of Wat Phichai Songkhram, now disappeared], then appointed Phra Jantakuman as his deputy ... like Phra Inthakuman at the plowing ceremony." Phra Jantukuman went in procession to a place where brahmans brought umbrellas made of rice stalks, which he set alight. Brahmans extinguished these flames, after which four groups from four directions fought to claim the burnt rice stalks, and the results of the contest contained predictions (presumably for the coming season). In another manuscript version (*Tamra phraratchaphithi kao*, 9–10), a representative of the king and other officials go in procession, each holding a candle and a bundle of straw. When they set light to the straw, a group of 50–70 men riding buffaloes charges in to seize the rice and scatter the officials away. These events probably took place on the crown ricefields known as the Hantra Plain, to the northeast of the city. In the chronicles of the early Borommakot reign, "royal sons, royal daughters, and all the palace ladies" drew carts of the new rice back from these crown fields to the palace, where the rice was made into umbrellas and *yaku*/yāgu (rice milk) for presenting to the monks, after which several sports and games were played. The ceremony had disappeared by the fifth reign (Chulachomklao, *Phraratchaphithi*, 81–83; Cushman, *Royal Chronicles of Ayutthaya*, 423–24; *Phraratchaphongsawadan ... mo bratle*, 404).

along the carriageway, the young folk court and spark
behind the cavalcade to send Phaisop along

a host of pure young girls seem made from one same mold   205
but, O, they do not capture me or fire my heart
from all the lands one goddess gold's my only love
the world admires these girls, I weep without relief

your limpid eyes shine brighter than the sun   206
did Indra, Brahma have designs on you, beloved?
and thus abandoned joy and sought this other realm
caught in the noose of love that demons set for gods

I watch a maiden goddess's full and pretty cheeks   207
my breast is bruised and pained as pierced by thorns
the feathered dancers weaving past in cavalcade
bring floods of tears and fires that torch my breast

a gem plucked from my heart brought parting's pain   208
did godly Phaisop lure my love to leave?
and was the trinity not watching three worlds here
so I must suffer, swimming, sorrow-struck?

a garland of nine-gems strung prettily   209
adorned, enhanced your face as smiling moon

204   **carriageway** รัถยา, *rathaya*, S: rathyā, a road for carriages, and the name of a street in
    old Ayutthaya, running southward from the palace, used for processions.
204   **cavalcade** ... This may be a parade with an image of the rice deity, but more likely is
    the procession back from the Hantra crown ricefields described in the v. 204 footnote
    on *thanyatho* above, and "Phaisop" here refers to the harvested rice personified by the
    deity.
206   **and thus abandoned joy** ... Meaning the gods abandoned the heavens and came to
    the world of sensual desire.
207   **goddess** เทพี, *thephi*, devī. Perhaps a woman in the procession.
207   **feathered dancers** ... พลแพนร่อนรำฉวาง, *phon phaen ron ram chawang*. Dancers clad in
    peacock feathers walk ahead, turning from side to side, imitating the gait of peacocks.
208   **trinity** ไตรฤทธิ, *trai ruetthi*, S: trai ṛddhi. Meaning Siva, Visnu, and Brahma.
209   **face** The face is assumed in this line.

I pine and yearn and supplicate all gods:
'O, gem unseen—not cheek, not head, nor hair!'

the god possessing heaven's finest form   210
perhaps has seized the peerless young princess
to go and be sole lady of his land
now lodged upon the god's divine physique

the rite of sending Phaisop now is done   211
a sizzling fire is searing withered lotus leaves
flames from the fire-pit's flowers blaze up bright
and O, my breast and belly shrivel into shreds

third month is almost past and flown   212
my heart, afloat upon a limpid sky
flies up so high it hides the golden moon
a new month comes, I hold on, wait, and dream

Month Four: Phagguna (February–March)

fourth month approaches fast, beloved   213
year-end, I'm heart-drunk, racked with loneliness
the sun shines bright above a pall of clouds
my chest is gaunt and gashed, my heart aghast

wherever crowds of people practice dhamma   214
I look—all through the earth and empty sky

---

210   **the god ...** สุนทรวรภาคย, *sunthon woraphak*, sundara vara bhāgya, "beautiful-best-fortune." Meaning Kāma, the god of love.

210   **now lodged ...** Perhaps reflecting the images of Hindu gods which include a consort, such as Laksmi sitting on Visnu's knee.

211   **sending Phaisop** See v. 204 note "cavalcade."

213   **year-end** ตรุษ, *trut*, cut(ting the year). The final day.

in all directions four till eyes no longer see
I do not find that face—face of little lotus love

in flicker-flash I seem to see your full-moon face   215
my breast is bruised, heart ripped, guts wrenched
beloved Si Julalak, adornment of my world
a new month comes—comes sorrow over you

some pretty girls who outshine heavens' maids   216
divinely decked in cloths and finery
hold jasmine flowers in hand for worshipping
and offer to the Triple Gem for merit hundredfold

your noble husband suffers many thousand ways   217
as many thousand fires increase the seething heat
your flawless face alone this young-king misses, cares
I raise clasped hands to pray, my breast awash

---

214 directions four The "directions" have to be inferred. "Watches" could be an alternative. Chanthit (*Thawathotsamat Khlongdan*, 301–2) followed a text with อรุณ, *arun*, dawn in place of จตุร, *jatun*, four, giving: through almost to dawn's light.

215 Si Julalak ศรีจุฬาลักษน, S: śrī cuḷalakṣana, holy-fine-features/beauty. In the civil list in the Three Seals Law (*Kotmai tra sam duang*, I, 221), the official name of one of the king's four primary consorts (นางท้าวพระสนมเอก, *nang thao phra sanom ek, sakdina* 1,000). In Sukhothai inscriptions, a lady named Si Julalak appears giving patronage to Wat Asokaram and Wat Bupharam. Phiset Jiajanphong (*Phra maha thammaracha*, 48–52) suggests she may have been a royal of Ayutthaya origin involved in marriage exchanges with the Sukhothai ruling clan. A lady of the same title appears in "Ocean Lament," a poem of the Narai era or after (Winai, *Kamsuan Samut*).

216 jasmine มุลิวรรณ, *muliwan* (มะลิวัน, *maliwan*). *Jasminum adenophyllum/bifarium/ gracilimum*, climbing jasmine.

216 some pretty girls ... The background here is probably สัมพัจฉรฉินท์, *samphatcharachin, saṃvacchara chinda*, "breaking/cutting the year," a three-day ceremony of bathing and merit-making for the new year which involved the entire palace household (Baker and Pasuk, *Palace Law of Ayutthaya*, 128–29, clause 191; Chulachomklao, *Phrarachaphithi*, 92–101; *Khamhaikan khun luang ha wat*, 106–7).

217 noble พิเศษ, *phiset*, visesa. Special, distinct, perhaps meaning "royal," perhaps meaning "unique."

217 young-king ... ยุพราช, *yupharat*, yuvarāja. See v. 14. Here the spelling differs, and Chanthit (*Thawathotsamat Khlongdan*, 6–9) argued the two words refer to two different people, but most likely it is a simple spelling variation or copying error.

heavy hardships heat me, slews of streams spill down   218
I miss the heaven's goddess, miss the pristine bud
when monks walk past to beg for alms of food
I clasp my hands and wail from wanting you

ten fingers raised and resting on my head   219
my heart spins round and blows away, I babble too
with eyes that stream like waterways in spate
I miss, I crave your heaven-crafted splendid form

some special girls surpassing *apsara*   220
wear bright breastcloths and walk as in the skies
hands holding golden candles upright overhead
as offering for the World Teacher in hope of fruit

your husband looks for you, O sole beloved   221
my heart is burnt, my breast must bear the heat
my heart wafts from my body left alone
cheeks dismal-dark, mind-fevered, fighting pain

O lady-love, full-figured and fresh-faced   222
the heart that you forsook now floats and spins
I miss your pure and perfect qualities
and seethe so hot I sicken, weep, and wail

I hurt as though my heart is baked in fire   223
the passions burn my breast, defy all words
this evening, graceful one, where have you disappeared?
I'd die by one sole cut, but still my gut would churn

---

219 **ten fingers** ... At the close of the year-end rite (see v. 216), the king presides over a large feast for the whole palace household before going for a ritual bath (Baker and Pasuk, *Palace Law of Ayutthaya*, 128–29, clause 191; Chulachomklao, *Phrarachaphithi*, 92–101). Perhaps that crowded scene is the setting of this passage.

220 *apsara* See v. 169.

220 **breastcloths** สไบ, *sabai*.

220 **World Teacher** สมเดจแสดงหล้า, *somdet sadaeng la*. The Buddha.

far from the lovely lotus, soft of skin   224
my quaking heart flies up, I'm wracked by fear
O, fulsome, precious, fresh-faced maiden fair
I miss your breasts, my breast's destroyed—where have you hid?

my sole heartstring, my utmost love   225
I think with loving heart of one lone flower
were ever you apart from me by half a thread?
I never failed to cherish, keep you close

I think with love about your every part   226
I daydream, pouring out my heart—you've gone
the flames of passion 'pass the fires that burn the earth
so who can douse this blaze destroying me?

hope gone, forsaken and forlorn, alone   227
love's fires now flame my heart, destroying me
alone long lonely, though this life may end
if there's a life ahead, there may I meet my love

through wisdom, fortune, faith in precepts pure   228
I start to make some merit, send the fruit to you
take part in Buddhist feasts and Vedic rites
may we be joined in joy, unparted till nibbana

Retrospect and summary

this year that's past, my heart's been burnt,
    my breast destroyed   229
fire-razed, nought left, in pain and pitiful

---

228 **send the fruit to you** ผลบุญจร ฝากแก้ว, *phon bun jon fak kaeo*. This is an action performed for the aid of the dead. See also v. 137.

228 **Vedic** สมเพท, *somphet*, S: sama veda, a Veda, meaning brahmanical.

228 **joined in joy** สมเสพย, *som sep*, "join/meet" and "consume/enjoy." Both words are used to mean lovemaking.

nought left, O golden lotus mine, no trace
the taste at watch-beat time will churn my gut ten thousand years

this year brought sorrow's deeply piercing pangs   230
my head goad-gouged by you, by parting's grief
the day you went away, world-adorning moon
old karma arrowed in the taste of loss

O, earth and sky are born again, yet is my merit hid?   231
far, far apart the clear bright-shining gem
the angel heavenly, the perfect partner mine
my breast is burnt by many thousand fires

the sun sends rays so hot and fierce   232
they raze the earth of all three worlds
yet equal not the punishment that parting brings
Lord Surya's light is only half as strong

through many eras, lives have ended, passed away   233
and lives reborn diminish and decline
all bodies suffer craving caused by loss
still more than during eras past and gone

afar I can't embrace, enfold, encircle you   234
my heart's bereft as died ten thousand deaths
in search of you alone, forsaken and forlorn
I think of love, the flower in you, and writhe

---

231 **earth and sky reborn** หล้าฟ้าพื้นฟึก, *la fa fuen fuek*. *Fa fuen* alludes to the rebirth of the world after the era-ending destruction. *Fuek* may mean "dawn."

233 **lives reborn** ชีพนิพนธ, *chip niphan*, jīva nibandha, "lives bound." A body or life is a collection of elements temporarily bound together. This line reflects a Buddhist belief that many things are in a process of diminution or atrophy over the long aeons of time—humans are becoming smaller, lives shorter, etc.

233 **craving** ดำฤษณ, *damritsana*, S: tṛṣṇa. Thirst, craving, desire.

have mercy, fine-skinned lady, my refuge 235
whate'er I do, you hold the center of my heart
you left to show your rank and grace elsewhere
your precious body floods my face and bathes my limbs

have mercy on a king long from the pillowed bed 236
I miss the finer taste in every single thing
so far away, who tends the little dancer now?
a pair of treetops lopped—forsaken and forlorn

this year began with heat that choked my breast, O love 237
my heart pursued you past the heavens' peaks
great seas of sorrow weighed upon my breast
the year has gone—gone like your face, unseen

I asked each month for news of you—did they not say? 238
the months all twelve have now passed by
I ask at every mountain, marsh, and stream
the lords of crags and hills just turn away

I've waited for the picture-pretty lotus bloom 239
the fragrant flower I've given all my heart
the lotus-lovely lily-lover mine
the climbing jasmine twined around my heart

days pass at speed, the sun revolves 240
the moon ascends to hide the sky

---

235 **refuge** นาถ, *nat, nātha.* Protector, refuge, used especially of the Buddha or a ruler.
235 **whate'er I do** นั่งฤๅนอน, *nung rue non,* sit or lie. Meaning at all times, whatever I am doing.
236 **king** นฤเบศ, *naruebet.*
236 **a pair** ... Obscure line. Alternatively, we are partners but I'm like a lonely treetop. Chanthit (*Thawathotsamat Khlongdan*, 325) interprets the couplet differently: with you there, who tends the king? / poking up like a lopped treetop, forsaken and forlorn.
238 **lords of crags and hills** หิมวาตเจ้าผา, *himawat jao pha, hima-vāsa,* living in the snow or the Hima(laya). These two lines refers to spirits residing in nature.

the days pass unconcerned, no word to you
the days don't tell the idle days I wait

the days pass by and by in cycles seven long 241
fine flower with filmy petals fitly formed
the days of joy are gone, my heart's aflame
O earth and sky pay heed and cry with me

the watch has come, the cloak of eventide 242
I think of begging answers from the flowers
night watch, I sorrow, feeble, fearful, sad
five aggregates burnt black by passing time

all watches four pass by till evening comes 243
each watch, the times of day, proceed in turn
the day you left I spoke and spilled my heart
and weeping held you weeping to my breast till gone

twelve months have passed, a year in full 244
and still I don't enjoy your body beautiful
Lord Indra, god supreme, and other gods
all still contrive to keep me from your charms

I beg to tryst my lissome sweet-voiced love 245
to fly through skies, through heavens high
to travel through the air, the firmament
to know, to share the taste one night again

the golden mount, cloud-topping, cleaves the sky 246
I reach the gods' abodes, the crystal wall

---

242 **five aggregates** เบญจสกนธ, *benjasakan*, S: pañca skanda. Five aggregates, the
components of existence: body, sensation, perception, volition, consciousness.

246 **golden mount** เขาทอง, *khao thong*. Perhaps Wat Phu Khao Thong to the northwest of
Ayutthaya, though the structure known today post-dates the composition of this
work. Perhaps Mount Meru. Alternatively, the line may start "Flying up as high as the
clouds." He is imagining flying to the heavens to plead with Indra.

246 **crystal wall** ฝั่งแก้ว, *fang kaeo*. The outer boundary of the universe.

Lord Kosiya, O three-eyed god, I plead
pray grant relief and let us tryst as two

Lord Surya drives his horses through the skies   247
his chariot as fine as sprays of jeweled flowers
I urge the god to join in joy the moon among the clouds
he trysts with her till dawn, but still I pine

the dark-hued peaks upon your lotuses   248
I covered, circled, clasping flesh with care
embraced, pressed to my breast with urgency
enjoyed the fragrant scent of womankind

to sky and earth and banks and waterways   249
to sun and moon, Mount Meru, and three worlds
as high and far as Indra, king of gods
I plead for moon-like you till mouth and tongue are tired

my single best beloved, pray have a care for me   250
your fragrance spreads, excites the five desires
the *apsara* that live in all three worlds
cannot compare, your face outvies the moon

Invocation and finale

all kings whose power o'er land and sky is like the sun   251
on earth come willingly to bow their heads

---

246 **Kosiya** See v. 65.

246 **three eyes** Three eyes are the distinguishing mark of Siva. Indra has a thousand.
Perhaps the poet has muddled the two and given Indra three eyes. Alternatively, the
line invokes both Indra and Siva.

246 **I plead** These two words have been moved from the fourth line.

247 **Surya** See v. 78.

248 **womankind** เศกสรี, *sek si*. Perhaps "created [by] woman," meaning by her or by
women in general. Chanthit (*Thawathotsamat Khlongdan*, 337) reads it as "bathe
[*aphisek*] holy," meaning the lustral water of consecration.

250 **five desires** ที่นท้า, *huen ha*. See v. 7.

before the lord of victory, might, and martial sway
and offer royal-flowers from their own hands

power famed in sixteen levels, heaven, earth, and netherworld 252
throughout three worlds below the skies
O may the emperor, the universe's sun-like crown
forever rule the world serene as king of premier rank!

may He be free of perils, sickness, sadness, pain 253
of all disease and lore-made maladies
enjoy the greatest treasures, everything
until enjoying bliss when to nibbana's realm!

through merit plenteous, the sovereign king 254
does govern, reign, and rule all other lords
may He be emperor high, upholder of the world
with kings in hundreds raising hands to offer flowers!

until the sun and earth and heavens disappear 255
may His great glory stand eternally
until Mount Meru cracks and crashes down
may His great merit shield and cleanse three worlds!

here ends this poem polished every part 256
alike a jeweled garland neatly strung

251   **royal-flowers** รัชมาลย, *ratchamalai*. Presumably, the "gold and silver flowers" of allegiance. See v. 4.

252   **sixteen** โสฬส, *solot*, soḷasa. Sixteen, meaning the sixteen Brahma levels at the summit of the Three Worlds cosmology (Reynolds and Reynolds, *Three Worlds*, 49–50).

252   **netherworld** (บา)ดาล, (*ba*)*dan*, pātāla. See v. 75.

252   **king of premier rank** อัครราช, *akkarat*, S: agra raja, "primary/topmost king." Perhaps this refers to King Trailokanat. See Afterword.

253   **lore-made maladies** โรคาคม, *rokhakhom*, roga āgama. Sickness induced by malicious magic. Āgama, meaning a text or discourse, is one of several terms referring to knowledge which in Thai mean knowledge of supernatural practices or magic. These terms include *wicha* (vijjā), from the same root as "witch." "Lore" has the same connotation.

a work sublime, melodious to hear
alike a jeweled garland tucked behind the ear

should any verse have meaning still unclear 257
O poets, please, amend and supplement
and any verse that's flawed, tell what's correct
so this may be a work of great auspiciousness

the cantos of this verse by one sole poet were composed 258
the young-king who's beside three worlds
illustrious Khun Phrom-montri, Si Kawirat
and San Prasoet helped polish and refine the verse

the glory of Ayutthaya is yoked to earth and sky 259
a city jubilant, a sovereign paramount

---

256 **garland ... ear** This same simile, and the appeal in the following verse, are echoed in
verses 57–59 of *Yuan Phai* (Baker and Pasuk, *Yuan Phai*, 33).

257 **and any verse ...** The last two lines of this verse have been transposed in the
translation.

258 **cantos** กานท์, *kan*, kaṇḍa. A piece or section.

258 **young-king** เยาวราช, *yaowarat*, yuvarājā. See v. 14.

258 **beside** สามนต, *samon*, sāmanta. Beside, in the neighborhood of.

258 **three worlds** ไตรแผ่นหล้า, *trai phaen la*. Probably a contraction of ไตรโลกนาถ,
trailokanat, "refuge of the three worlds," a common epithet of Ayutthaya kings, and
the ruling title of the king reigning 1448–88 CE.

258 **illustrious** This word has been moved from the fourth line as it probably refers to all
three of the assistants.

258 **Khun Phrom-montri** ขุนพรหมมนตรี, brahma mantri. Possibly a brahman in the
medical department since this department had a deputy with the official name of
Phrom-thewi, and departments often used similar-sounding official names (Chanthit,
Thawathotsamat Khlongdan, 45; *Kotmai tra sam duang*, I, 262).

258 **Si Kawirat** ศรีกวิราช, S: śrī kavirāja, "the royal poet." In the Bangkok second reign,
someone with this title helped to edit a revision of an elephant manual from the Narai
reign (Chanthit, *Thawathotsamat Khlongdan*, 46).

258 **San Prasoet** สารประเสริฐ, S: sāra praśreṣṭha. Excellent substance. Title of a deputy in
the department of royal scribes, given as Khun Son Prasoet in the civil list but as Phra
San Prasoet when he recorded additions to the Law on Judging (Chanthit,
Thawathotsamat Khlongdan, 47; *Kotmai tra sam duang*, I, 272; II, 159).

259 **yoked** โยค, *yok*, yoga. Probably meaning that the glory will last as long as earth and
sky remain.

this *Twelve* is twelve of wretchedness
but love and happiness are found throughout the world

enjoy felicity   260
have great authority
until the moon and sun
the earth and sky expire
have always perfect joy
your glory sung by every lord!

259   *Twelve* ทวาทศ, *thawathot,* dvādasa. Meaning twelve months or a reference to the title
of the work.
260   **enjoy** ... This verse alone is in ร่าย, *rai* meter. It is a blessing for the king, but that is
not explicit in the wording.

Afterword

Twelve Months (*Thawathotsamat*) is a poem of 1,042 lines probably written in the late fifteenth century. Among the early works of Thai literature, it is the least well-known and least discussed, partly because the language is obscure, and partly because the work does not fulfill the role assigned to literature by the court and the old literary establishment. This translation was made possible by a major landmark in the poem's history—a new annotated Thai edition prepared by a team under Trongjai Hutangkura and Winai Pongsripian, published in 2017.[1] In this Afterword, we review the research on the poem's origins, trace the history of its publication and academic study, and follow the curious attempts to assign the poem to various genres. We then examine in detail the structure and content of the work, before comparing it with the Western elegy.

---

1. Trongjai, *Upathawathotsamat*. In Jindamani, a manual of prosody authored by the Chief Astrologer (*phra horathibodi*) during the reign of King Narai (1656–88), the poem is called อุปทวาทศ, *upathawathot*, "enter/through twelve." The team that produced Trongjai, *Upathawathotsamat* thus proposed the title of *upathawathotsamat*, a Thai version of Pali-Sanskrit: upa + ā + dvā + dasa + māsa, enter-all-two-ten-month, meaning "through all twelve months" (Trongjai, *Upathawathotsamat*, 4).

Dating and Authorship

Early attempts to date the work ranged from the fifteenth to seventeenth century, but there is now a rough consensus that it was written in or around the reign of King Trailokanat (1448–?88), for several reasons.[2] The meter used was designed for the form of Thai language in use before the "great tone shift" that probably happened before the seventeenth century (see Note on Translation above). The language is similar to other works that can be dated more securely to the late fifteenth century, especially *Yuan Phai* and *Mahachat Khamluang*.[3] The finale of *Twelve Months* states that a *yaowarat/yuvaraja* "young-king"[4] composed

---

2. Samoe ("Si prat khue kawi phu taeng 'Thawathotsamat'") argued that *Twelve Months* was written in the reign of King Narai by the poet known as Si Prat. He suggested that the figure mentioned among the four authors in verse 258 as "Si Kawirat" is Si Prat holding the title of the royal poet, and that Si Prat, in fact, authored the whole work on the grounds that the quality of the verse is very high and very consistent throughout. Samoe's major evidence was that *Twelve Months* and the work conventionally called *Kamsuan Si Prat* both have a leading lady called Si Julalak and both share stylistic similarities, such as the repeated use of words and the play on words. His case, however, was not strong since Si Julalak is an official title that would have been held by a succession of women, and the stylistic points are characteristic of most Thai verse. Besides, some authorities now contend that "Si Prat" and the romantic stories of his exploits at the court of King Narai are not grounded in any secure sources and are fictions invented in later decades. Samoe has abandoned this view of the dating.

3. *Yuan Phai* recounts a battle fought in 1475/76 and was probably composed soon after (Baker and Pasuk, *Yuan Phai*, 1). The composition of *Mahachat Khamluang* is mentioned in the Luang Prasoet chronicles for 1482/83 (*Phraratcha phongsawadan krung kao*, CS 844, 19; Cushman, *Royal Chronicles*, 18).

4. In the Ayutthaya Palace Law, clause 3, *phra yaowarat* is the title of a son of the king "born of a royal consort" (Baker and Pasuk, *Ayutthaya Palace Law*, 79; *Kotmai tra sam duang*, I, 70–71). As Michael Vickery points out, the titles given in this clause refer to "the royalty who were in the king's presence at the moment of proclamation of the law the moment when this law was drafted," rather than being prescriptions for all time. He shows that royal titles were used very differently at different times ("The Constitution of Ayutthaya," 156–60). In this work, *yaowarat* may mean the son of a consort, as in the Palace Law, but may just be a looser term for a young royal.

the whole work with the help of three men whose titles suggest they were official court poets.[5]

> the cantos of this verse by one sole poet were composed
> the young-king who's beside three worlds
> illustrious Khun Phrom-montri, Si Kawirat
> and San Prasoet helped polish up the verse (258)

This verse could be a later insertion. Old Thai texts were not considered sacrosanct and were often "improved" by later authors or copyists. From the text, however, it is clear that the speaker, the "I" of the poem, is a royal person who is resident in Ayutthaya, the old capital of Siam, and who plays a presiding role in royal ceremonies.

Who was the "young-king who's beside three worlds"? According to the chronicles, in 1463/64 King Trailokanat, whose name translates as "refuge of the three worlds," "went to rule the realm in Phitsanulok and had a king rule the realm in Ayutthaya with the royal title of King Boromracha."[6] The Trongjai-Winai team suggests that the "young-king who's beside three worlds" in this verse is Boromracha, who ruled in Ayutthaya while Trailokanat went to rule in Phitsanulok. This identification is not conclusive because "refuge of the three worlds" was a standard part of kingly titles in this era, but certainly the identification is plausible. Boromracha is often assumed to have been a son of Trailokanat, but Trongjai argues that he was a younger brother on the grounds that their respective sons were ordained at the same time and thus the fathers were probably of similar age.[7]

There is another possibility. In the Luang Prasoet chronicle, King Trailokanat died in 1488/89. However, in the Chinese records, a

---

5. On the court poets, see the notes on v. 258.
6. *Phraratcha phongsawadan krung kao*, CS 865, 17; Cushman, *Royal Chronicles*, 17.
7. Trongjai's introduction in *Upathawathotsamat*, 8.

Siamese envoy attended the Chinese court in July 1482 to request enfeoffment (i.e., imperial recognition) of a new king. A Chinese envoy was duly dispatched to enfeoff "the heir to the king of the country of Siam," suggesting the incumbent king was still alive and had abdicated.[8] According to a contemporary Chinese poem, "The Son of Heaven [Chinese emperor] took pity on the king of the country [of Siam] who was very aged and had wearied of duties, and hastily issued orders enfeoffing his heir as king."[9] This accords with the account of the end of Trailokanat's reign in the historical-cum-religious chronicle, *Sangitiyavamsa* (*Sangkhittiyawong*, chronicle of Buddhist Councils): "He ruled for twenty years, then bestowed the kingdom on his son called Somdetphra Intharacha, and himself entered the monkhood." According to Van Vliet's account, which closely resembles this passage in *Sangitiyavamsa*, Intharacha was sixteen years old at the time.[10] Both sources report that he reigned thereafter for thirty-seven years.[11]

---

8.   Wade, *Southeast Asia*, online nos. 2721, 2722.

9.   Wade, "The *Ming shi-lu* as a source for Thai history," 267, quoting from Ma Zhong-xi, *Dong-tian wen-ji*.

10.   *Wannakam samai rattanakosin lem 3: Sangkhittiyawong*, 222. In Van Vliet's version: "He ruled twenty years. He lay down his royal functions and became a religious person to the grief of his subjects. He did not encumber himself any more with worldly affairs, but remained studious, religious, and devout. He died a monk.... After the aforementioned king set down his crown, he was succeeded in the kingdom by his son who was a young man of sixteen years. He was called Phra Intharacha" (Baker et al, *Van Vliet's Siam*, 207–8). The "twenty years" matches the time since Trailokanat went to rule in Phitsanulok. According to the Luang Prasoet chronicle, in 1482/83 there was a fifteen-day festival at Wat Phra Si Ratana Mahathat and the king composed the *Mahachat*, which might have marked Trailokanat's entry into the monkhood (Cushman, *Royal Chronicles*, 18; *Phraratcha phongsawadan krung kao*, CS 844, 19–20). This Intharacha is clearly different from the son named Intharacha who fought alongside Trailokanat earlier in the reign. This Intharacha is probably the prince named Chettha in the chronicle, who was ordained in 1484/85 (when he would have been about eighteen). Gilles Delouche ("Quelques réflexions," esp. 18–21) argues that *Thawathotsamat* and *Lilit Phra Lo* were written by the unnamed son of Trailokanat who traveled to Sri Lanka around 1465 (Baker and Pasuk, *Yuan Phai*, 37).

11.   In the Luang Prasoet chronicle, Boromaracha appears to have acted as king at Ayutthaya from 1482 onwards, succeeded Trailokanat in 1488/89, died three years later,

Perhaps then the author was Intharacha. Verse 5 on a "new-come king" may refer to his installation in 1482. The work may have been written between then and 1488/89 when Trailokanat passed away. The passion of the poem seems quite compatible with someone aged between sixteen and twenty-two.[12]

Hence the work was probably written by a relative of King Trailokanat, either his younger brother at some time after 1463 or, more likely, by his son Intharacha between 1482 and 1488.

Who was the audience? At the end, there are two verses vaunting the quality of the poem, and inviting other poets to suggest improvements:

> here ends this poem polished every part
> alike a jeweled garland neatly strung
> a work sublime, melodious to hear
> alike a jeweled garland tucked behind the ear
>
> should any verse have meaning still unclear
> O poets, please, amend and supplement
> and any verse that's flawed, tell what's correct
> so this may be a work of great auspiciousness (256-57)

---

and was succeeded by Phra Chettha (=Intharacha) who ruled as Ramathibodi until 1529 (Cushman, *Royal Chronicles*, 18; *Phraratcha phongsawadan krung kao*, CS 844, 19). The *Sangitiyavamsa* seems to have merged the two sons of Trailokanat into one person, and the Luang Prasoet chronicle appears to have erased Trailokanat's abdication.

12. Delouche ("Le Lilit Phra Lo," "Quelques réflexions," and "Une hypothèse d'attribution") proposes that the poem, along with *Lilit Phra Lo* and *Kamsuan Si Prat*, was composed by an unnamed son of Trailokanat who traveled to Sri Lanka around 1465, as reported in *Yuan Phai* (Baker and Pasuk, *Yuan Phai*, 37); that the title *yaowarat* indicated a son by a concubine who could not have had a relationship with Si Julalak (but see fn. 4 above); and that therefore he and the three court poets composed the poem on behalf of Boromracha.

This suggests the work was exposed within the palace circle. The title is listed with other literary works as exemplary models of versification in *Jindamani*, a literary manual from the Narai reign,[13] suggesting that it circulated in the same way as other literary works. It was not private and hidden.

Publication and Academic Study

The National Library of Thailand holds nine manuscript versions of which only three are complete. All appear to stem from a single original, though there is a great deal of minor variation that has probably arisen in the process of copying.

Twelve Months was among the old literary work known and applauded from the early Bangkok era. Two early nineteenth-century poets, Phraya Trang and Nai Narintharathibet, mentioned *Twelve Months* in verses that reflect the language and phrasing of the original—a clear display of appreciation and respect.[14] In the late nineteenth century, two manuscripts of *Twelve Months* were lodged in the palace library. In 1904, a text of *Twelve Months* was printed in *Wachirayan*, the journal of the court intellectual elite.[15] In that year or the next, this edition of *Wachirayan* was reprinted as a booklet.[16] Another text of the poem was edited by Prince Sommot Amoraphan, a son of King Mongkut, who had managed King Chulalongkorn's

---

13. Fine Arts Department, *Jindamani*, 46.

14. Chanthit, *Thawathotsamat Khlongdan*, 51. Phraya Trang was a leading poet in the Bangkok second reign. The mention of *Twelve Months* appears in Trang, *Khlong nirat tam sadet thap lamnam noi*, 176. Nai Narintharabet (In) was a page in the Front Palace during the second reign. The mention of *Twelve Months* comes in Narintharabet, *Khlong nirat narin*, 124.

15. *Wachirayan*, vol. 114, March 1904. Many other old texts first appeared in print in this journal. The text used is incomplete, missing from verse 230 onwards.

16. Wachirayan, *Thawathotsamat*.

finances and been a leading figure in the court's literary elite.[17] Over 1907–12, three more manuscripts were acquired by the library, one by gift and two by purchase.[18]

In 1925, *Twelve Months* was printed in the same format as many other works at this time—as a cremation book[19] printed by a private press but with a preface by Prince Damrong Rajanubhab and the seal of the Wachirayan Library on the title page.[20] Such publication usually signaled a work's status as a classic of Thai literature, part of the canon. But here the story changes. Prince Damrong's contribution to the book is labeled as a "Note" rather than a preface,[21] is dated the day before the book was distributed at a cremation ceremony, and devotes only one short paragraph to the work:

> *Khlongdan nirat thawathotsamat* is an old poem long considered as a manual. In a verse at the end it is said to have been jointly composed in the Ayutthaya era by three poets, (Khun) Phrommontri, (Khun) Si Kawirat, and (Khun) San Prasoet. It seems it was composed for presentation to *somdetphra yupharat* [his majesty the young king] in

17. This edition was printed by Chulalongkorn University in 1962; Publication History below.

18. Trongjai, *Upathawathotsamat*, 102.

19. To promote the printing of books, Prince Damrong encouraged members of the elite to print and distribute books as gifts at cremation ceremonies. The practice has continued down to the present.

20. *Khlong Thawathotsamat* (1925). Distributed at the 100-day rite for Prince Phrommaworanurak, who was a son of King Mongkut, a newspaper editor, and literary scholar. The Wachirayan Library evolved from the Palace Library and became the National Library.

21. In the other two paragraphs of this Note, Damrong explains that the widow of Prince Phrommaworanurak had asked the Wachirayan Library to choose texts for printing in commemoration and the library committee had chosen *Nirat Hariphunchai* for the 50-day ceremony and *Thawathotsamat* for the 100-day rite.

some reign, and is supposed to have been composed after *Khlong nirat hariphunchai*, but in what year there is no hint.

Prince Damrong seems to have misread the verse in which the "young-king" claims sole authorship of the work, with the three poets as assistants, though this is difficult to believe as this verse is not obscure.[22]

Patrick Jory noted, "As much as the works of literature or history they accompany, many of these prefaces [by Prince Damrong] have themselves become 'classics', reproduced time and time again in subsequent publications of the same work by the Fine Arts Department as well as by private publishers."[23] This preface may be the shortest and the least recopied of the many that Prince Damrong wrote. Jory also noted, "The influence of the Wachirayan Library Editions has long outlived their original publication. They have been (and continue to be) reprinted, usually with no change to the original edited text, for the use of schools, universities and the general reading public."[24] This Wachirayan Library edition of *Twelve Months* seems to have had limited distribution, was reprinted only once (by a private publisher), and is now very hard to find. The only library holdings in Thailand are in the National Library and Prince Damrong's own library.[25]

In 1914, King Vajiravudh established the *Wannakhadi samoson*, the Literary Society, and assigned it the task of identifying works of literary excellence to stand as exemplars and to make them better

---

22. So Thammayot (*Sinlapa haeng wannakhadi*, 118) suggested that the word อาทิ in the first line of the verse was miscopied from อาธิ, so the line reads not as "by one sole poet was composed" but as "was composed by the poet named Athi."

23. Jory, "Books and the Nation," 371.

24. Jory, "Books and the Nation," 372.

25. The only holding of the book listed in WorldCat is at Yale; the Library of Congress and ISEAS Singapore have microform.

known.[26] *Lilit Phra Lo* was among the first batch given this accolade in 1916, but *Twelve Months* never received this recognition.

An edition was published by Tai Press (undated, probably prior to 1934), but now cannot be traced in any library.[27] In 1954, a private press reprinted the 1925 text along with two other works as a cremation volume, and the Fine Arts Department contributed a preface wrongly attributing the 1925 edition to the Royal Society (which was not founded until the following year).[28]

In 1948, Phra Worawet Phisit, first head of the Thai department at Chulalongkorn University, published a short reading guide for students because "if they know good literature, it will help them become persons of good character."[29] The selection of books included three of the other early Thai works, but not *Twelve Months*. In 1953, Phra Worawet produced one of the first textbooks for the study of old Thai literature. It mentions *Twelve Months* but with no description while allotting at least a page to each of the other early works.[30] Plueang na Nakhon's *Prawat wannakhadi thai* (History of Thai literature), a history-cum-anthology which was first published in 1952 and became the

26. Thanapol, "The Royal Society of Literature," 44–45.

27. Chanthit (*Thawathotsamat Khlongdan*, 58) had a copy. The publisher, Rongphim Tai, was founded before 1913 by Nai He from Chanthaburi, who graduated from proof reader to pioneering press owner, and who moved closely with the literary elite of the time, including Khun Wichitmatra, Phraya Anuman Rajadhon, and Tri Nagaprathip. He printed several works from the Wachirayan Library, and was given the title of Khun Sophit Aksonkan by King Rama VII. He died in 1934, and probably the press closed at that time. See Matichon, *Sayam phimphakan*, 37–40, 272–74.

28. *Nirat Suphan, Khlong Nirat Hariphunchai, Khlong Thawathotsamat.* The preface also reproduced part of Prince Damrong's 1925 "Note" without attribution. There is another printing, bundled with four other old literary works, found in the Chulalongkorn University Library, missing the early pages with publication information, and wrongly identified in the catalog as the 1925 edition.

29. Worawet, *Nangsue*, preface.

30. Worawet, *Wannakhadi thai*, 55. As in Prince Damrong's "Note," the citation here ascribes the authorship to the three court poets alone.

standard textbook, contained three pages of extracts from *Twelve Months*, and noted that "the poetry is of the highest standard," but made no comment on the poem's authorship or content.[31]

In 1962, Chulalongkorn University printed the text of *Twelve Months* under a policy "to print books of literature, which have not been widely printed and distributed, for use in the Faculty of Arts."[32] The publication was a bare text with no introduction or annotations, and was intended for internal faculty use only. There is no copy in the National Library and none listed in WorldCat, a central catalog of world libraries (www.worldcat.org).

The first scholarly edition emerged not from the universities but from a self-taught scholar from the provinces who was working for the Oil and Fuel Organization (the precursor of PTT, the Petroleum Authority of Thailand). Chanthit Krasaesin[33] began work on the text in the 1950s, after completing editions of other early works of Thai literature.[34] His edited and annotated version of the first hundred

---

31. Plueang, *Prawat*, 131–32.

32. *Thawathotsamat* (1962), preface. The edition used the text edited by Prince Sommot Amoraphan (1860–1913).

33. Chanthit is a fascinating example of the self-taught scholars of this era. He was born in Hua Hin in 1908, before the railway came and the palace was built, when Hua Hin was a little fishing village. His father ran a liquor business that went bankrupt. Chanthit studied for only seven years at the local school but was also acquainted with Thai literature by his father. After a short spell in the police, he left for Bangkok in 1932, got a job in the Oil and Fuel Organization, and started writing for newspapers. Within a few years he was writing short stories, poetry, features on literature and history, and astrology columns for many newspapers and magazines, using about twenty pen-names. He also did radio broadcasts on amulets, and became a well-known performing musician, specializing in the so fiddle and violin. In 1956, he was commissioned by the army to identify the date of King Naresuan's famous elephant duel in 1593, which became the annual Army Day on 25 January (later moved to the 18th). His edition of *Twelve Months* is one of his ten books on literature and history. He was appointed an advisor to the prime minister's office. See Prayong, "Chanthit krasaesin."

34. "... as I had decided I would try to pursue this work with all pieces of the nation's literature that I have time for, and have done several works already such as *Kamsuan Si Prat*,

verses was published as a cremation book in 1961.[35] At the urging of friends, he completed the editing four years later.[36] Although he published other texts with the major academic publishers of the time, he seems to have abandoned hope of publishing the full edition of this work, lamenting "it is a pity that *Twelve Months* is neglected, like a jewel buried in mud, or something hidden away in old manuscripts that one day will crumble into dust with the passage of time."[37] Lakkhana Dusadiwijai, owner of Trimit Press decided to print the book "even though it will make a loss ... and even though I have never printed such a hugely valuable book before."[38] The book was published in 1969. Chanthit commented on Lakkhana's decision in his preface:

> The occupation of Lakkhana Dusadiwijai is a jobbing printer of books and other items on the order of her customers. Her printing of a major work of national literature, which even the great and major printing houses of Thailand have not printed, is a very interesting matter .... When Lakkhana Dusadiwijai approached me, I objected that printing such a book for sale in the pursuit of profit was a vain hope ... even the great printing houses which directly

---

Phra Lo Lilit, and the *Eulogy of King Narai*, and am working on *Yuan Phai*." Foreword (3). His edition of *Yuan Phai* appeared a year later.

35. At the cremation of Thanphuying Klip Mahithon, wife of La-o Krairiksh, Chaophraya Mahithon.

36. "...completed on Sunday 11 April 2508/1965 at 13.37 at the Oil and Fuel Organization's oil depot in Chiang Mai while I had gone to attend a seminar as representative of the Oil and Fuel Organization on 8 April" (Chanthit, *Thawathotsamat Khlongdan*, 350, last page).

37. Preface, 2. Chanthit's first two literary studies of *Phra Lo Lilit* and *Kamsuan Si Prat* were both published by the major publishing house, Thai Watthanaphanit, in 1954 and 1957 respectively; his edition of the eulogy of King Narai appeared from another major publisher, Akson Prasoet, in 1961, and his *Yuan Phai* from Mitr Siam in 1970. It would appear that these presses declined to publish his edition of *Twelve Months*.

38. "Reason for the decision" by Lakkhana in the front matter of Chanthit's 1969 edition.

dominate the market for student publications do not dare to publish this. Why was she risking a certain loss? But Khun Lakkhana Dusadiwijai stated that ... leaving such a book buried in the mud was something she could not bear. She said she was worried that the book would become a repository of linguistic mysteries that nobody would want to touch, and would eventually disappear from neglect.[39]

Under an ASEAN literature project, Maneepin Phromsuthirak[40] published an edition with a version in modern Thai in 1996, and an English translation (done with Panit Boonyavatana) in 1999.

Until very recently, academic work on the poem was very sparse. The first academic study did not come until 1973 in a Chulalongkorn University master's thesis by Duangmon Paripunna[41] on "The beauty of *Thawathotsamat*." It seems to be the only thesis on the subject, and was published in reduced form as an article.[42] There appears to have been no other academic article until Maneepin Phromsuthirak, editor and translator of the poem for the ASEAN project, published "*Twelve Months: Nirat* or Manual of Poetics" in a Silpakorn University journal in 2005.[43]

39. Foreword (1)–(2)

40. Maneepin Phromsuthirak studied at the Faculty of Arts, Chulalongkorn University, earned a PhD from SOAS, University of London in 1980 with a thesis on "Hindu myths in Thai literature with special reference to the Narai Sip Pang," and spent her teaching career at Silpakorn University. Her research has focused mainly on Indian influences, including the genealogy of various versions of the Ramayana in Southeast Asia.

41. Duangmon (Paripunna) Jitjamnong earned her BA, MA, and PhD from the Faculty of Arts, Chulalongkorn University, taught in the Department of Thai Language at the Pattani campus of Prince of Songkhla University from 1969 until retirement, and published studies of Thai literary works, Thai prosody, and the theory of literary criticism.

42. Duangmon, "Khwam ngam nai thawathotsamat" (1973, 1982). Photocopied versions of the thesis are found in some libraries.

43. Maneepin, "Khlong thawathotsamat." Manot, "Wikhro thawathotsamat" is a short course guide for students, not an academic study.

The Trongjai-Winai 2017 edition has significantly expanded the academic appreciation of the poem through an editorial introduction and three essays on different aspects of the poem, on which we draw below.[44]

Classification

In the introduction to this 2017 edition, Trongjai Hutangura defines *Twelve Months* as "one of the great works of old literature," which "expresses the emotion of love through interplay between the joy of love and the pain of loss."[45] Samoe Bunma adds that *Twelve Months* "breaches the boundaries of the manuals of Thai literature in the poet's powerful expression of love and desire, including lovemaking."[46] This was a breakthrough. Earlier, the work had been classified in several ways, all seemingly evading this obvious definition.

Royal Ceremonial

Twelve Months has often been categorized as an account of the annual round of royal ceremonial. The best-known example of this genre is King Chulalongkorn's "Royal ceremonies of the twelve months" (Chulachomklao, *Phrarachaphithi sipsong duean*), which is a prose treatise, but there are others in verse, including one from the fourth reign which has *thawathotsamat* in its title.[47] The Fine Arts Department assigned *Twelve Months* to this genre by stating that this fourth reign work, which is a very detailed account of the ceremonies,

---

44. Samoe, "Thawathotsamat wipak"; Sasithorn, "*Upathawathotsamat* khlongdan"; Trongjai and Jakkri, "'Withi chao ban—withi chao wang.'"
45. Trongjai, *Upathawathotsamat*, 1.
46. Samoe, "Thawathotsamat wipak," 29.
47. Bamrap, *Khlong phraratchaphithi thawathotsamat*. This text was first printed in serial form in *Wachirayan wiset*, beginning in 1888.

is "exactly like the old *Twelve Months*, differing only in detail."[48] A literary scholar told us that the account of royal ceremonies was the core of *Twelve Months* and the rest was of no importance.[49] The English-language Wikipedia page on "Thai literature" classifies *Twelve Months* in this genre. The author, editor, and pundit Sujit Wongthes wrote that "*Twelve Months* is literature for ceremonies of the royal court," adding sternly, "it is not literature to be read for pleasure."[50]

Scholars who have studied *Twelve Months*, such as Chanthit and Duangmon,[51] deny this classification—with good reason. Royal ceremonies are clearly not the focus of the poem. They figure in only 31 of the poem's 260 verses. Only four ceremonies are named and eight or nine others can be identified by allusion, often very brief. The ceremony for chasing away the monsoon waters, for example, is referenced in a single line: "The season's come to make the floods recede" (128). In the case of the Sārada festival, the name alone is mentioned in passing. No ceremony is described in any detail. They are part of the background, not the foreground, of the poem. Perhaps because "twelve months" appears in the title of King Chulalongkorn's work, and of others in the genre, it has been assumed that *Twelve Months* must belong to the genre.

48. Bamrap, *Khlong phraratchaphithi thawathotsamat*, preface.
49. At a seminar in Ayutthaya in late 2017.
50. Sujit, "Thawathotsamat nirat 12 duen."
51. Duangmon, "Khwam ngam nai thawathotsamat," 2–3

Month	Ceremony	Wording in the poem	Explanation	1st verse
8	rains-retreat	พรรษา, phansa	Buddhist merit-making	71
10	Sarada	ศารท, sat	A harvest festival, also honoring the consorts of Hindu deities	97
11	Assayuja	(description only)	A ritual boat-race	111
12	chasing the waters	ไล่ชล, lai chon, chase the waters	A ceremony to lower the flood waters to facilitate the harvest	128
12	Jong Priang	โคมถวาย, khom thawai, offering lanterns	"Raising fat," a lantern festival probably derived from Dipavali	130
1	kite flying	ดูว่าว, du wao, watching kites	Flying kites to summon the seasonal wind	149
1	Trīyampawāi	ตรียามพวาย, triyamphawai	Propitiation of Siva; the Swinging Festival	154
2	Flower Anointment	บุษยาภิเษก, butsayaphisek	A re-enactment of the ceremony of royal installation, including a head anointment (murathaphisek) and fireworks	160
3	Sivaratri	ไตรเพท, trai phet, Triple Veda	A celebration of Siva by a ritual washing of the lingam	197
3	rice deity	ส่งพระไพสพ, song phra phaisop, sending the rice deity	Propitiating the rice deity to secure a good harvest	203
3	Thanya tho	(description only)	ธานยเทาะห์, thanyatho, S: dhānya daha, burning rice; a harvest festival with prediction of the coming season	204
4	Cutting the year	(description only)	สัมพัจฉรฉินท์, samphatcharachin, saṃvacchara chinda, cutting the year. Ceremony of year end	216

Nirat

Twelve Months is sometimes classified as a *nirat*, a word derived from Pali-Sanskrit, ni-rasa, meaning "without the taste (of love)," and hence separation or loss.[52] In this genre, the speaker is separated from a loved one on a journey and is prompted by sights and incidents along the way to remember her and lament the separation. The form became popular in the nineteenth century, primarily through the works of Sunthon Phu.[53]

Twelve Months is sometimes seen as a precursor of the genre and also a variant as the journey is through time rather than space. Duangmon takes this view, even though she notes that the *nirat* genre was not defined until several hundred years after *Twelve Months* was composed.[54] Damrong adopted this classification by titling the work *Khlongdan nirat thawathotsamat* in his 1925 preface, even though the word *nirat* did not appear on the cover or title page of the book in which his preface appeared. The Wachirayan Library labeled the work as a "a poem in the form of a *nirat*."[55] Prince Bidyalabh Bridhyakon, who contributed a preface to Chanthit's edition, did not use the term *nirat* but described *Twelve Months* in a similar way as "literature describing nature ... in sequence ... in each month describing the changes in nature along with accounts of the game of love."[56] In his history of Thai literature, Plueang Na Nakhon defined *Twelve Months*

---

52. Manas, "Emergence and Development."

53. *Nirat Hariphunchai*, which probably dates to the early sixteenth century, is often cited as the earliest work in the genre. Sunthon Phu (1786–1855) was the leading poet of the early to mid-nineteenth century, initially under the patronage of King Rama II. He wrote several *nirat*, a picaresque epic, *Phra Aphaimani*, and manuals on polite behavior.

54. Duangmon, "Khwam ngam nai thawathotsamat," 1–9.

55. "Preface" at vajirayana.org/โคลงทวาทศมาส/คำอธิบาย.

56. "Wijan thawathotsamat," in Chanthit, *Thawathotsamat Khlongdan*, ฌ.

as "a poem in the form of a *nirat* with a taste of love and passion."[57] Sujit Wongthes called it the "*nirat* of twelve months."[58]

This classification as a *nirat* has had a subtle effect. While early examples of *nirat* may have been based on a genuine experience of loss, later ones were clearly works of imagination. Sunthon Phu admitted that the lamented ladies in his later *nirat* were "put in for taste," like a cook spicing a curry, because "poetical tradition" demanded this convention.[59] Several other *nirat* were composed around old stories, such as Rama's separation from Sita, where there was clearly no personal experience involved. King Chulalongkorn and friends whiled away their time on a ship journey to Europe by composing *nirat*, with each contributing a line in turn.[60]

The *nirat* became a form in which poets showed off their talent for writing verse with no necessary connection to real experience. Perhaps as a result, several writers have wondered whether the situation of the king and his lover in *Twelve Months* is real or a work of imagination, a personal statement or a salon exercise. Duangmon believes the set-up is imaginary: "The lamenter and the lady in *Twelve Months* are probably not based on particular individuals, but are people molded from the imagination of the poets. The emotional distress in *Thawathotsamat* is thus more generalized than particular, whether intentionally or not."[61]

The prominent litterateur Sujit Wongthes went further: "In the literature of the Ayutthaya period ... the poet's passages of lamentation about a beloved woman are not real. The poet is not really separated.

57. Plueang, *Prawat wannakhadi thai*, 131.
58. Sujit, "Thawathotsamat nirat 12 duen."
59. Manas, "Emergence and Development," 154–55.
60. Manas, "Emergence and Development," 135–36. By the late nineteenth century, the term nirat was applied to travel poems with no theme of love and separation.
61. Duangmon, "Khwam ngam nai thawathotsamat," 19.

It is a literary convention to make an appearance of undergoing suffering to acquire merit."[62]

The classification as *nirat* deflects attention onto the background, the events that trigger the poet's emotions. The preface to the Chulalongkorn University edition announces that *Twelve Months* is "an old work of the Ayutthaya era ... that gives knowledge on many of the customs and traditions of the Thai at that time."[63] Maneepin noted, "the poet also inserts the way of life of Ayutthaya folk over the course of a year."[64] But while these phenomena do indeed appear, they are part of the background and there is little in the way of "information" about them. For example, verse 63 tells of people "speeding out to plow," but nothing further.

Twelve Months differs significantly from the classical *nirat*. In the works by Sunthon Phu and his contemporaries, the traveling poet is reminded of the loved one in two ways: by a visual image, such as a flower that recalls her hair; or by a place name that triggers an association—passing through Mango Village, he remembers her hands slicing a mango. This second type was the most common, using several variants that Manas termed as "puns" and "transfers."[65] In *Twelve Months*, there is only one verse that resembles the first technique (62, where a flower recalls her eyes), and none of the second. The devices that appear throughout *Twelve Months* are different: the poet remembers the same event in previous years when they were together; he is visited by memories of her body in the past; or he has illusions

62. Sujit, "Khwam rak phuea bamphen phawana."

63. *Thawathotsamat* (1962), preface.

64. Maneepin, "Khlong thawathotsamat," 90. See also Trongjai and Jakkri, "Withi chao ban—withi chao wang."

65. Manas, "Emergence and Development," 157–65

that she is visiting him in the present. None of these devices are characteristic of classical *nirat*.

Manual of Poetics

A third interpretation classifies *Twelve Months* as a "manual" (*tamra*) of poetics. The root of this interpretation is the citation of *Twelve Months* as a good example of *khlong* poetry in *Jindamani*, a manual of the literary arts from the Narai era.[66] In his 1925 preface, Prince Damrong stated that *Twelve Months* "was considered a manual from long ago," probably in reference to *Jindamani*. Plueang na Nakhon wrote, "Poets of later generations when dealing with love and loss did not stray from the ideas laid down by *Twelve Months*."[67] Chanthit noted that Phraya Trang and Nai Narin, writers of the early nineteenth century, both referred to *Twelve Months*, "because for a poet not having read *Twelve Months* is like not yet having entered the world of literature."[68] Prince Bidyalabh Bridhyakon[69] remarked of *Twelve Months* that "its striking feature is the quality of the poetry."[70] Maneepin Phromsuthirak's article on the poem is titled with the question, "Twelve Months: *Nirat* or Manual of Poetics?" On the grounds of the *Jindamani* citation, Maneepin ended the article saying, "this writer wishes to conclude that the author of *Twelve Months* composed this work mainly to be a manual of poetics."[71]

---

66. Fine Arts Department, *Jindamani*, 46.
67. Phlueang, *Prawat*, 132.
68. Chanthit, *Thawathotsamat Khlongdan*, 51–52.
69. Better known as Prince Dhani Nivat, the title he held from 1922 until his elevation to this title in 1950.
70. "Wijan thawathotsamat," in Chanthit, *Thawathotsamat Khlongdan*, ฆ.
71. Maneepin, "Khlong thawathotsamat," 96.

Emulation of Indian Literature

Maneepin's article also suggests another classification for *Twelve Months*—as an emulation of Indian literature.

Maneepin completed a thesis at SOAS about Indian influence on Thai literature in the Narai era. She then produced a modern Thai version and English translation of *Twelve Months* for an ASEAN literature project, and hence was intimately familiar with the text. The first half of her article is a general survey of the influence of Indian literature on early Thai literature, much of this influence coming via Cambodia, and including vocabulary, prosody, and literary conventions. She argues that authors of early Thai works were clearly aware of Sanskrit epic literature as there are many references to the Mahabharata, Ramayana, and Puranic works. Maneepin then wonders whether *Twelve Months* was influenced by Sanskrit love poetry, particularly the works of Kalidasa who probably lived in the fourth or fifth century CE.

In Kalidasa's *Meghadūta* or "The Cloud Messenger," a *yaksa* in exile persuades a cloud to take a message to his separated wife at Mount Kailash by describing the beautiful sights along the way. The first half of the work is a journey, and the second is about missing a loved one—the two elements of a *nirat* although assembled in a different way. Kalidasa also composed *Ritusamhara* or "Cycle of Seasons," which uses the framework of a year like *Twelve Months*, but is a celebration of the enjoyment of love through the changing seasons rather than a lament over the loss of love. Maneepin also suggests that *Twelve Months* may be structured on the Sanskrit code of *kāmadasa* or the ten stages of lament over lost love, namely longing, anxiety, memory, praise of virtues, agitation, prattling, hysteria, physical malady, swooning, and finally death.[72]

---

72. Hudak, *"Kamadasa"*; Maneepin, "Khlong thawathotsamat," 89–90.

While it is possible to match verses in *Twelve Months* to these stages, it is difficult to find the code's sequence. *Twelve Months* shows awareness of Indian aesthetics, epecially the concept of *rasa*, taste or experience, but this is found in other forms of literature that traveled from South to Southeast Asia. It is hard to trace a parallel between a line in *Twelve Months* and anything in either of these two works of Kalidasa.

Discourse on Man and Nature

In the sole thesis on *Twelve Months*, Duangmon Paripunna dismisses issues over dating, authorship, context, and the identity of the poem's characters, and focuses on the text without context, following the "close reading" method of I. A. Richards.[73] Much of the thesis is about expression in the poem—about figures of speech, choice of words, use of sound, and double meanings. Duangmon suggests that the foreground story of parting is not a real, personal experience but a construction on which to hang poetic exercises and philosophic themes. She concentrates on a subtext which she finds running throughout the work about man's relationship to nature (*thammachat*). Man dominates nature, but equally nature dominates man. The poem portrays the insecurity of man within a natural universe that is both unknowable and unreliable, particularly through a recurring image of the great fire that destroys the universe at the end of a Buddhist era. She concludes, "In times of greatest hardship, as shown in *Twelve Months,* the deep part of humanity is revealed unconsciously." The desire that is the focus of the plot "may be the unconscious desire to

---

73. I. A. Richards (1893–1979) was an English critic and poet who contributed to the New Criticism, a movement in literary theory that emphasized the close reading of a literary text, especially poetry, in an effort to discover how a work of literature functions as a self-contained, self-referential æsthetic object.

reproduce and sustain the human race together with the world and nature within the universe."[74]

Summary on Genre

Twelve Months has been categorized as a treatise on royal ceremonies, a *nirat*, a salon exercise, a philosophical discussion of man and nature, an emulation of Indian literature, and a manual of poetics. Literary scholars have been reluctant to accept what the work itself clearly claims to be— an erotic love poem written by a king.[75]

The barriers to accepting the poem are multiple. First, it does not conform to the role assigned to the "national literature" to promote morality.

Second, it celebrates the expression of strong emotions in defiance of the Buddhist teaching to keep such feelings under control. The king is overcome by passion and by despair, and he seems to revel in exposing his situation for others to share.

Third, it invites the reader to a view of the king too intimate for the conventions of the present day. In the seventeenth century, the Ayutthaya monarchy invested growing revenues from trade in developing a form of royal absolutism similar to monarchies in Europe and elsewhere. By various techniques, royalty was mystified and elevated to a superhuman status. The royal body was concealed. The court was shrouded in brahmanical ritual. The palace walls, royal language, ritual performance, and infusions of foreign culture (Persian, French) distanced the monarchy from the masses.[76] A French visitor

---

74. Duangmon, "Khwam ngam nai thawathotsamat," 197, 198.

75. An "analysis" of the poem (Manot, "Wikhro"), probably prepared as a course guide, displays the reluctance in a stark form. It skips past the early segment remembering past love as if it was not there; skips past the later retrospective segment in the same way; and quotes the verse on authorship without discussing what it means.

76. Baker and Pasuk, *A History of Ayutthaya*, 139–50.

in the 1680s commented, "In the Indies there is no state that is more monarchical than Siam."[77] After the fall of Ayutthaya in 1767 and the emergence of a new dynasty and new capital, the ritual elevation of the monarchy was somewhat relaxed, and in the high colonial era, the styling of the Siamese monarchy was influenced by European models. Through the twentieth century, however, as the monarchy had to adjust to democratizing trends, the ritual elevation was gradually reinforced. In the words of the current constitution, "The King shall be enthroned in a position of revered worship and shall not be violated." The conventions of the present are applied to the past. In historical films and television series, royal characters behave much like their present-day counterparts and ordinary people interact with them similarly. In *Twelve Months*, the king presents himself as physically and emotionally naked, completely at odds with the suprahuman image of royalty.

Fourth, Samoe Bunma suggests that neglect of *Twelve Months* is due partly to its linguistic difficulty but also partly because

people call it 'erotic literature' [สังวาสวรรณกรรม, *sangwat wannakam*] as it deals with inappropriate matters such as the private organs of men and women, and uses words for erotic effect in some verses. This is too much for Thai society, even though the poet disguises these with double meanings that the modern reader may not understand.[78]

In an essay in the Trongjai-Winai volume, "*Through Twelve Months:* A Poem of Emotion and Passionate Love," Sasithorn Sinvuttaya, an

---

77. Gervaise, *Natural and Political History*, 53.
78. Samoe, "Thawathotsamat wipak," 21.

anthropologist, cuts through these barriers. She starts by summarizing Norbert Elias's thesis on the way that the range of behavior once considered publicly acceptable in Europe was gradually narrowed over time by self-restraint, especially in the seventeenth century with the rise of a sense of shame and codes of gentility. She implies that Siam would have been similar—that the range of emotions considered publicly acceptable would have been wider in the past than today. She then concludes:

> It's nothing strange that parts of *Through All Twelve Months* portray the passion for a lover by relaying memories of times experiencing the joy of sex, the emotion called passionate love, described with "non-erasure of emotion." However, at present the "custom of Thai society" is bound up with a moralistic frame of thought, with the result that the poet's unrestrained portrayal of passionate love has been criticized for causing the work to be "erotic literature." In fact, the work is a good example of a poem that reflects the mindset of Ayutthaya society so that present-day society may see and understand about the display of "passionate love."[79]

Structure and Content

Several toponyms indicate that *Twelve Months* is set in Ayutthaya, the capital of Siam. The speaker is the "young-king." His lover is also of royal status, as he refers to her with royal terminology, including *somdet*, *narit*, and *narintharanarit*,[80] and uses pronouns and verbs reserved for royalty. At one point he calls her Si Julalak, the title of

---

79. Sasithorn, "*Upathawathotsamat* khlongdan," 80.
80. See verses 43, 45, 132, 170, and associated notes.

one of the king's four major queens in the *Three Seals Law*,[81] though we cannot be precise about her status since the meaning of such titles changed over time. The speaker also calls her the "little dancer" (*nutchanat*) but this is probably a term of endearment, recognizing her elegance, rather than a description. He tells us she is young, slight, very beautiful, fine-skinned, and well-spoken. None of this description is particularly distinctive except that in two places he implies her eyes are a deep-blue color (62, 175), and once refers to her complexion as "foreign gold" (61). The eyes of almost all Southeast Asians are black unless they have some exotic blood.[82]

The structure of the poem is as follows:

No.	Section	Verses
1	Invocations	1–5
2	Preface: love remembered	6–20
3	Literary comparisons	21–27
4	Twelve months (9–28 verses per month)	28–228
5	Retrospect and summary	229–250
6	Closing invocations	251–260

Invocations and Literary Comparisons

Invocations of the gods and the ruler were an obligatory part of poetic composition. What is striking about the invocations in *Twelve Months* is that they are rather short and distinctively erotic in theme. The opening invocation of the king is limited to two verses and the closing invocation to five. In *Yuan Phai* from the same era, the opening invocation is fifty-two verses. The invocation of the gods refers only

81. *Kotmai tra sam duang*, I, 221.
82. Was she a consort, presented in the course of foreign diplomacy? Persians and others were present in Ayutthaya from its early years.

to the Hindu gods, with no trace of anything Buddhist. The erotic theme of the poem intrudes into the invocation from verse two, where Visnu is honored in his pleasure-loving incarnation as Krisna "who savors worldly joys," and where Kama, the god of love, and his consort are introduced. The third verse invokes Siva "trysting tender lissome flower-girls."

Allusions to other literary works were a feature of court poetry where professional authors showed off their scholarship. Here the six verses cite six works with a theme of love lost and regained. These allusions have been important to historians of Thai literature, but this segment seems awkward in context. The style differs from the rest, and the transitions from the prior section (from verse 20 to 21) and into the following section (from verse 27 to 28) are jarring. Perhaps these verses were contributed by the court poets to conform to expectations of the time. In *Nirat Hariphunchai,* a work from the same era, there is a very similar passage.[83]

Love Remembered

In these fifteen verses, the speaker recalls their lovemaking in the past. In the first few verses, he describes her beauty and his love, with the treatment becoming gradually more graphic and physical. On the surface, the description depends on an array of symbols. Many of these are universal in meaning—flowers, bodies of water, snakes. Others are more local. The image of bees taking pollen from a flower is a metaphor for lovemaking borrowed from Indian poetry. Besides

---

83. The passage in *Nirat Hariphunchai* is also of six verses (173–77) and in a similar meter, but appears at the end of the poem rather than near the beginning, as here. It mentions eight couples, four of whom are the same as the six in *Twelve Months*: Rama-Sita, Sudhanu-Cirappa, Samuddaghosa-Vindumati, and Pa/Aniruddha-Usa. *Nirat Hariphunchai* was probably written in 1517 CE, shortly after *Twelve Months*, but the dating of neither work is secure (Prasert, *Khlong Nirat Hariphunchai*, 172–77; Winai, *Ruthiratramphan*, 310–14).

its meaning as a flower, the lotus offers a symbol for young breasts through the shape of its buds. The beating of a drum at a tower in central Ayutthaya to tell time had acquired multiple meanings—evening time, repetition, rhythm, and hence lovemaking. Other references are disguised in double meanings. Samoe suggests that a verb meaning "to fly" may also mean a clitoris; Meru may mean a vagina; and a Khmer word for medicine may mean an aphrodisiac.[84] Such double meanings are accessible only to those with the appropriate knowledge.

The Year

The main body of the poem is structured by the calendar—a lament of 201 verses extending over a year, beginning with a month that corresponds to March–April. Each month forms a kind of canto: the arrival of the new month is usually announced in the first verse, and the passing is sometimes noted in the last. The number of verses per month varies from nine to twenty-eight. Each verse is like a message addressed to her.

The year can be divided into three phases, each with its distinctive themes and motifs. These three phases are not discrete. They overlap, but the first theme is dominant in the opening three months, the second through the middle of the year, and the third towards the end. In the analysis below, "his first month" means the first month of the year described in the poem, as shown in the first column of the table.

---

84. Samoe, "Thawathotsamat wipak," 29–32.

"His year"	Month[1]	Thai[2]	Pali name	Modern calendar	1st verse	Verses
1st	5	เจตร, *jet*	Citra	March–April	28	22
2nd	6	ไพศาข, *phaisak*	Vesākha	April–May	50	8
3rd	7	เชษฐ, *chet*	Jeṭṭha	May–June	58	10
4th	8		Āsāḷha	June–July	68	14
5th	9		Sāvana	July–August	82	13
6th	10	ภัทรบด, *phatrabot*	Bhadda	August–September	95	15
7th	11	อาสยุช, *atsayut*	Assayuja	September–October	110	16
8th	12	กรรดึก, *kantuek*	Kattika	October–November	126	15
9th	1	มฤค, *maruek*	Māgasira	November–December	141	19
10th	2	บุษยา, *butsaya*	Phussa	December–January	160	28
11th	3		Māgha	January–February	188	25
12th	4		Phagguṇa	February–March	213	16

1. Month as numbered in the Thai calendar
2. Thai, as it appears in the text

Phase 1: Nature and Numbness

In the verse before the twelve months begins, the speaker tells us that he and his lover have been parted and asks, "must this, my only breast where rested once your flesh / now hurt as we're apart, and must my heart collapse" (27).

In the first two months, the weather is the dominant motif. The poem opens at the height of the hot season. The pain he feels inside is compared to the searing heat, the parched streams, the fissured earth, and the dying vegetation.

> the earth, the breast of Dharaṇi, is cracked apart
> the waterworld below there seethes and quakes
> the pain of parting fragrant love of mine
> O, perish earth and sky, this pain won't pass (32)

The speaker builds an association between the seasonal heat and the catastrophic fire that incinerates the world at the end of a Buddhist era.

> the heat that sears three worlds and ages four
> and makes the world of men a molten mass
> the heat I hide inside's a hundred thousand more
> as three fires burn and boil and burst my breast (35)

As Duangmon notes, this image of the destruction of civilization associates the poet's grief with the insecurity of humankind at the mercy of nature's power. This motif recurs throughout the poem.

At the transition to the second month, the rains arrive. For the next two and a half months, the monsoon storms, lowering skies, and rumbling thunder reflect the speaker's inner turmoil, and the rains are similes for his tears.

> the breezes blow, bring flowing, flooding rains
> the heavens' restless rage compounds my grief (52)

> as heaven's greenish belly growls and groans
> dream-dazed I wail and weep in welling streams (59)

The speaker's focus in this phase is almost entirely internal. He describes his mental anguish, and also its effect on his physical state: "alone, my skin and hair are dry and red / my breast is hot and withered, back a board" (59). At one point, he is so distressed that he throws up (66). He is tormented by images of her that leap into his mind, especially graphic images of their lovemaking:

> I miss the taste of love, your body's every part
> the pause before possessing you, on fire (45)

> I miss the flowers, garlands, places of yours
> this season's love, your belly, utmost joy
> my belly hot and hurt against your navel's bud (50)

Through these three and a half months, the speaker scarcely notices the world around him. He remarks on people going out to plow; notices the birds are silent; and briefly chases after a plow. But these events take up only a handful of lines. There is no mention of any royal ceremony, although the plowing ceremony and others fall in this period.

In this phase of the poem, each verse is distinct. There is virtually no continuation of a theme from one verse to the next. The focus flits from one verse to another, and often shifts between the opening and closing couplets, seeming to reflect his chaotic mental state. This whole phase of the poem feels like an outpouring of grief, with little thematic organization beyond the symbolism of the weather's violence.

Phase 2: Denial and Re-engagement

Midway through his fourth month, June–July, the climate comparisons dwindle away to a minor theme, and the poem enters its second phase.

The reason for their separation is never directly explained. As the poem progresses, however, it becomes increasingly probable that she has died. The first hint comes in the first verse of the year where Yama, the god of death, is included among the gods who "hamper your return" (28). Through the early part of the year, however, the speaker addresses her as if she is merely "far away," and repeatedly longs for her return. In his fourth month, however, he sees an omen that is associated with death (83). At the mid-point of his year, he mentions fear for the first time: "deep in my navel down, I'm wracked with fear" (109). The same phrase is repeated regularly from here on.

Soon after, at the lantern festival in the twelfth month, the speaker shares with his beloved the merit he has made, a common practice for assisting the passage of a deceased to a future life (137). He may also cry out, "O may you not be dead" (133), but the clause can be read in other ways. Early in the following month, he refers to himself as "widowed" (145), though the Thai term is ambiguous. In his eleventh month, he mentions that her departure was sudden, hinting at a sudden death, perhaps from illness (200). In the retrospect, he appears to recall the day of her passing:

> the day you left I spoke and spilled my heart
> and weeping held you weeping to my breast till gone (243)

In this second phase of the poem, as the likelihood of her death becomes gradually apparent, the speaker seems engaged in efforts to deny this reality. This denial has three main themes.

Accusing the Gods

First, the speaker accuses the gods of taking her away, and begs for their help to bring her back. In the first verse of the opening month, he suggests that "Indra, Brahma, Yama hamper your return" (28).

Later, he makes the same accusation against the sun god, Surya (78), accuses the gods of rain and wind of carrying her off under cover of the rain clouds (88–89), speculates that the gods have "kidnapped" her (109), rails at Kama, the god of love, for spiriting her away to be "sole lady of his land" (210), and makes a similar accusation against Phaisop, the rice deity (208). He draws all gods into his accusation (70), and offers them a reward of "a hundred thousand maidens" if they will return her to him (77). He reminds the gods that he has made merit and complains that they have not rewarded him (104). Towards the end of his year, he raises the question

> did Indra, Brahma have designs on you, beloved?
> and thus abandoned joy and sought this other realm
> caught in the noose of love that demons set for gods (206)

In the retrospect after the end of the year (244–49), in a sequence of verses betraying desperation, he repeats his accusations against the gods, and imagines himself traveling to the heavens to plead with them "till mouth and tongue are tired."

Sending Messages

Second, the speaker calls on the gods, spirits, birds, and kites flying in the sky to send a message for her to return. He grumbles that all these couriers fail him, and addresses her, "the word I send each day, have you not seen?" (82)

Seeing Visions

Third, the speaker is visited by graphic visions of her body. He continues to evoke memories of their lovemaking, but also has flashes of memory that are striking because they are mundane. He remembers a time when she grasped at petals blown by the wind, "your fingernails up high like nine-gems glittering / I see each nail, my jewel, paint-patterned gold" (64). He recalls her eyes when prompted by a flower (62). He remembers a garland lying on a seat before she put it on—a trifling image that somehow appeared in his mind (94).

He is visited by false visions of seeing her in the present day. He mistakes a trembling leaf and a flag fluttering on a plow for her waving hand. His eyes swim and her image seems to flash before his eyes (96, 215). He sees her likeness in the moon, in a wooden image of a goddess, and in young ladies in festival processions. He imagines she is approaching him:

> I muse that you have come, my ladyship divine
> my eyes are streaming tears, my heart is thrilled (194)

At the height of the rainy season, his sexual longing peaks. Water becomes a symbol not only of tearful sorrow but also of erotic play. Boats slide down waterways (138); "foamy waters froth" (118); he speaks directly of his lust (61, 95, 119, 133); and he spins an elaborate word-play on erotic, emotional, and geographic qualities of water:

> the waters of your love and of my lust once fused
> why have the waters of your kindness dried?
> the northern waters flow to join the greater stream
> waters meeting waters thus—thus should matters be (136)

Re-engaging

Through this middle phase of the poem, the speaker gradually re-engages with the outside world, beginning with Buddhist ceremonies for the "rains-retreat" (71–73). He passes comments on fish, deer, birds, paddy ripening, and the beauty of the palace buildings. In his seventh month, he begins to participate in the annual round of royal ceremonial, starting with the ritual boat race of Assayuja (111).

In parallel, the subjects treated in the verses start to lengthen. In his fifth month, a passage on the moon extends over four verses (91–94). In his seventh month, his account of the Assayuja boat races extends over five (111–15). In his eighth month, the lantern festival is the subject of two passages, each of four verses (130–33, 137–40). In his ninth month, four verses dwell on kite flying (149–52).

At the same time, there is gradually more artifice in the poetry, more deliberate development of metaphor and symbolism. At the lantern festival, his heart "hangs" like the lanterns, and burns like the candle inside (133). Fish bones can stab a wary eater the way her parting has stabbed his heart (147). His heart spins and lurches like the kites tugged by strings to send them upwards (149).

The most elaborate of these symbols is the moon, which appears for the first time fleetingly at the end of his first month, but is developed at the end of his fourth (91–94). From this point forward, the moon reappears every ten verses or so. He compares her beauty to a full moon. He uses the whiteness of the moon as a metaphor for her purity, and complains that the image of a rabbit seen on the face of the moon is a blemish. He compares the sun's heat to his inner turmoil, and poses the moon as a contrastive rival. He compares her departure to the setting of the moon, and complains that she has failed to rise again.

Phase 3: Ritual and Acceptance

Through the middle of his year, the height of the rainy season, the weather is mentioned in only a scattering of verses (84, 95, 123). As the monsoon retreats in late October, however, the speaker notes the clouds dispersing, the sky growing brighter, and the moon shining with greater intensity (126–27). This announces the third phase.

In this phase, his involvement in ritual activities increases. In each of the five months from the 11th to the 3rd (his 7th to 11th), he describes his involvement in one major ceremony—the Assayuja boat race, Jong Priang lantern festival, Triyampawai swinging festival, Flower Anointment, and rice-burning harvest festival. He is emerging from his numbness. He begins to notice other women. He watches women dancing as *kinnari* at Triyampawai (156), young girls in the procession for the harvest festival (205), and noble ladies making merit at year-end (220). He rejects them all as inferior to his love, but these observations show he has begun to thaw.

Ceremonies

Even during the five months when festivals figure in the poem, many more verses are devoted to recalling her body, remembering their parting, and expressing his distress. In the passages on Buddhist observance and court ceremonial, the speaker scarcely describes these events at all, but describes *himself* during these events, recalling her presence at the same ceremonies in previous years, searching for her face in the crowds, and grieving terribly. He cannot get his lover out of his mind, and is intent on conveying that fact rather than any details of the ceremony.

On his first appearance at a Buddhist event, he confesses "when listening to the dhamma, still I pine for you" (72). At the lantern festival, he recounts: "I offer trays of food as alms to monks / and pray to tryst with lithe young lissome you" (138). At the swinging festival, "I watch the rites as love burns up my heart" (157). At the new year, "when monks walk past to beg for alms of food / I clasp my hands and wail from wanting you" (218).

During a ritual boat race that is part of the annual round of royal ceremonial, the energetic plunging strokes of his paddlers, and their canted oars, remind him of their first bout of lovemaking (113). Viewing the river stirred to foam by racing boats, he bursts out, "I ache to taste the flower inside a flower soon" (119). At the lantern festival, when the lanterns are hauled to the top of the post, the sound of the pulleys remind him of her moans during lovemaking (140). The vibrations of kite strings and the creaking of ropes during the swinging festival have a similar effect (155). The flat wooden images used in the swinging festival remind him of "your navel-belly flower" (155). A lantern-like firework recalls their bedside lamp and triggers memories:

> I watch Celestial Lanterns float above
> with flags, pipe-flags that flutter in the sky
> they're like the lulling-lamp at times of making love
> of supping passion's super senses hundred five (184)

The speaker presides at *Butsayaphisek*, the Flower Anointment, an annual reprise of the ceremonial bathing of the king during the coronation ceremony. While the brahmans carry out the anointment with all the court nobles prostrate before him, he howls inside, "O, I care for you—where have you gone?" (162) While undergoing another bathing rite soon after, he confesses "I swallow my desire" (164). In the retrospect, he sums up his state of mind during these ceremonies,

> ten fingers raised and resting on my head
> my heart spins round and blows away, I babble too (219)

In royal rituals, the king's role is to personify royalty. He is bathed, or weighed, or venerated. He presides or he performs some formulaic actions. He is passive and symbolic. In *Twelve Months*, the speaker does not conform to this role.

Firework Crisis

In the tenth month of his year, twelve verses are devoted to a firework display that is probably part of the Flower Anointment ceremony. This is the longest passage on a single theme, and seems to mark a crisis or turning point. The fireworks offer him similes for falling tears, illusions of her eyes, and another medium for sending messages to her. A flower motif brings together the name of the ceremony, the names of most of the fireworks, and his similes for her and the parts of her body. The erotic symbolism is obvious. Two other factors, however, seem to give this event such prominence. First, the sights and sounds of the fireworks seem the perfect reflection of his inner turmoil.

> Fire-Lilies thunder in the sky
> the sound of fireworks spreads across the earth
> the rockets rise with sparkling colors, sizzling sounds
> or is this noise my breast on fire, my heart ablaze? (179)

Second, the ephemeral nature of the fireworks, the intensity of sound and color that is so startling and then so quickly gone, seems to mirror the intensity of their love followed by the finality of his loss—"pin-wheels spin up, then fall and fade—like love" (177). The two verses following the firework passage are among the most poignant on the theme of loss:

> of you I miss each single thing, of you
> and seethe and sob with no relief
> your perfect body's every part still flays my heart
> should all three worlds expire, this feeling would not fade (187)

In the remaining verses, his description of his pain becomes more physical and more intense. The references to fire continue on from

the firework passage, recurring every few verses, associating his pain
with the era-ending fire.

> I tear the karma from my breast and tip it on a fire (203)

> flames from the fire pit's flowers now blaze up bright
> and O, my breast and belly shrivel into shreds (211)

> the flames of passion 'pass the fires that burn the earth
> so who can douse this blaze destroying me? (226)

Merit and Karma

In the final month, following this firework crisis, the dominant
theme is one that has gradually grown more prominent through the
poem—merit and karma.

In his fourth month, the speaker wonders for the first time "perhaps
your karma made us part—mine too" (80, see also 100, 163), but the
thought is effaced in the next line by the memory of her flesh. In a
motif that is common in *jātaka* tales, he wonders if their parting is
punishment for causing the separation of a pair of birds or deer in a
previous life (76). In his eighth month, he mentions making merit and
sending the fruit to her (137).

After the firework crisis, he seems briefly to contemplate suicide—
"I'd die by one sole cut, but still my gut would churn" (223). He asks
himself whether he can live alone. In this portion of the poem, the
focus again flits from subject to subject. Then, in the very last two
verses of the year, he comes to terms with her death by imagining a
future life (227–28):

> hope gone, forsaken and forlorn, alone
> love's fires now flame my heart, destroying me
> alone long lonely, though this life may end
> if there's a life ahead, there may I meet my love

through wisdom, fortune, faith in precepts pure
I start to make some merit, send the fruit to you
take part in Buddhist feasts and Vedic rites
may we be joined in joy, unparted till nibbana

In the retrospect, the speaker reviews the year, meditates on the passage of time, and reflects on mortality.

through many eras, lives have ended, passed away
and lives reborn diminish and decline
all bodies suffer craving caused by loss
still more than during eras past and gone (233)

The Year in Summary

There is a clear emotional progress through the year, in three overlapping phases. In the first, the speaker is numb to the outside world, and draws on metaphors from the climate to express his inner turmoil. In the second, he accuses the gods of abducting her, appeals to gods, kites, and birds to send messages to her and assist in securing her return, and is visited by memories of their past and illusions of seeing her in the present. He cannot accept the reality of her death, and is using various devices to block this out. In the third phase, he becomes more involved in the world around him, and takes on board the discourse of merit and karma to come to terms with reality. A firework display serves as a turning point because of its visual-aural violence and its ephemeral beauty. His final resolution is announced in the poem's penultimate verse:

this *Twelve* is twelve of wretchedness
but love and happiness are found throughout the world (259)

Elegy

... the death then of a beautiful woman is, unquestionably, the most poetical topic in the world, and equally is it beyond doubt that the lips best suited for such topic are those of a bereaved lover (Edgar Allan Poe).[85]

Nowhere in the poem is there an explicit indication of the beloved's death. No commentator has addressed the possibility that she may have died. In our view, this interpretation is highly probable, for several reasons. First, as detailed above, there are many references to the god of death, to merit-making rituals associated with a death, and to the prospect of a future life which are consistent with this interpretation, and suggest that the speaker intends to communicate exactly this point. Second, down the ages and across the world, poets have crafted poems as part of managing their own grief, including Tennyson, "I do but sing because I must" (see below). Perhaps the best explanation of why a king created such a remarkable, revelatory work is that he had to. Third, there are multiple and striking parallels between *Twelve Months* and elegies, poems of lament for the dead, primarily found in the Western tradition but also less prominently in the East. Placing *Twelve Months* within this worldwide genre illuminates the interpretation of the poem.

The Western Elegy

Laments over the dead and departed are a major genre in most languages and cultures. In Western tradition these are elegies. The term comes from Greek, and the genre was popular in classical

85. Poe, "The Philosophy of Composition" (1846), 19.

literature. It was taken up in Europe in the Renaissance and became perhaps the most prominent of all poetic genres.[86] The subjects were mostly lovers, friends, relatives, and public figures, but the form was expanded to mourn the passing of a collectivity, an era, a place, or an idea.

Many elegies are really eulogies or epitaphs, focused wholly on memorializing and praising the deceased. More interesting for our comparison here are those elegies that are "poems about being left behind,"[87] about mourning and the experience of loss. Among these works are several that were composed over a period of time, and record what Sigmund Freud called the "work of mourning,"[88] the process by which the loss is gradually accepted. These include some of the most famous of the genre: Tennyson's *In Memoriam* on the death of his friend, Arthur Hallam; Milton's *Lycidas* on the death of a friend and cleric; Dante Alighieri's *Vita Nova* on Beatrice; Shelley's *Adonais* on John Keats; Ralph Waldo Emerson's *Threnody* on his son; and Walt Whitman's "When Lilacs Last in the Dooryard Bloom'd" on President Abraham Lincoln.[89] A modern adaptation is cycles of poems on the death of a wife or lover, such as those written by Thomas Hardy in 1912–13, Douglas Dunn in 1981–85, and the Italian poet Eugenio Montale in 1963–66, or Allen Ginsberg's long memorial to his mother, written over 1957–59.[90]

Elegies are also found in Eastern literary cultures, particularly those of China and Japan. In 1675, the Osaka poet and novelist Ibara Saikaku

---

86. Kennedy, *Elegy*, 10–34.
87. Cavitch, *American Elegy*, 1.
88. Freud, "Mourning and Melancholia," esp. 255–58.
89. Tennyson, "In Memoriam A. H. H."; Milton, "Lycidas"; Alighieri, *Vita Nova*; Shelley, "Adonais"; Emerson, "Threnody"; Whitman, "When Lilacs Last in the Dooryard Bloom'd."
90. Hardy, "Poems of 1912–13"; Dunn, *Elegies*; Montale, *Xenia*; Ginsberg, "Kaddish."

composed *A Thousand Haikai Alone in a Single Day* as a requiem for his wife who had died six days earlier at the age of twenty-four.[91]

Like *Twelve Months*, almost all these great elegies mourn a death that was sudden and untimely—from sickness, murder, or war. What has been lost is the remainder of the expected life. The weight of this great loss drives the speaker to chronicle the experience of loss as part of the "work of mourning."

Twelve Months has parallels with these works in at least three ways: in the general setting; in the structure or sequence; and in the use of some distinctive poetic techniques and figures of speech.

Setting

In the heyday of the English elegy, the genre was fused with a tradition of "pastoral" poetry that set events in a rustic setting and drew heavily on images from nature. Even when this format became over-stylized and was consciously rejected, later elegies were still suffused with nature. Tennyson set his celebration of Hallam in a portrait of the English landscape, and Whitman placed Lincoln in its American equivalent. In the cycles by Hardy and Dunn, almost all the poems draw heavily on imagery from nature.

Many elegies also highlight the passage of time through references to nature. *In Memoriam* tracks the seasons through three years after Hallam's death. Dunn's cycle has poems marking the winter, spring, and summer following his wife's death. According to Peter Sacks, author of a classic study of elegies, the natural cycle of the seasons contains a reassurance of regeneration and renewal, of the continuity of the mourner's life beyond the shock of bereavement, of the ability

---

91. Drake, "The Collision of Traditions" and "Saikaku's Haikai Requiem."

to master nature rather than be its victim.[92] Saikaku's *A Thousand Haikai* is packed with images of nature's continuities—rivers flowing onward, blossom reappearing, crops ripening, recurrent tides, and migrating birds.[93]

In *Twelve Months*, the cycle of seasons provides the framework of the whole poem, and nature is dramatically present throughout. The retrospect celebrates the relentless passage of time: "days pass at speed, the sun revolves ... the days pass by and by, in cycles seven long ... all watches four pass by till evening comes ... twelve months have passed, a year in full" (240–44).

Three Stages

Peter Sacks wrote, "The elegy follows the ancient rites in the basic passage from grief or darkness to consolation and renewal."[94] John B. Vickery noted that Milton's *Lycidas* had the "conventional elegiac triad of lamentation-confrontation-consolation."[95] As we have analyzed above, *Twelve Months* has a three-part progression from numb despair, through agonized denial, to acceptance and consolation.[96] Several studies of Western elegy relate this threefold pattern to a 1917 article by Sigmund Freud about the "work of normal mourning."

Freud argued that a bereaved person has to manage grief or else fall into "melancholy" or depression. This "work of normal mourning" has three stages. The first stage is marked by

---

92. Sacks, *The English Elegy*, 18–21.

93. Drake, "Saikaku's Haikai Requiem."

94. Sacks, *The English Elegy*, 20.

95. Vickery, *The Prose Elegy*, 2.

96. This analysis of the poem was developed in early 2018, and presented at SOAS in June 2018, before we began to examine the parallels with the elegy.

a profoundly painful dejection, cessation of interest in the outside world, loss of the capacity to love, inhibition of all activity … a turning away from reality … and a clinging to the object through the medium of a hallucinatory wishful psychosis.[97]

In this first stage of *In Memoriam*, Tennyson wrote, "This year I slept and woke with pain, / I almost wish'd no more to wake" (28), and his despair bursts out in exclamations such as "And Time, a maniac scattering dust, / And Life, a Fury slinging flame" (50). Dante wrote, "And then I call for death / so mild and sweet a moratorium" (21). Douglas Dunn feels "That the large percentage of me that is water / Is conspiring to return to the sea" (11). Hardy, similarly, "I seem but a dead man held on end" (308). Saikaku exclaims, "Am I night-blind? / I can't see any birds" (836). In this first stage in *Twelve Months*, the speaker shows scant interest in the outside world, and dwells on images of decay and destruction, especially the annihilation of the world in the era-ending fire. Very like Hardy and Dunn, he notes, "I fear this body seems to pass away" (69).

In the second stage of "normal mourning," Freud suggests, the bereaved repeatedly summons up the memory of the deceased. This work "absorbs all the energies of the ego" until

each single one of the memories and situations of expectancy which demonstrate the libido's attachment to the lost object is met by the verdict of reality that the object no longer exists. (255)

---

97. Freud, "Mourning and Melancholia," 244. Melancholy differs from "normal mourning" in displaying also a loss of self-regard, leading to self-accusation and feelings of worthlessness.

Tim Armstrong summarized this process "as involving a repeated confrontation of loss; anger and perhaps denial; a recapitulation of the relationship with the dead; the creation of a satisfactory internal image of the dead; and a giving up of the dead to the larger forces of nature."[98] This process is clearly dramatized in Tennyson's *In Memoriam.* Over a period of three to four years,[99] Tennyson repeatedly summons up Hallam—by sitting at his grave, visiting places they had been together (Cambridge, a walk, a garden), and recalling incidents from the past. In addition, the poet dreams of the deceased, has visions of him appearing in the present, and imagines meeting him in heaven. Dante recounts every encounter with Beatrice from first seeing her when both were children until hearing of her death. In his cycle of *Elegies*, Douglas Dunn recalls his late wife at their home, in a supermarket, and on holidays in France. In all but three of the twenty-one poems in his cycle, Hardy conjures up a specific memory of his late wife (at home, at a party, on horseback in the rain), or visits places associated with her (a hillside, a cliff, a castle, a town, their old home), especially from their time of happy courtship. In "Kaddish," Allen Ginsberg summons up memory after memory of his mother, ending, "O Mother / what have I left out / O mother / what have I forgotten / O mother / farewell."

In the second phase of *Twelve Months*, the speaker repeatedly evokes memories of their lovemaking, of her body, of her presence at events in the past, and of trite details like her fingernails or a garland. These memories recur metronomically while the speaker is gradually

---

98. Armstrong, "Thomas Hardy," 361.
99. The poem narrates three celebrations of Christmas, and the cycle of seasons in between. The poem was not completed and published until sixteen years after the death, delayed possibly until the marriage of the author's sister who had been betrothed to the deceased subject of the poem.

re-entering the outside world. He is also visited by visions of her appearing in the present day.

In the third stage of Freud's scheme, the bereaved accepts the reality of loss and achieves some consolation. Tennyson finally sighs, "My pulses therefore beat again," and hears "A hundred spirits whisper 'Peace.'" In the great European elegies, this consolation is generally found in Christianity's promise of heaven and redemption. Modern elegies are more mixed and ambivalent. Walt Whitman's *Lilacs* climaxes with the poet's acceptance of death, including his own. Ginsberg finds "the key is in the sunlight at the window."

Although couched in a Buddhist rather than Christian idiom, *Twelve Months* follows the classic pattern of finding both consolation and optimism in the finale: "if there's a life ahead, there may I meet my love" … "this *Twelve* is twelve of wretchedness / but love and happiness are found throughout the world."

Literary Devices

Besides the role of nature and this overall three-stage pattern, there are also parallels between *Twelve Months* and the Western elegy in the use of literary devices. These include the pathetic fallacy, apostrophe, outbursts of anger and cursing, blaming the gods, conscious rejection of other women, copious use of repetition, and a final coda or summary.

Pathetic fallacy is a technical term for attributing human emotions and actions to non-human elements of nature "when, for example, clouds seem sullen, when leaves dance, or when rocks seem indifferent."[100] In *Twelve Months*, birds, winds, and kites are summoned to serve as messengers. The months somehow spirit the lost love away.

---

100. Wikipedia on pathetic fallacy.

The sky and earth have swallowed her up: "an eerie sky proclaims that we must be apart" (164). The sky cries down rain.

Apostrophe is an exclamation, addressed to an absent person, abstract quality, or inanimate object—someone or something that cannot answer. In the classic European elegies, the speaker frequently breaks off to invoke the gods, muses, love, time, and so on. "O grief, can grief be changed to less?" (*In Memoriam*, 78). Modern elegies avoid this device as old-fashioned and trite, yet Douglas Dunn still bursts out, "Why? Why? Why?" (34). In *Twelve Months*, there are eighteen such exclamations, roughly one every twelve lines.[101] These are addressed to various gods, the moon, earth, sky, wind, kites, and time. "O moon, destroy the sun, so I see her again!" (78).

Classical elegies also characteristically have outbursts of anger and cursing. Milton famously cursed the clergy. Shelley blamed the death of Keats on a harsh critic. As Sacks explains, both the apostrophic exclamations and the cursing are techniques "to set free the energy locked in grief and rage … the mourner succeeds in shifting the focus from the lost object or from himself and turns outward to the world" (22). In Freud's scheme, there is a risk that the mourner will allow feelings of anger and revenge to turn inwards, leading to melancholy (depression) rather than eventual consolation. These literary devices are thus part of the "work of mourning," deflecting potentially self-destructive emotions outwards.

In *Twelve Months*, the speaker vents his anger at the gods: "and was the trinity not watching three worlds here / so I must suffer, swimming, sorrow-struck?" (208). While listening to a sermon, the speaker suddenly bursts out, "but you don't care so what's the point of prayer?"

---

101. There are also around twenty-three "O" exclamations addressed to her, and another nine bemoaning his own state.

(72). In the last three of the twelve months, the tone becomes more petulant and aggrieved: "O fair-coiffed lady, why make me like this?" (190); "… do you have mercy none?" (191); "… must I lie and weep?" (195).

Many classical and Pagan gods appeared in the pastoral elegies. Shelley's *Adonais* has a string of them appear to praise the deceased. Milton's *Lycidas* allots a prominent role to Phoebus, the sun god. Tennyson invokes the Muses. As noted above, throughout *Twelve Months* the gods are accused of engineering the separation, and are cursed, begged, and bribed. Interestingly, Surya, the equivalent of Phoebus, is mentioned often, even though he is generally not prominent in Thai cosmology.

As Freud noted, the mind is so hamstrung in the initial phase of loss because an object of attachment has been suddenly withdrawn, and no substitute is thinkable at this stage. As, however, the reality of loss is gradually accepted, so the libido gradually becomes more insistent again. In the Western elegies, this impulse is sublimated in various ways, such as passages denying any interest in desire and explicit rejection of alternate partners. This latter theme is a striking element in the third stage of *Twelve Months*. At the Trīyampawāi swinging festival, the speaker watches the pretty dancers but instantly declares "I see their faces aren't like yours—this month's a bore" (156). In the next month at the end of the Flower Anointment, he again watches the dancers but announces, "this festival won't soothe my ruined heart" (169). Two months later he eyes girls in the procession for Phaisop "but, O, they do not capture me or fire my heart / from all the lands one goddess gold's my only love" (205). A few lines later, he admires a dancer's "full and pretty cheeks" but rejects her too (207). At the lunar new year, he sees "some pretty girls who outshine heavens' maids" and "some special girls surpassing *apsara*" (216, 220) but does not make any explicit rejection—perhaps because it is no longer necessary, perhaps because it is no longer felt.

Repetition, and especially repetitive questioning, were prominent features of the classical elegies, and are retained in several more modern examples, especially Whitman's *Lilacs*. The device seems to be used in several ways—to convey the insistent quality of the pain caused by loss, and to mimic the chanting of religious or spiritual music. Repetition is also prominent in *Twelve Months*, especially repeated questioning.[102] There are sixty-two questions spread through the poem, roughly one every four lines. The query "where have you gone to hide?" or "where are you hid?" is repeated eight times. Certain descriptions of himself are repeated, including "wracked by fear" six times, and "forsaken and forlorn" five times. Appellations of the lost love are repeated, including "fount of fortune" five times, and "little dancer" five times. There is also repetition in the initial words of lines. The same word is used to begin two and sometimes three of the four lines in forty-two verses, roughly one in six.[103]

During the "work of mourning," the speakers in many Western elegies imagine or invoke their own deaths. Tennyson wrote of "the life that almost dies in me" (18). Most startlingly, Whitman appears to invoke his own death as the resolution of his grief over Lincoln. Near the end of his cycle, Dunn concludes, "I would rather that I could die/ In the act of giving, and prove the truth of us / Particular, eternal ...." (58). In *Twelve Months*, the speaker interprets an omen as meaning

---

102. See the discussion of rhetorical devices in Duangmon, "Khwam ngam nai thawathotsamat," ch. 7.

103. In addition, the same word begins two, sometimes three, and once four consecutive verses in a total of ten occasions. The same word begins the last line of one verse and the first of the next in two cases. Some similar and slightly more complex patterns also appear. These word repetitions are not well reflected in the English translation because of the constraints of conveying the sense.

he is "marked to die" (83); senses "I fear this body also seems to pass away" (69); and briefly seems to contemplate suicide (223).

Many Western elegies end with a coda, a review or summary of the whole poem. This is also true of *Twelve Months*. Beginning at verse 229, the speaker sums the main themes of the poem—his loss, her beauty, the destruction of the world, his memory of her, his attempt to send messages to her, the relentless passage of time, her comparison to the moon, the malevolent role of the gods—ending with a final appeal to them. Peter Sacks notes "the elegist's need to draw attention, consolingly, to his own surviving powers."[104] The coda is a statement of this triumph.

There are some other parallels on points of detail. In several Western elegies, the deceased is associated with a planet or star. In Whitman's *Lilacs*, this is Venus, the evening star. In Milton's *Lycidas*, it is the "day-star," the sun. In *Twelve Months,* the lost love is associated with the moon. Many also have a motif of weaving; this appears fleetingly in *Twelve Months* in the image of her weaving flower garlands (64). In "Kaddish," the elegy for his mother, Allen Ginsberg used the word "lacklove."[105] This closely approximates the confected word นิราศ, *nirarot*, which appears five times in *Three Months*,[106] and appears to be unknown elsewhere—not found in any dictionary and scoring zero hits on Google.

While sharing many similarities with Western elegies, *Twelve Months* is also different. Western elegists cannot avoid some awareness of writing within a great genre of poetry, and may consciously embrace

---

104. Sacks, *The English Elegy*, 2.

105. Ginsberg, "Kaddish," in line 24 of the first canto, "no fear radiators, lacklove, torture even toothache in the end…." The word "lack-love" appears in Shakespeare's *A Midsummer Night's Dream* (act 2, scene 2, line 83, spoken by Robin) with a slightly different meaning of someone who does not give love.

106. See note on v. 20.

or avoid certain features of the tradition. Jahan Ramazani notes, "all elegies stylize mourning to some degree, permitting something less than 'the effusion of real passion.'"[107] *Twelve Months* belongs in no tradition or lineage. Indeed, it seems to be the only old Thai poem that might be called an elegy. As a result, the poem has a clarity, simplicity, and innocence that would be difficult for a Western elegist to achieve.

Finally, elegies are a self-conscious exercise. They are composed as part of the "work of mourning," the working through of grief. Tennyson explains, "I do but sing because I must" (21). In considering why Saikaku wrote *A Thousand Haikai Alone in a Single Day*—a work that, like *Twelve Months*, is unique within its own literary tradition—Christopher Drake surmises: "One reason for this iconoclastic act was surely that his love for his wife was simply too large and too intense to be contained within the decorous or ceremonial grief expected of the males of his age."[108] Perhaps the best explanation of why a king should have written such a candid poem is that he could not do otherwise.[109]

Genre

These parallels between Western elegies and *Twelve Months* cannot, of course, be the result of "influence." *Twelve Months* was probably written before the elegy became popular in early modern Europe. The similar threefold pattern attests to the commonality of human experience, as investigated in Freud's article. The similarity in the use of literary devices arises because speakers in different cultures and

---

107. Ramazani, *Poetry of Mourning*, 31. The "effusion of real passion" comes from Samuel Johnson's critique of Lycidas.

108. Drake, "Collision of Traditions," 10–11.

109. Here too, perhaps, lies the main reason for doubting that the poem was a salon exercise, a work of imagination, perhaps by someone other than a king.

languages discover similar solutions to the problems of converting emotion into expression.

The literary establishment asserts that Thai literature is unique and thus can and should be studied on its own terms. The categorization of genres, developed since the seventeenth century, has evolved a few thematic genres—*nirat*, *sepha*, royal eulogy—and defines other works by their metrical form—*khlongdan*, *lilit*, and so on. *Twelve Months* has been categorized in various of these ways. It seems to have been difficult to embrace the work as a contribution to one of the great genres of world poetry.

Perhaps it is time to push *Twelve Months* and *Lilit Phra Lo* "out over the parapets of Thai society"[110] and into a wider world.

---

110. The phrase was coined by Thongchai Winichakul and discussed in Harrison, *Disturbing Conventions*, xviii, 233–39.

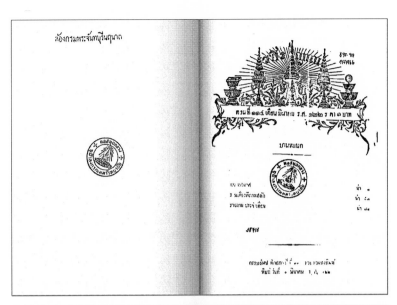

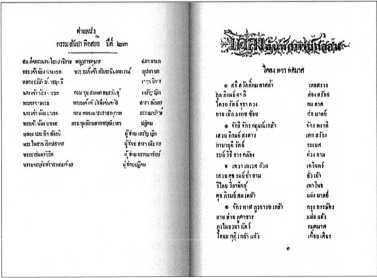

Fig. 2. *Thawathotsamat*, title and first page of 1905 booklet version from Wachirayan Library.

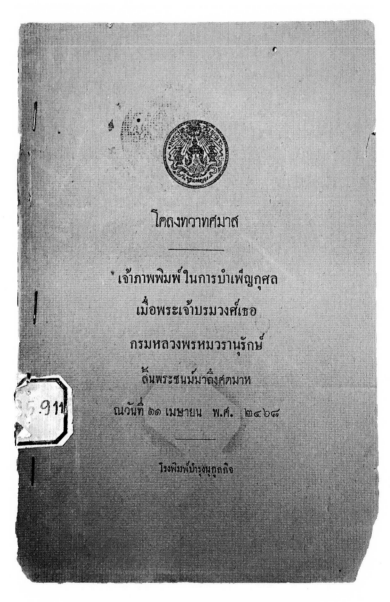

Fig. 3. *Khlong Thawathotsamat*, first book printing, 1925.

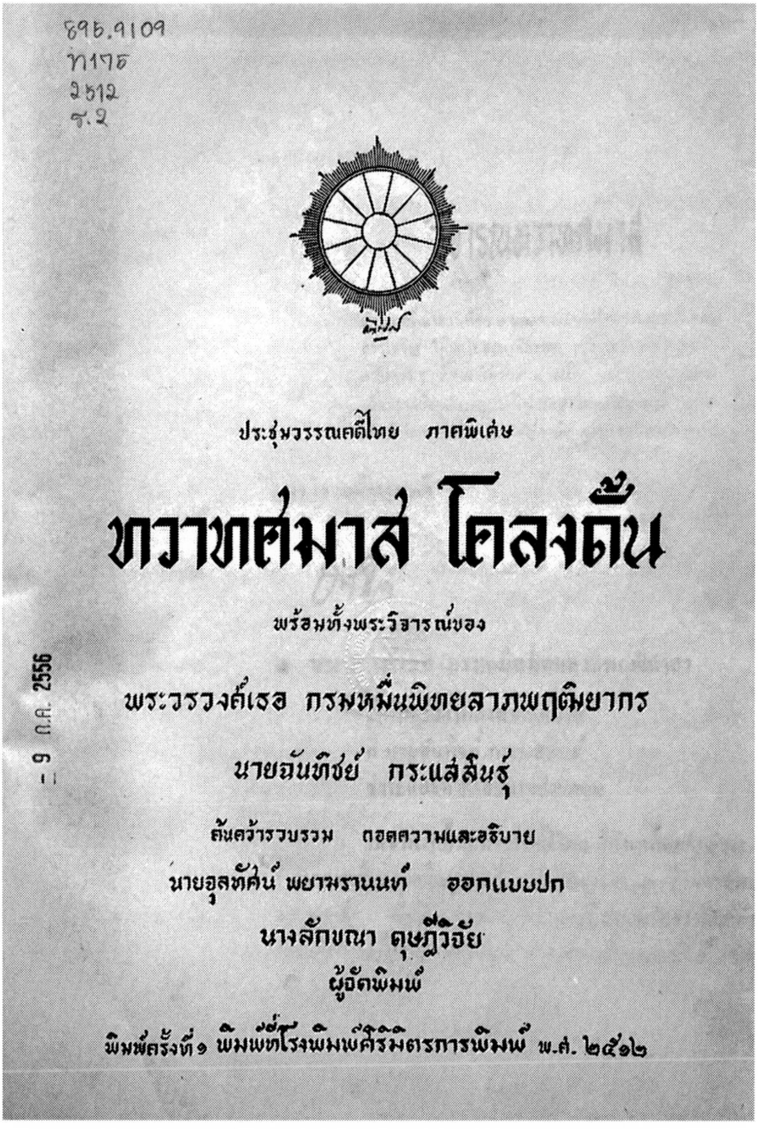

ประชุมวรรณคดีไทย ภาคพิเศษ

ทวาทศมาส โคลงดั้น

พร้อมทั้งพระวิจารณ์ของ

พระวรวงศ์เธอ กรมหมื่นพิทยลาภพฤฒิยากร

นายฉันทิชย์ กระแสสินธุ์

ค้นคว้ารวบรวม ตอดความและอธิบาย

นายอุลทัศน์ พยามรานนท์ ออกแบบปก

นางลักขณา ดุษฎีวิจัย
ผู้จัดพิมพ์

พิมพ์ครั้งที่ ๑ พิมพ์ที่โรงพิมพ์ศิริมิตรการพิมพ์ พ.ศ. ๒๕๑๒

Fig. 4. Chanthit Krasaesin, *Thawathotsamat Khlongdan*, Sirimit Press, 1969.

Publication History

Wachirayan journal, vol. 114, March 1904. [The ending, from v. 230 onwards, is missing.]

Thawathotsamat Ramakian jaruek thi sila salak pen phap ramakhian thi phanak rop ubosot wat phra chetuphon. [Twelve Months and Ramakian Verses Engraved with Murals in the Cloister of the Ordination Hall at Wat Phra Chetuphon]. Bangkok: Wachirayan, 1904 or 1905. [Facsimile reproduction of the 1904 *Wachirayan* journal (fig. 2).]

Khlong Thawathotsamat [Twelve Months], printed on the 100-day rite for the death of Prince Phrommaworanurak, April 11, 1925. Bangkok: Bamrung Nukunkit Press. [Wachirayan Library edition with the Wachirayan Library crest on the title page and a "Note" by Prince Damrong (fig. 3).]

Edition printed by Tai Press (โรงพิมพ์ไท), date unknown. [Chanthit Krasaesin had a copy and showed that it differed in detail from the Wachirayan Library edition. Tai Press was founded in 1913 by Nai He (Khun Sophit Aksonkan) and possibly disappeared after his death in 1934 (Matichon, *Sayam phimphakan*, 37–40, 272–74). We cannot locate an extant copy.]

Nirat Suphan, Khlong Nirat Hariphunchai, Khlong Thawathotsamat. Bangkok: Rap Phim Press, 1954. Cremation volume for Ro O Tho Sa-at Thammasarot at Wat Makutkasatriyaram, March 22. [A reprint of three old texts with no annotation or commentary.]

Wannakhadi samai ayutthaya: Khlong Nirat Hariphunchai, Thawathotsamat, Nirat Suphan khong nai mi, ed. Muen Phromphatson (Mi). Bangkok: Department of Teacher Training, 1961. [Found in WorldCat; not seen.]

Chanthit Krasaesin, ed. *Khlong Thawathotsamat* [Twelve Months]. Printed for the cremation of Thanphuying Klip Mahithon. Bangkok: Siwaphon, 1961. [Chanthit's edition of the first one hundred verses only.]

Thawathotsamat. Bangkok: Borikan Thong Press for the Faculty of Fine Arts, Chulalongkorn University, 1962. [Printed for internal faculty use, using a text edited by Prince Sommot Amoraphan (1860–1915), with no annotations. Seal of the Fine Arts Department on the title page. V. 49 is missing.]

Chanthit Krasaesin, ed. *Thawathotsamat Khlongdan: phrom thung phrawijan khong phraworawongthoe krommuen phithayalap phuethiyakon* [Twelve Months, with Commentary by Prince Bidyalabh Bridhyakon]. Bangkok: Sirimit Press, 1969. [Chanthit's complete edition, with interpretation in modern Thai, and a long introduction (fig. 4).]

Khlong Thawathotsamat [Twelve Months]. 4th printing. Bangkok: Faculty of Arts, Silpakorn University, 1979.

Maneepin Phromsuthirak. "Khlong thawathotsamat thot khwam" [Twelve Months Interpreted]. In *Wannakam samai ayutthaya chabap thot khwam* [Literature of the Ayutthaya Era Interpreted], ed. Kunlasap Ketmaenkit, 71–155. Bangkok: ASEAN Literature Project, Thailand, 1996. [With a preface by Sittha Phinitphuwadon, the Thai text, and Maneepin's version in modern Thai.]

Panit Boonyavatana and Maneepin Phromsuthirak. "Khlong Thawa Thotsamat." In *Anthology of ASEAN Literatures, Volume IIa, Thai Literary Works of the Ayutthaya Period, Translated Version,* 127–99. Bangkok: Amarin for ASEAN, 1999.

"Khlong Thawathotsamat" [Twelve Months]. In *Wannakam samai ayutthaya lem 2* [Literature of the Ayutthaya Era, vol. 2], 679–770. Bangkok: Fine Arts Department, 2002.

Trongjai Hutangkura, ed., *Upathawathotsamat Khlongdan* [Through All Twelve Months]. Bangkok: Sirindhorn Anthropology Center, 2017.

Glossary

baisi บายศรี. A representation of a food offering, crafted from folded banana leaves and flowers, used in many ceremonies.

balustrade ราชวัติ, *ratchawati*. A fence or railings to demarcate a ritual area for a cremation or other ceremony, often made of wood or metal in lattice design, with openings midway along the sides, ritual umbrellas at the corners, and a covering of paper or cloth.

betel(nut) หมาก, *mak*. Areca nut, chewed as a mild stimulant.

britches สนับเพลา, *sanap phlao*. Close-fitting trousers ending below the knee, often with a flared cuff, now seen mostly as part of the costume for traditional dance.

crore โกฏิ, *kot*. Ten million.

CS จุลศักราช. Chula Sakkarat, "lesser era," a lunisolar calendar; add 638 to convert to Common Era.

era-destroying fire ไฟกัลป์, *fai kan*. A fire that consumes the world at the close of an era in the Three Worlds cosmology. The fire starts after seven suns rise in succession and burns not only the realm of mankind but all four realms of loss and woe below and ten of the realms above.

Garuda ครุฑ, *khrut*. A mythical bird with a human body and the head, wings, and talons of an eagle; the mount of Vishnu.

gaur กระทิง, *krathing*. *Bos gaurus*, a massive wild buffalo of dark gray or black color, weighing around a ton when fully grown.

Indra พระอินทร์, *phra in*. King of the gods, presiding over Tāvatiṁsa, the heaven of the thirty-three gods; the most prominent of the Hindu gods in Thai tradition, closely associated with kingship, able to intervene directly in the world, often known as Amarin.

Jataka ชาดก, *chadok*. A story of one of the Buddha's past lives, as remembered and recounted by him.

karma กรรม, *kam*. The accumulated effect of good and bad deeds done in the past and past lives which affects the course of this life and future births.

khun ขุน. A title, once used by rulers, and gradually degraded over time; here meaning a middle-ranked officer.

krajae กระแจะ. Fragrant water made by steeping the bark of the *krajae* tree, *Hesperethusa crenulata*, used like eau de cologne. It might come as a powdered extract for dissolving, sometimes combined with sandal and other ingredients.

lion-lord พญาไกรสรราชสีห์, *phya kraison ratchasi*. Lord of the mythical lions in the Himavanta Forest; a simile for power.

lore คุณ *khun*, คุณไสย *khunsai*, ไสยเวท *saiwet*, ไสยศาสตร์ *saiyasat*, อาถรรพณ์ *athan*, วิชา *wicha*. Knowledge of and ability with supernatural powers.

mandala มณฑล, *monthon*. An area or space, here especially an area with a symmetrical plan of sacred power.

mantra มนตร์, *mon*. A formula or prayer. The term is sometimes used more generally to mean supernatural, supernaturalism.

maprang มะปราง. *Bouea macrophylla*, a fruit related to the mango, the size and shape of a small chicken egg, with a fine smooth skin that turns from yellow to orange when ripe; sometimes called a Marian plum or mango plum; common simile for a good complexion.

meru เมรุ. Funeral pyre, modeled on Mount Meru, the mountain at the center of the Three Worlds cosmology.

Mount Meru พระสุเมรุ, *phra sumeru*. In Buddhist cosmology, the center of the universe. At a royal funeral, the cremation pyre is set on a representation of this mountain.

muen หมื่น. Ten thousand; a title or rank of a middle-level officer.

musth ซับมัน, *sap man*. A frenzied state of some male animals, including elephants.

nak นาก. An alloy of gold, silver, and copper with an appearance similar to silver, known among European traders as tutenague.

nibbana นิพพาน, *nipphan*. Nirvana, release from suffering.

nine jewels/gems เนาวรัตน์, นพรัตน์, *naowarat, nopparat*. A conventional term conveying extreme riches. The nine are usually listed as diamond, ruby, emerald, topaz, garnet, sapphire, moonstone, zircon, and lapis lazuli.

nirat นิราศ. "Being without," a poetic lament for an absent lover.

overseer มูลนาย, *munnai*. An officer in charge of a unit of men.

soul ขวัญ, *khwan*. In Thai traditional belief, the body and its various elements, usually numbered as thirty-two, all have a *khwan* or spiritual representation. In cases of illness or psychological trouble, the *khwan* is believed to have deserted the body for some reason and has to be called back by ceremony.

stupa เจดีย์, *jedi*. A monument to enshrine a relic of the Buddha or ashes after cremation.

Thorani (แม่)ธรณี, *dharani*. The goddess of the earth.

Three Worlds ไตรภูมิ, *traiphum, S: tribhumi*. The cosmology of Theravada Buddhism. The three are the world of sensual desire, including the human world along with the heavens of the gods above and the netherworlds and hells below; the world with a remnant of material factors containing sixteen levels inhabited by *brahma* of diminishing substance; and the world without material factors which has four realms with only space and mentality, no substance. The phrase "all three worlds" is often used to mean everywhere, everything.

wai ไหว้. A gesture of greeting and respect by joining the palms in front of the chest or face.

wat วัด. A Buddhist monastery.

yang, yung ยาง, ยูง. Two dipterocarp species, used conventionally as a pair to denote deep forest.

yantra ยันต์, เลขยันต์, *yan, lekyan*. A graphic device, made by an adept, combining several powerful symbols, usually to provide protection.

Bibliography

Alighieri, Dante. *Vita Nova*, tr. Andrew Frisardi. Evanston: Northwestern University Press, 2012. digitaldante.columbia.edu/text/library/la-vita-nuova-frisardi/

Armstrong, Tim. "Thomas Hardy: Poems of 1912–13." In *A Companion to Twentieth-Century Poetry*, ed. Neil Roberts, 359–68. Oxford: Blackwell, 2001.

Baker, Chris and Pasuk Phongpaichit. *From the Fifty Jātaka: Selections from the Pannāsa Jātaka*. Chiang Mai: Silkworm Books, 2019.

—————. *A History of Ayutthaya: Siam in the Early Modern World*. Cambridge: Cambridge University Press, 2017.

—————. *The Palace Law of Ayutthaya and the Thammasat: Law and Kingship in Siam*. Ithaca: Cornell University Press, 2016.

Baker, Chris and Pasuk Phongpaichit, tr. and ed. *The Tale of Khun Chang Khun Phaen*. Chiang Mai: Silkworm Books, 2010.

—————. *Yuan Phai, the Defeat of Lanna: A Fifteenth-Century Thai Epic Poem*. Chiang Mai: Silkworm Books, 2016.

Baker, Chris, Dhiravat na Pomberja, Alfons van der Kraan, and David K. Wyatt, eds. *Van Vliet's Siam*. Chiang Mai: Silkworm Books, 2005.

Bamrap Porapak, Somdetphra Chaofa Kromphraya. *Khlong phraratchaphithi thawathotsamat* [Poem on the Royal Ceremonies of the Twelve Months]. Bangkok: Thai Watthanaphanit, 1966.

Bickner, Robert John. *An Introduction to the Thai Poem 'Lilit Phra Lor' (The Story of King Lor)*. DeKalb, Illinois: Northern Illinois University Center for Southeast Asian Studies, 1991.

Bidyalabh Bridhyakon, Prince. "Wijan thawathotsamat" [Critique of *Twelve Months*]. In *Thawathotsamat khlongdan* [Twelve Months], ed. Chanthit Krasaesin. Bangkok: Sirimit Press, 1969.

Boonsong Lekagul and Edward Cronin. *Birds of Thailand*. 2nd ed. Bangkok: Association for the Conservation of Wildlife, 1974.

Breazeale, Kennon. "Portuguese Impressions of Ayutthaya in the Late Sixteenth Century." In *500 Years of Thai-Portuguese Relations: A Festschrift*, ed. Michael Smithies, 50–58. Bangkok: Siam Society, 2011.

Cavitch, Max. *American Elegy: The Poetry of Mourning from the Puritans to Whitman*. Minneapolis: University of Minnesota Press, 2007.

Chanthit Krasaesin. *Prachum wannakhadi thai phak 2 phra lo lilit* [Collected Thai literature, pt 2, Phra Lo Lilit]. Bangkok: Thai Watthanaphanit, 1987 [1954].

—————. *Thawathotsamat Khlongdan* [Twelve Months]. Bangkok: Sirimit Press, 1969.

—————, ed. *Khlong Thawathotsamat* [Twelve Months]. Printed for the cremation of Thanphuying Klip Mahithon. Bangkok: Siwaphon, 1961.

—————. *Thawathotsamat Khlongdan: phrom thung phrawijan khong phra-worawongthoe krommuen phithayalap phuethiyakon* [Twelve Months, with Commentary by Prince Bidyalabh Bridhyakon]. Bangkok: Sirimit Press, 1969.

Chehabi, H. E. and Allen Guttmann, "From Iran to All of Asia: The Origin and Diffusion of Polo." In *Sport in Asian Society: Past and Present*, ed. Fan Hong and J. A. Mangan, 309–21. London: Routledge, 2005.

Cholada Ruengruglikit. *An lilit phra lo chabap wikhro lae thot khwam* [Reading Lilit Phra Lo: Analytic Edition]. 3rd printing, revised, Bangkok: Cholada Ruengruglikit/Thanapress, 2016 [2001].

—————. "Lilit phra lo dai ma jak tamnan rak nai mueang phrae jing rue" [Did Lilit Phra Lo Really Come from a Folktale of Phrae?]. Presentation, Faculty of Arts, Chulalongkorn University, March 7, 2019.

—————. "The Thai Tale of *Aniruddha*: Popularity and Variations." In *Thai Literary Traditions*, ed. Manas Chitakasem, 170–85. Bangkok: Chulalongkorn University Press, 1995.

Cholthira Kladyu (Satyawadhna). "Sunthariyaphap nai lilit phra lo" [Aesthetics in Lilit Phra Lo]. In Cholthira Kladyu (Satyawadhna), *Wannakhadi khong puangchon* [Literature of the People], 71–112. Bangkok: Chulalongkorn University Students Association, 1974.

Chulachomklao Jaoyuhua, Phrabat Sompetphra [King Chulalongkorn]. *Phrarat-chaphithi sipsong duean* [Royal Ceremonies of the Twelve Months]. Bangkok: Sinlapa Bannakan, 2009 [1911].

Chulalongkorn University. *Thawathotsamat*. Bangkok: Borikan Thong Press for Faculty of Fine Arts, Chulalongkorn University, 1962.

Coedès, George. *Inscriptions du Cambodge*. 6 vols. Hanoi, various years.

Cushman, Richard D. *The Royal Chronicles of Ayutthaya*. A synoptic translation by Richard D. Cushman, ed. David K. Wyatt. Bangkok: Siam Society, 2000.

Damrong Rajanubhab, Prince. "Kham winitchai rueang phra lo lilit" [Verdict on Phra Lo Lilit], *Nangsue banthuek samakhom wannakhadi* [Annals of the Literary Society], 1, 5 (1932). Available at www.vajirayana.org/ลิลิตพระลอ (accessed June 10, 2018).

Delouche, Gilles. "Le Lilit Phra Lo et l'Âge d'or de la littérature classique siamoise." *Moussons*, 2 (2000).

——————. "Quelques réflexions à propos de la datation du Lilit Phra Lo." *Moussons*, 3 (2001).

——————. "Une hypothèse d'attribution: Phra Yaowarat (พระเยาวราช), unique auteur du « Poème du roi Lo » (ลิลิตพระลอ), du « Poème des Douze Mois » (ทวาทศมาสโคลงดั้น) et de la « Lamentation de Sri-Prat » (กำสรวลศรีปราชญ์)." *Peninsule*, 74 (2017): 117–40.

Dhammapada: The Buddha's Path of Wisdom, translated from the Pali by Acharya Buddharakkhita. *Access to Insight (BCBS Edition)*, November 30, 2013 [1966], www.accesstoinsight.org/tipitaka/kn/dhp/dhp.17.budd.html.

Drake, Christopher. "The Collision of Traditions in Saikaku's Haikai." *Harvard Journal of Asiatic Studies*, 52, 1 (1992): 5–75.

——————. "Saikaku's Haikai Requiem: *A Thousand Haikai Alone in a Single Day* The First Hundred Verses." *Harvard Journal of Asiatic Studies*, 52, 2 (1992): 481–588.

Duangmon Paripunna. "Khwam ngam nai thawathotsamat" [The Beauty of *Thawathotsamat*]. MA thesis, Chulalongkorn University, 1973.

——————. "Khwam ngam nai thawathotsamat" [The Beauty of *Thawathotsamat*]. In *Aksonsatniphon 2: ruam botkhwam thang phasa lae wannakhadi thai* [Arts Writings: Collected Articles on Thai Language and Literature], eds. Trisin Bunkhajon, Cholada Rueangruglikhit, and Phonthip Phukphasuk, 139–84. Bangkok: Faculty of Arts and Alumni, Chulalongkorn University, 1982.

Duangmon (Paripunna) Jitjamnong. *Bot wikhro lilit phra lo nai choeng wannakhadi wijan* [Literary Critical Analysis of Lilit Phra Lo]. Bangkok: Krung sayam, 1978.

Dunn, Douglas. *Elegies*. London: Faber and Faber, 1985.

Emerson, Ralph Waldo. "Threnody." In *Poems*, 148–57. Boston and New York: Houghton, Mifflin, 1904, en.wikisource.org/wiki/Poems (Emerson, Household Edition, 1904).

Fine Arts Department. *Chumnum rueang phra lo* [Collected Dramas on the Phra Lo Story]. Bangkok: Fine Arts Department, 2003.

——————. *Jindamani lem 1 lae jindamani chabap yai boribun* [Jindamani, vol. 1 and Jindamani, complete edition]. Bangkok: Fine Arts Department, 2018.

——————. *Wannakam samai ayutthaya lem 1* [Literature of the Ayutthaya Era, vol. 1]. Bangkok: Fine Arts Department, 1997.

Freud, Sigmund. "Mourning and Melancholia." In *The Standard Edition of the Complete Psychological Works of Sigmund Freud*, ed. James Strachey, vol. XIV (1914–16): 243–58. London: Hogarth Press, 1957.

Gervaise, Nicolas. *The Natural and Political History of the Kingdom of Siam*. Bangkok: White Lotus, 1998 [1688].

Ginsberg, Allen. "Kaddish." www.poetryfoundation.org/poems/49313/kaddish (accessed June 10, 2018).

Griswold, A. B. and Prasert na Nagara. "The Pact Between Sukhodaya and Nān: Epigraphic and Historical Studies no. 3," *Journal of the Siam Society*, 57, 1 (1969): 57–107.

Hardy, Thomas. "Poems of 1912–13." In *The Collected Poems of Thomas Hardy*, ed. Michael Irwin, 307–25. Ware, Hertfordshire: Wordsworth Editions, 1994.

Harrison, Rachel V. "Introduction." In *Disturbing Conventions: Decentering Thai Literary Cultures*, ed. Rachel V. Harrison, 1–33. London and New York: Rowan and Littlefield, 2014.

Hau, Caroline S. *Necessary Fictions: Philippine Literature and the Nation, 1946–1980*. Quezon City: Ateneo de Manila University Press, 2000.

Hudak, Thomas J. "The *Kamadasa* in Classical Thai Poetry." In *Thai Literary Traditions*, ed. Manas Chitakasem, 158–69. Bangkok: Chulalongkorn University Press, 1995.

Indrayuth [Atsani Pholajan]. "Lilit phra lo … wannakhadi sakdina" [Lilit Phra Lo … Feudal Literature]. *Aksonsan*, 2, 1 (April 1950). Reprinted in *Kho khit jak wannakhadi* [Reflections on Literature], Project on reading Nai Phi, no. 7, 73–90, Bangkok: Aan, 2016.

——————. "Niyai phuenban pen kaen samkhan ying nai chiwit sangkhom khong pracharat." [Local Tales Are Very Important in the Social Life of the People]. *Aksonsan*, 2, 2 (May 1950). Reprinted in *Kho khit jak wannakhadi*

[Reflections on Literature], Project on reading Nai Phi, no. 7, 97–104, Bangkok: Aan, 2016.

Jory, Patrick. "Books and the Nation: The Making of Thailand's National Library." *Journal of Southeast Asian Studies*, 31, 2 (September 2000): 351–73.

—————. "*Khunatham jariyatham thai* (Thai Morals and Manners): A Historical Perspective." Unpublished paper presented at the 13th International Conference on Thai Studies, Chiang Mai, July 2017.

—————. "Thailand's Politics of Politeness: Qualities of a Gentleman and the Making of 'Thai Manners.'" *South East Asia Research*, 23, 3 (2015): 357–75.

Kalidasa. "The Cloud Messenger." In Kalidasa, *Translations of Shakuntala and Other Works*, tr. Arthur W. Ryder. London: J. M. Dent and Sons, 1933 [1914]. www.gutenberg.org/files/16659/16659-h/16659-h.htm (accessed June 10, 2018).

—————. *Ritusamhara: The Garland of Seasons*, tr. Rajendra Tandon. New Delhi: Rupa, 2008.

Kennedy, David. *Elegy*. London: Routledge, 2007.

Khamhaikan chao krung kao [Testimony of the Inhabitants of the Old Capital]. Bangkok: Chotmaihet Press, 2001 [1924].

Khamhaikan khun luang ha wat [Testimony of the King Who Entered a *Wat*]. Bangkok: Sukhothai Thammathirat University, 2004.

Khlong Thawathotsamat [Twelve Months], printed on the 100-day rite for the death of Prince Phrommaworanurak, April 11, 1925. Bangkok: Bamrung Nukunkit Press.

Khlong Thawathotsamat [Twelve Months]. 4th printing, Bangkok: Faculty of Arts, Silpakorn University, 1979.

"Khlong Thawathotsamat" [Twelve Months]. In *Wannakam samai ayutthaya lem 2* [Literature of the Ayutthaya Era, vol. 2], 679–770. Bangkok: Fine Arts Department, 2002.

Kotmai tra sam duang [Three Seals Law]. 5 vols. Bangkok: Khurusapha, 1994 [1805].

Kreangkrai Kirdsiri. "Sathapattayakam sinlapa lae patimakamasin haeng phaendin ayutthaya wa duai lak ban prathan mueang" [Architecture, Art, and Sculpture of the Major Sites of Ayutthaya]. In *Ayothaya siramathepnakhon boworathawarawathi: moradok khwam songjam haeng siam prathet* [Ayodhya: Siam's Heritage of Memory], ed. Winai Pongsripian, vol. II, 297–327. Bangkok: Thailand Research Fund, 2016.

La Loubère, Simon de. *A New Historical Relation of the Kingdom of Siam*, tr. A. P. Gen. London, 1793.

Lagirarde, François. "Un pèlerinage bouddhique au Lanna entre le XVIe et le XVIIe siècle d'après le Khlong Nirat Hariphunchai." *Aséanie*, 14 (2004): 69–107. www.persee.fr/doc/asean_0859-9009_2004_num_14_1_1829.

"Lilit ongkan chaeng nam" [Water Oath]. In *Wannakam samai ayutthaya lem 1* [Literature of the Ayutthaya era, vol. 1], 1–23. Bangkok: Fine Arts Department, 1997.

Lilit Phra Lo. Bangkok: Tai Press, 1915.

Lilit Phra Lo: nangsue an kawi niphon. Bangkok: Krom Sueksathikan, 1947.

Lom Phengkaeo. *Bot lakhon rueang phra lo chabap mueang phetchaburi* [Phra Lo Play, Phetchaburi Edition]. Phetchaburi: Phetchaburi Provincial Cultural Center Project to Publish Local Literature, 1982.

Luce, H. G. *Phases of Pre-Pagan Burma: Languages and History*. 2 vols. Oxford: Oxford University Press, 1985.

Manas Chitakasem. "The Emergence and Development of the Nirāt Genre in Thai Poetry." *Journal of the Siam Society*, 60, 2 (1982): 135–68.

—————. "Nation-building and Thai Literary Discourse: The Legacy of Phibun and Luang Wichit." In *Thai Literary Traditions*, ed. Manas Chitakasem, 29–55. Bangkok: Chulalongkorn University Press, 1995.

Maneepin Phromsuthirak. "Khlong thawathotsamat thot khwam" [Twelve Months Interpreted]. In *Wannakam samai ayutthaya chabap thot khwam* [Literature of the Ayutthaya Era, Interpreted], ed. Kunlasap Ketmaenkit, 71–155. Bangkok: ASEAN Literature Project, Thailand, 1996.

—————. "Thawathotsamat: nirat rue tamra kan praphan" [Twelve Months: Nirat or Manual of Poetics?]. In *Phasa-jaruek 10*, ed. Kusuma Raksamani *et al*, 79–97. Bangkok: Silpakorn University, 2005.

Manot Dinlansakun. "Wikhro thawathotsamat khlongdan" [Analysis of *Twelve Months*]. In Manot Dinlansakun, *Wannathat*, 121–62. Bangkok: Thaksin University, 2004.

Matichon. *Sayam phimphakan: prawatisat kan phim nai prathet thai* [Siamese Printing: History of Printing in Thailand]. Bangkok: Matichon Press, 2006.

Mattani Mojdara Rutnin. *Dance, Drama, and Theatre in Thailand: The Process of Development and Modernization*. Tokyo: Centre for East Asian Cultural Studies for UNESCO, 1993.

McGovern, Nathan. "Balancing the Foreign and the Familiar in the Articulation of Kingship: The Royal Court Brahmans of Thailand." *Journal of Southeast Asian Studies*, 48, 2 (June 2017): 283–303.

Milton, John. "Lycidas." www.poetryfoundation.org/poems/44733/lycidas (accessed June 10, 2018).

Ministry of Education. *Lilit Phra Lo*. Bangkok: Sophon Phiphatanakon, 1926.

—————. *Nangsue an kawi niphon rueang lilit phra lo* [Reading Text of the Poetic Composition, Lilit Phra Lo]. Bangkok: Khurusapha, 1957.

Montale, Eugenio. *Xenia*, tr. Mario Petrucci. Todmorden: Arc Publications, 2016.

Nai Tamra na Mueang Tai (Plueang na Nakhon). *Lilit Phra Lo*. Bangkok: Thai Watthanaphanit, 1994.

Nai Tamra na Mueang Tai and Hem Vejakorn. *Phra Lo*. Bangkok: Thai Watthana-phanit, 1994.

Narintharabet, Nai. *Khlong nirat narin*. www.vajirayana.org/โคลงนิราศนรินทร์

National Library. *Lilit Phra Lo chabap ho samut haeng chat* [Lilit Phra Lo, National Library Edition]. Bangkok: Sinlapa Bannakhan, 1965 [1926].

Nirat Suphan, Khlong Nirat Hariphunchai, Khlong Thawathotsamat. Bangkok: Rap Phim Press, 1954. Cremation volume for Ro O Tho Sa-at Thammasarot at Wat Makutkasatriyaram, March 22. www.car.chula.ac.th/rarebook/book/av_00099.

Nittaya Natayasunthon. *Rak thi thuk moen* [Love Abandoned]. Bangkok: Klang Withaya, 1972.

Niyada Lausunthorn. "Lilit phra lo: kan sueksa choeng prawat" [Lilit Phra Lo: Historical Study]. In Niyada, *Phinit wannakam: ruam botkhwam wichakan dan wannakhadi lae phasa* [Collected Articles on Literature and Language], 43–52. Bangkok: Mae Khamphang, 1992.

—————. *Jitakam phap sat himaphan phrawihan luang wat suthat thepworaram* [Murals of the Himavanta Animals in the Main Preaching Hall of Wat Suthat]. Bangkok: Amarin, 2016.

Oertel, F. O. *Note on a Tour in Burma: in March and April 1892*. Bangkok: White Orchid, 1995 [1893].

Ousa (Sheanakul) Weys and Walter Robinson, tr. "Phra Law Lilit: A Siamese Poem of Tragic Love." Unpublished manuscript, London, 1960.

Pairote Gesmankit, Rajda Isarasena, and Sudchit Bhinyoying. "Lilit Phra Lo: Ayutthaya Literary Work." In *Anthology of ASEAN Literatures, Volume IIa: Thai Literary Works of the Ayutthaya Period, Translated Version*, 332–545. Bangkok: Amarin for ASEAN, 1999.

Pallegoix, Jean-Baptiste. *Dictionarium linguae thai sive siamensis interpretatione latina, gallica et anglica illustratum*. Paris, 1854.

Panit Boonyavatana and Maneepin Phromsuthirak. "Khlong Thawa Thotsamat." In *Anthology of ASEAN Literatures, Volume IIa: Thai Literary Works of the Ayutthaya Period, Translated Version*, 127–99. Bangkok: Amarin for ASEAN, 1999.

Parthasarathy, R. *Erotic Poems from the Sanskrit: An Anthology*. New York: Columbia University Press, 2017.

Patravadi Mejudhon. "Lilit Phra Lo 2019." Staged in Bangkok and Hua Hin, 2019. www.youtube.com/watch?v=j0vBSMWuNNg&fbclid=IwAR3N_gigAOFj3I EW0ZhKLdSQiJvAcgwn94jC0ZU6lCa4ETKVD1iU-DVRiH4.

Pei Xiaorui and Xiong Ran. 帕罗赋>翻译与研究，北京：北京大学出版社燃 [A Translation and Study on Lilit Phra Lo]. Beijing: Peking University Press, 2013.

Phiset Jiajanphong. *Phra maha thammaracha kasatrathirat: kan mueang nai prawatisat yuk Sukhothai-Ayutthaya* [King Maha Thammaracha: Politics in the History of the Sukhothai-Ayutthaya Era]. Bangkok: Sinlapa Watthanatham, 2003.

Phra Lo Lilit. Bangkok: Wat Sangwet Printers for the Ministry of Education, 1934. Reprinted under the title *Nangsue an kawi niphon rueang lilit phra lo khong krasuamg sueksathikan* [Ministry of Education Edition of the Poem *Lilit Phra Lo*].

Phraratcha phongsawadan chabap phraratchahatthalekha [Royal Chronicles, Royal Autograph Edition]. 2 vols. Bangkok: Fine Arts Department, 1999.

Phraratcha phongsawadan krung kao: chabab luang prasoet [Royal Chronicles of Ayutthaya, Luang Prasoet Edition]. Bangkok: Saengdao, 2001.

Phraratcha phongsawadan krung si ayutthaya chabap mo bratle [Royal Chronicles of Ayutthaya, Dr Bradley Edition]. Bangkok: Kosit, 1963.

Plueang na Nakhon. *Prawat wannakhadi thai* [History of Thai Literature]. 13th printing, Bangkok: Thai Watthanaphanit, 2002 [1952].

Plueang na Nakhon and Hem Vejakorn. *Phra lo phap vijit* [Phra Lo Illustrated]. Bangkok: Thai Watthanaphanit, 1963.

Poe, Edgar Allan. "The Philosophy of Composition" (1846). In Edgar Allan Poe, *Essays and Reviews*, ed. G. R. Thompson, 13–25. New York: Library of America, 1984.

Poramin Khruathong. "An phra lo" [Reading Phra Lo]. In Poramin Khruathong, *Wannakhadi thi songsai* [Wondering about Literature], 10–29. Bangkok: An, 2015.

Prachum phongsawadan phak thi 72 tamnan mueang suwannakhomkham [Collected Chronicles, pt 72, Legend of Suwanna Khomkham]. Bangkok, 1939.

Prasert na Nagara. *Khlong Nirat Hariphunchai: sop kap ton chabap chiang mai* [Nirat Hariphunchai: Examined with the Chiang Mai Original]. 3rd printing, Bangkok: Phrajan, 1973.

Prayong Anantawong. "Chanthit krasaesin prat phu pen phet hua hin" [Chanthit Krasaesin, the Scholar-Gem of Hua Hin]. n.d. www.identity.opm.go.th/identity/doc/nis02945.pdf.

Prem Chaya (Prem Purachatra, HH Prince). *Magic Lotus, A Romantic Fantasy: An Adaptation for the English Stage of the Fifteenth Century Siamese Classic Pra Law.* Bangkok: Krungthep Bannakan, 1937. Reprint, Chatra Press, 1946.

Ramazani, Jahan. *Poetry of Mourning: The Modern Elegy from Hardy to Heaney.* Chicago: University of Chicago Press, 1994.

Reynolds, Frank E. and Mani B. Reynolds, *Three Worlds According to King Ruang: A Thai Buddhist Cosmology*, Berkeley: University of California Press, 1982.

Roveda, Vittorio. *Images of the Gods: Khmer Mythology in Cambodia, Thailand and Laos.* Bangkok: River Books, 2005.

Ruenruethai Satjaphan. "Wannakhadi sueksa choeng pramoen khunkha: prasoppakan jak kan tatsin rangwan wannakam" [Research on Evaluating Literature: Experience from the Award of Literary Prizes]. In *Prathet thai nai khwam khit khong methi wijai a-wuso lem 2* [Thailand in the Thinking of Distinguished Research Scholars, vol. 2], 122–45. Bangkok: Thailand Research Fund, 2019.

Sacks, Peter M. *The English Elegy: Studies in the Genre from Spenser to Yeats.* Baltimore, Maryland: Johns Hopkins University Press, 1985.

Samoe Bunma. "Si prat khue kawi phu taeng 'Thawathotsamat'" [Si Prat was the Author of *Twelve Months*], *Warasan phasa thai lae wannakam thai* [Journal of Thai Language and Literature], 3, 5 (2009): 71–89; www.baanjomyut.com/library_2/extension-4/sri_guru_is_poet/index.html (accessed June 10, 2018).

―――――. "Thawathotsamat wipak" [Critique of *Twelve Months*]. In *Upathawathotsamat Khlongdan*, ed. Trongjai Hutangkura, 19–68. Bangkok: Sirindhorn Anthropology Center, 2017.

Sanderson, Alexis. "The Śaiva Religion among the Khmers." *Bulletin de L'École française d'Extrême-Orient*, 90–91 (2003–4): 349–463.

Sasithorn Sinvuttaya, "*Upathawathotsamat* khlongdan: bot kawi duai arom lae phitsawat rak' [*Through All Twelve Months*: A Poem of Emotion and Passionate Love]. In *Upathawathotsamat Khlongdan*, ed. Trongjai Hutangkura, 69–82. Bangkok: Sirindhorn Anthropology Center, 2017.

Sathiankoset (Phraya Anuman Rajathon). *Kan tai* [Death]. Bangkok: Sayam, 1996.

Shelley, Percy Bysshe. "Adonais: An Elegy on the Death of John Keats." www. poetryfoundation.org/poems/45112/adonais-an-elegy-on-the-death-of-john-keats (accessed June 10, 2018).

Siriphot Laomanajaroen, "Triyamphawai-tripawai phian ma jak triwempawai-trippawai" [Triyamphawai-Tripawai Modified from Triwempawai-Trippawai], and "Lo chingcha prapheni pradit mai mai khong phram sayam" [Great Swing: A Festival Newly Crafted by Siamese Brahmans]. In *Lo chingcha: phithikamduekdamban khong suwannaphum mai chai phithi phram chomphuthawip* [The Giant Swing: An Ancient Festival from Suvarnabhumi Not a Brahman Festival from India], 7–22. Bangkok: Bangkok Metropolitan Authority, 2007.

So Thammayot. *Sinlapa haeng wannakhadi* [The Art of Literature]. Bangkok: Mingkhwan, 1937.

Soison Sakolrak. "Thai Literary Transformation: An Analytical Study of the Modernization of *Lilit Phra Lor*." PhD diss., SOAS, University of London, 2003.

Souneth Phothisane. "The Nidān Khun Borom: Annotated Translation and Analysis." PhD diss., University of Queensland, 1996.

Sujit Wongthes. "Khwam rak phuea bamphen phawana khong khon chan sung" [Love as Meditation of the Upper Class]. *Matichon*, February 14, 2016. www.matichon.co.th/entertainment/news_37339.

————. "Thawathotsamat nirat 12 duen mai chai nangsue an len phloen phloen" [Thawathotsamat, *Nirat* of 12 Months is not a Book to be Read for Pleasure]. *Matichon Weekly*, March 5, 2017. www.matichonweekly.com/culture/article_26971.

Sumali Wirawong. *Withi thai nai lilit phra lo* [Thai Ways in Lilit Phra Lo]. Bangkok: Sathaporn Books, 1994.

Sumonajati Svastikul, MR. "Sopsuan rueang kan taeng phra lo" [Investigating the Composition of Phra Lo]. *Warasan haeng samakhom wicha prathet thai chabap phasa thai* [Thai Academic Journal, Thai Language Edition], 3 (1945): 70–119. Reprinted in *Phasa lae wannakhadi thai* [Thai Language and Literature], 11 (1994).

Sun Laichen. "Military Technology Transfers from Ming China and the Emergence of Northern Mainland Southeast Asia (c. 1390–1527)." *Journal of Southeast Asian Studies*, 34, 3 (2003): 495–517.

Sunait Chutintaranond, "Lilit ongkan chaeng nam lae phraratchaphithi thue nam phraphiphat sataya" [*Ongkan chaeng nam* and the Royal Ceremony of the Water Oath of Loyalty]. *Warasan thammasat* [Thammasat Journal], 9, 1 (1979): 32–52.

Suphon Bunnag. "Kan yatyiat pom wiparit rueang phet hai kae wannakhadi thai" [Stuffing Sexual Complexes into Thai Literature]. *Phasa lae nangsue* [Language and Books], 8 (1973): 9–40.

————. "Phra Lo." *Pakkai chabap wannakam wipak* [Literary Criticism Review]. Bangkok: Thailand Writers Association, 1975.

Tamra phraratchaphithi kao [Manual of old Royal Ceremonies]. Printed by Phrajaoborommawongthoe Kromluang Phrommaworanuk. Bangkok: Sophon Phiphanthanathon, 1923.

Temple, R. C. *Notes on Antiquities in Ramannadesa (the Talaing Country of Burma).* Bombay: Education Society, 1894.

Tennyson, Alfred Lord. "In Memoriam A. H. H." In *Alfred Lord Tennyson Selected Poems*, ed. Christopher Ricks, 96–199. London: Penguin, 2007.

Terwiel, Barend J. "Rice Legends in Mainland Southeast Asia: History and Ethnography in the Study of Myths of Origin." In *Rice in Southeast Asian Myth and Ritual*, ed. Anthony R. Walker, *Contributions to Southeast Asian Ethnography*, 10 (1994): 1–36.

Thak Chaloemtiarana. *Read Till It Shatters: Nationalism and Identity in Modern Thai Literature.* Canberra: ANU Press, 2018.

Thammathibet, Chaofa. "Bot he ruea" [Boat Songs]. In *Wannakam samai ayutthaya lem 3* [Literature of the Ayutthaya Era, vol. 3], 201–206. Bangkok: Fine Arts Department, 2002.

Thanapol Limapichart. "The Royal Society of Literature, or, the Birth of Modern Cultural Authority in Thailand." In *Disturbing Conventions: Decentering Thai Literary Cultures*, ed. Rachel V. Harrison, 37–62. London and New York: Rowan and Littlefield, 2014.

Thawathotsamat. Bangkok: Borikan Thong Press for Faculty of Fine Arts, Chulalongkorn University, 1962.

Thein Lwin and U Min Han. "Images of Brahma in the Buddhist Art of Bagan (circa 11–13th century)." Paper from SOAS Southeast Asian Art Education Programme, 2017.

Thommayanti. *Rak thi tong montra* [Love by Magic]. Bangkok: Ruamsan, 1969.

Trang, Phraya. *Khlong nirat tam sadet thap lamnamnoi* [Poem Following the Royal Army to Lamnamnoi]. www.vajirayana.org/วรรณกรรมพระยาตรัง/โคลงนิราศ ตามเสด็จทัพลำน้ำน้อย

Trongjai Hutangkura, ed. *Upathawathotsamat Khlongdan* [Through All Twelve Months], Bangkok: Sirindhorn Anthropology Center, 2017.

Trongjai Hutangkura and Jakkri Phothimani. "'Withi chao ban—withi chao wang' pathisamphan nai khlong thawathotsamat" [Folk Ways—Palace Ways: Relations in *Twelve Months*]. In *Upathawathotsamat Khlongdan*, ed. Trongjai Hutangkura, 83–96, Bangkok: Sirindhorn Anthropology Center, 2017.

Vajirayana. n.d. Preface. www.vajirayana.org/โคลงทวาทศมาส/คำอธิบาย

Vickery, John B. *The Prose Elegy: An Exploration of Modern American and British Fiction.* Baton Rouge: Louisiana State University Press, 2009.

Vickery, Michael. "The Constitution of Ayutthaya: The Three Seals Code." In *Thai Law: Buddhist Law. Essays on the Legal History of Thailand, Laos and Burma*, ed. A. Huxley, 133–210, Bangkok: White Orchid, 1996.

Wachirayan. *Thawathotsamat Ramakian jaruek thi sila salak pen phap ramakian thi phanak rop ubosot wat phra chetuphon* [Twelve Months and Ramakian Verses Engraved with Murals in the Cloister of the Ordination Hall of Wat Phra Chetuphon]. Bangkok: Wachirayan, 1904 or 1905.

Wachirayan journal, vol. 114, March 1904.

Wachirayan Library. *Khlong Thawathotsamat* [Twelve Months], printed on the 100-day rite for the death of Prince Phrommaworanurak, April 11. Bangkok: Bamrung Nukunkit Press, 1925.

—————. *Lilit Phra Lo.* Bangkok: Sophonphiphit-thanakon, 1926.

Wade, Geoff. "The *Ming shi-lu* as a Source for Thai History—Fourteenth to Seventeenth Centuries." *Journal of Southeast Asian Studies*, 31, 2 (2000): 249–94.

—————. *Southeast Asia in the Ming Shi-lu: An Open Access Resource*, Singapore: Asia Research Institute and the Singapore E-Press, National University of Singapore. http://epress.nus.edu.sg/msl/. [Wade, *Southeast Asia* online]

Wales, H. G. Quaritch. *Siamese State Ceremonies.* London: Quaritch, 1931.

Wannakam samai rattanakosin lem 3: Sangkhittiyawong [Literature of the Bangkok Era, vol. 3: Sangitiyavamsa]. Bangkok: Fine Arts Department, 2001.

Wannakhadi samai ayutthaya: Khlong nirat hariphunchai, Thawathotsamat, Nirat suphan khong nai mi, ed. Muen Phromphatson (Mi). Bangkok: Department of Teacher Training, 1961.

Whitman, Walt. "When Lilacs Last in the Dooryard Bloom'd." www.poetry-foundation.org/poems/45480/when-lilacs-last-in-the-dooryard-bloomd (accessed June 10, 2018).

Wibha Kongkananda. *Phra Lo: A Portrait of the Hero as a Tragic Lover*. Bangkok: Silpakorn University, 1982.

—————. "Thatsana rueang phra lo kap phuchao samingphrai" [Viewpoint on Phra Lo and Old Lord Tiger Spirit]. *Lok nangsue* [Book World], 5, 8 (1982).

Wibha Senanan. *The Genesis of the Novel in Thailand*. Bangkok: Thai Watthanaphanit, 1975.

Winai Pongsripian. *Ayutthaya: phannana phumisathan phranakhon si ayutthaya ekkasan jak ho luang (chabab khwam sombun)* [Ayutthaya: Description of Ayutthaya, Documents from the Palace Library (Complete Version)]. Bangkok: Thailand Research Fund, n.d.

Winai Pongsripian, ed. *Kamsuan Samut: sut yot kamsuansin* [Ocean Lament: Ultimate of the Lament Genre]. Bangkok: Thailand Research Fund, 2010.

—————. *Ruthiratramphan (Khlong Nirat Hariphunchai) lae jaruek wat phra yuen moradok khwam songjam haeng aphinawaburi-si hariphunchai* [Ruthirat-ramphan (Nirat Hariphunchai) and the Inscription of Wat Phra Yuen, Heritage of Chiang Mai–Lamphun]. Bangkok: Princess Maha Chakri Sirindhorn Foundation, 2019.

Worawet Phisit, Phra (Seng Siwasiyanon). *Khumue lilit phra lo* [Manual for Lilit Phra Lo]. 2 vols. Bangkok: Chulalongkorn University for Khurusapha, 1970 [1961].

—————. *Nangsue prawat kawi lae wannakhadi thai* [History of Thai Poetry and Literature]. Bangkok: Chulalongkorn University, 1948. www.digitalrarebook.com/index.php?lay=show&ac=cat_show_pro_detail&pid=74296.

—————. *Wannakhadi thai* [Thai Literature]. Bangkok: Chulalongkorn University, 1953. www.car.chula.ac.th/rarebook/book2/clra60_0129.

Wright, Michael. "Phraratchaphithi triyampawai lo chingcha sapson kwa thi khrai khrai khit" [The Royal Ceremony of Triyamphawai, Swinging Festival, More Complex than Anyone Thought]. *Sinlapa watthanatham* [Art and Culture], 16, 11 (February 1993): 162–71.